COMMITTING TO PEACE

Committing to Peace

THE SUCCESSFUL SETTLEMENT OF CIVIL WARS

Barbara F. Walter

PRINCETON UNIVERSITY PRESS

PRINCETON AND OXFORD

Library of Congress Cataloging-in-Publication Data

Walter, Barbara F.
Committing to peace : the successful settlement of civil wars / Barbara F. Walter.
p. cm.
Includes bibliographical references and index.
ISBN 0-691-08930-2 (cl : acid-free paper) — ISBN 0-691-08931-0 (pb : acid-free paper)
1. Civil war.   2. Low-intensity conflicts (Military science)   3. World politics—20th
century.   I. Title.
U240 .W35 2002
303.6'4—dc21   2001036379

British Library Cataloging-in-Publication Data is available

To Zoli

CONTENTS

FIGURES

TABLES

ACKNOWLEDGMENTS

I HAVE BEEN the beneficiary of much support and assistance throughout the writing of this book. David Laitin read every version of this work, from its distant beginning as a graduate school paper to the final book manuscript. He offered invaluable guidance throughout the process and made the whole experience more enjoyable as a result. No one could ask for a better mentor. James Fearon and Stephen Walt were equally important in my training as a scholar. Both read numerous versions of the manuscript and were always generous with their time and advice. I owe a great deal of thanks to each of them.

I was also extremely fortunate to go through graduate school with a cohort of friends much smarter than I. Stacey Bergstrom, Dale Copeland, Hein Goemans, Andrew Grant-Thomas, Atsushi Ishida, Stathis Kalyvas, Barbara Koremenos, Andy Kydd, Alicia Levine, Walter Mattli, Stu Romm, Ivan Arreguin Toft, Monica Duffy Toft, and Yael Wolinsky discussed various parts of this manuscript with me and helped formulate many of its important ideas. I will always look back at those years as a particularly stimulating time in my life.

Sammy Barkin, Rachel Bronson, Allan Castle, Bruce Cronin, Charles Glaser, Roy Licklider, Dan Lindley, John Matthews, Dan Philpott, Ken Pollack, Dani Reiter, Beth Rodgers, Don Rothchild, and Duncan Snidal offered helpful comments on all or parts of the manuscript and helped clarify my arguments. Neal Beck, Curt Signorino, Mike Tomz, and Richard Tucker answered numerous questions about research design and improved the empirical analysis in valuable ways. Paul Papayoanou walked me through the game theory and showed unending patience in answering simple questions. Page Fortna sent me a copy of her exceptional dissertation, which served as my model of how social science should be conducted. Bob Jervis and Jack Snyder will always hold a special place in my heart for taking me under their wings and serving as role models during my transition from graduate student to full-fledged academic.

The University of California at San Diego has provided the most nurturing of homes. For lunches and dinners and hallway conversations I thank Liz Gerber, Peter Gourevitch, Steph Haggard, Michael Hiscox, Miles Kahler, David Lake, Skip Lupia, Andrew McIntyre, John McMillan, Barry Naughton, Susan Shirk, Matt Shugart, and Chris Woodruff. I have grown much as a scholar from my interactions with each of them. Thanks also to Risa Brooks and Stephanie McWhorter, my excellent research assistants, and to Matt Baum who taught me more than I ever taught him. It was my good fortune to work with each of them while they were graduate students at UCSD.

This book has also benefited from the generous financial support of numerous institutions. I am most grateful to The Smith Richardson Foundation for their Junior Faculty Grant Program, which supported this work during a critical stage in its writing. The Harry Frank Guggenheim Foundation and the Andrew Mellon Foundation helped fund this project in its early years. The Olin Institute for Strategic Studies at Harvard University, the War and Peace Institute at Columbia University, the Institute on Global Conflict and Cooperation at the University of California, and UCSD's Academic Senate also helped fund the project at various stages and provided wonderful places to work.

My family, Lynn, Rudolf, Christine, Joe, Marc, Elke, Vivian, Zoltan, and Catherine have provided many hours of fun away from the book and have helped bring balance and contentment to my life. My biggest debt, however, is to my husband, Zoltan Hajnal. Zoli read every word of every chapter and never let me doubt myself or the project. His careful hand and intelligence are present throughout the book. He is my intellectual partner, my soul mate, my most fun playmate, and the source of an extraordinarily happy marriage. Those who know him understand how supremely blessed I am to pass through life with this man. I dedicate this book to him.

PART ONE

Theory

1. Introduction

WHY DO SOME CIVIL WARS end peacefully, while others are fought to the finish? Why, for example, did the Sandinistas and Contras in Nicaragua stop their war with a negotiated settlement, while the Sandinistas and the Somoza regime did not? Why were the Sudanese able to end their conflict in 1972 in a settlement, but not the Nigerians? Why did negotiations in Bosnia bring peace, while negotiations in Rwanda brought genocide?

Between 1940 and 1992, only a third of all negotiations to end civil wars resulted in a successfully implemented peace settlement. In most cases, combatants chose to walk away from the negotiating table and return to war. In fact, civil war combatants almost always chose to return to war unless a third party stepped in to enforce or verify a post-treaty transition. If a third party assisted with implementation, negotiations almost always succeeded, regardless of the initial goals, ideology, or ethnicity of the participants. If a third party did not, these talks almost always failed.

This book tries to explain why combatants in some civil war negotiations choose to sign and implement peace settlements, while others choose to return to war. I argue that successful negotiations must do more than resolve the underlying issues over which a civil war has been fought. To end their war in a negotiated settlement, the combatants must clear the much higher hurdle of designing credible guarantees on the terms of the agreement—a task made difficult without outside assistance. The biggest challenge facing civil war opponents at the negotiating table, therefore, is not how to resolve disagreements over land reform, majority rule, or any of the underlying grievances that started the war. These are difficult issues, but they are not the most difficult. The greatest challenge is to design a treaty that convinces the combatants to shed their partisan armies and surrender conquered territory even though such steps will increase their vulnerability and limit their ability to enforce the treaty's other terms. When groups obtain third-party security guarantees for the treacherous demobilization period that follows the signing of an agreement, and obtain power-sharing guarantees in the first postwar government, they will implement their settlement. When groups fail to obtain such guarantees, the warring factions will eventually reject a negotiated settlement and continue their war.

I have four aims in this book. The first is to uncover why so many civil wars fail to end in successfully negotiated settlements and why third-party enforcement or verification of the post-treaty implementation period is critical for success. The second is to reconceptualize the resolution of civil wars as a three-step process during which combatants must decide whether to (1) initiate negotiations, (2) compromise on goals and principles, and (3) implement the terms of a treaty. By understanding resolution as composed of three distinct stages, I hope to demonstrate that the factors held up in the scholarly literature to explain the settlement of civil wars omit a key problem. Groups who agree to meet at the negotiating table and who manage to resolve their grievances still worry that their enemy will take advantage of them after they sign a peace agreement and begin to demobilize. In the end, it is the implementation phase, long ignored by scholars, that is the most difficult to navigate and the reason so many negotiations to fail. My final aim is to collect and analyze the data necessary to test a range of competing explanations in order to draw appropriate lessons.

Before continuing, I should mention what this book does not aim to do. It does not take a stand on whether the United States should have intervened in Rwanda or Bosnia or should intervene in any country seeking a settlement to a civil war. It makes no judgment about the practicality of providing peacekeeping services around the globe, or the ethics of intervening to help stop a civil war.[1] It also does not discuss the difficulties world leaders face obtaining domestic political support for post-treaty interventions.

What it does lay out are the conditions under which peace negotiations succeed, the type of outside intervention that is necessary to get combatants through the difficult implementation period, and the timing during which third-party intervention is most valuable. This book leaves it up to policymakers to decide whether the benefits of peace are worth the money, manpower, and support needed to launch such missions.

The rest of this chapter is divided into five sections. The first presents the empirical puzzle driving the book, namely that combatants frequently choose to return to civil wars even after they have signed comprehensive peace agreements. The second section summarizes the main argument: civil war peace negotiations frequently fail because combatants cannot enforce or credibly commit to treaties that produce enormous uncertainty in the context of a highly dangerous implementation period. The third section reviews other explanations for why civil war

---

[1] For an analysis of these issues see Lori Fisler Damrosch and David J. Scheffer, *Law and Force in the New International Order* (Boulder: Westview Press, 1991); and Laura W. Reed and Carl Kaysen, eds., *Emerging Norms of Justified Intervention* (Cambridge, Mass.: American Academy of Arts and Sciences, 1993).

negotiations may break down. In the next section I explain the methodology used to test these competing explanations. The final section gives a brief summary of the rest of the book.

The Puzzle

A close examination of all civil war negotiations between 1940 and 1992 shows that getting combatants to the bargaining table and resolving their grievances does not guarantee peace.[2] As figure 1.1 shows, 62 percent of all negotiations during this period led to a signed bargain.[3] Yet as figure 1.2 reveals, almost half of these treaties were never implemented. Contrary to common expectations, combatants do not have the greatest difficulty resolving underlying conflicts of interest and reaching bargains. They have the greatest difficulty implementing the resulting terms. In short, the conditions that encourage groups to initiate negotiations and sign settlements do not appear sufficient to bring peace.

The Argument

An important and frequent reason why civil war negotiations fail is because it is almost impossible for the combatants themselves to arrange credible guarantees on the terms of the settlement. Negotiations frequently do not fail because the conditions on the ground are not "ripe for resolution," as many have argued. Combatants in most civil wars seek a negotiated settlement at some point during the conflict. Nor do negotiations frequently fail because bargains cannot be struck, as many others have argued. Adversaries often compromise on the basic issues underlying their conflict, and they often find mutually acceptable solutions to their problems. Negotiations fail because combatants cannot credibly promise to abide by terms that create numerous opportunities for exploitation after the treaty is signed and implementation begins. Only if a third party is willing to enforce or verify demobilization, and only if the combatants are willing to extend power-sharing

[2] Fifty-one percent of all civil wars that started between 1940 and 1992 experienced formal peace negotiations at some point during the conflict. See appendix 1 for the list of cases.

[3] Only those agreements that included a political as well as a military solution to the conflict were defined as comprehensive peace agreements. See chapter 3 for a discussion of how peace agreements were defined and coded.

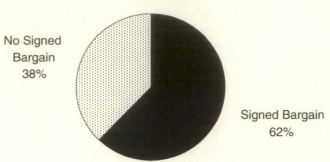

Fig. 1.1. Percentage of civil war negotiations that led to signed bargains,
1940–1992

guarantees, will promises to abide by the original terms be credible and
negotiations succeed. I call this theory the *credible commitment theory*
of civil war resolution.

In what follows, I show that resolving a civil war requires much more
than negotiating a bargain and establishing a cease-fire. A successful
peace settlement must integrate the previously warring fractions into a
single state, create a new government capable of accommodating their
interests, and build a national, nonpartisan military force. This process
of integration, however, creates a transition period during which combatants become less and less able to survive a surprise attack and
enforce subsequent terms. Thus, even under the very best conditions—
when combatants have initiated negotiations and signed a mutually
agreeable treaty—the desire for peace clashes with the realities of implementation, and groups frequently choose the safer, more certain option
of war.

The fact that combatants have such difficulty enforcing and credibly

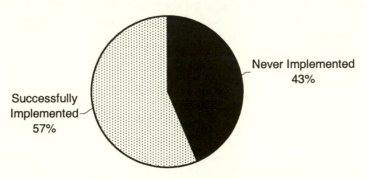

Fig. 1.2. Percentage of signed bargains that were successfully implemented,
1940–1992

committing to the terms of their own peace settlements, however, does not mean that the resolution of civil wars can be traced to a single cause, outside security guarantees. Combatants have no chance to settle their wars unless they are willing, first, to meet at the negotiating table and, second, to resolve their underlying grievances and strike a deal. Both of these steps are likely to be driven by a variety of factors that come into play long before third parties arrive on the scene. Although the credible commitment theory says almost nothing about these additional conditions for peace, the focus here on enforcement and commitment does serve a purpose. By emphasizing the structural problems of implementation I hope to show that in important ways, issues of post-treaty security are likely to pervade all decisions leading to settlement and play a critical role in the final outcome of civil wars. In the end, enforcement will matter a great deal.

Current Theories of Civil War Resolution

Six additional theories of civil war resolution can be found in the literature, and I present them for several reasons. The first is to give skeptical readers a better sense of the many variables purported to take combatants from war to peace and allow these readers to come to their own conclusions about the efficacy of my argument. My second purpose is to begin to identify the full range of factors that are likely to play a role in each of the three stages of the peace process. This tactic is designed to impose greater conceptual rigor on the study of civil war resolution and enable me to determine what factors are doing what work at each of step along the way. My final aim is to determine whether third-party security guarantees and power-sharing pacts really do play critical, independent roles in the peaceful resolution of civil wars, or are only the end result of these other, more important, conditions.

Current theories of civil war termination can be roughly grouped into one of two camps. The first views negotiated settlements primarily as a function of the economic, military, or political conditions that exist on the ground and are likely to encourage combatants to initiate negotiations. This set of theories tends to assume that once these conditions favor negotiation, successful settlement is likely.[4] The second set of theories views negotiated settlements primarily as a function of combatants' ability to resolve underlying conflicts of interest. This camp assumes

[4] See especially I. William Zartman, *Ripe for Resolution: Conflict and Intervention in Africa* (New York: Oxford University Press, 1989); and Stephen John Stedman, *Peacemaking in Civil War: International Mediation in Zimbabwe, 1974–1980* (Boulder: Lynne Rienner Publishers, 1991).

that once a bargain has been reached, successful settlement should follow. Both camps stand in contrast to the credible commitment theory, which argues that even if combatants reach a mutually agreeable bargain they will not implement its terms unless credible guarantees on the terms of the treaty are included.

Conditions That Affect "Ripeness for Resolution"

The most popular explanation for the success or failure of negotiations focuses on the importance of situational factors, conditions that make civil wars "ripe for resolution."[5] Three conditions in particular are believed to make war less attractive and encourage combatants to pursue compromise solutions: high costs of war, military stalemate, and certain domestic political institutions.

COSTS OF WAR

Expected utility choice theorists have long assumed that the decision to fight or negotiate is determined by the relative costs and benefits of a unilateral victory or a compromise settlement.[6] Proponents of this view argue that combatants carefully estimate their chances of winning a civil war, the amount of time it will take to achieve this victory, how much it will cost, and their relative payoffs from winning versus accepting a settlement. Settlement occurs when combatants believe they can do no better by continuing to fight than by bargaining.

There are good theoretical reasons to believe the costs of war have a significant effect on the process by which civil wars end. First, incumbent governments and rebels have a finite base of resources on which to draw and are forced to pursue alternate solutions to violence as war coffers dry up. Second, a full military victory becomes less attractive as the costs of achieving it increase. Third, leaders are likely to come under increasing domestic pressure to end violence as civilian suffering increases and war fatigue sets in. Peter De Vos, former U.S. ambassador to Liberia, Guinea-Bissau, Mozambique, Tanzanian, and Costa Rica,

---

[5] The term "ripe for resolution" was coined by I. William Zartman in his book by that title.

[6] See, for example, Donald Wittman, "How a War Ends: A Rational Model Approach," *Journal of Conflict Resolution* 23, no. 4 (1979): 743–63; Bruce Bueno de Mesquita and David Lalman, *War and Reason: Domestic and International Imperatives* (New Haven: Yale University Press, 1992); T. David Mason and Patrick J. Fett, "How Civil Wars End: A Rational Choice Approach," *Journal of Conflict Resolution* 40, no. 4 (1996): 546–68; and T. David Mason, Joseph P. Weingarten, Jr., and Patrick J. Fett, "Win, Lose, or Draw: Predicting the Outcome of Civil Wars," *Political Research Quarterly* 52, no. 2 (1999): 239–68.

points out that "the participants are not ready to settle until they're just too weary. If you look at Mozambique, if you look at Angola, that's what's happened."[7] The costs of continuing a war, therefore, should be directly related to combatants' willingness to pursue a negotiated settlement.

BALANCE OF POWER

Theorists of international relations have long argued that the decision to go to war (or remain at peace) is strongly affected by the relative balance of power between adversaries.[8] A. F. K. Organski, for example, has argued that a balance of power produces peace because "no one side can achieve a great enough superiority to be sure that aggressive action would be crowned with success."[9] This logic should apply equally well to the resolution of civil wars. Combatants who are fairly equal on the civil war battlefield should be more likely to negotiate a settlement for at least two reasons. First, military stalemates often, although not always, indicate a determined opponent who promises a costly war of attrition. Second, military stalemates produce uncertainty as to the eventual winner, making each side less willing to risk a decisive loss.[10] "Stalemate," according to George Modelski, "is easily the most important condition of a settlement. Without it, one or both of the parties may hold justified hopes of an outright win and therefore have the incentive to go on fighting."[11] This theory, therefore, predicts that

---

[7] From Dana Francis, ed., *Mediating Deadly Conflict* (Cambridge, Mass.: World Peace Foundation, 1998), 34–35.

[8] See A. F. K. Organski, *World Politics*, 2d ed. (New York: Random House, 1968); Inis L. Claude, *Power and International Relations* (New York: Random House, 1962); Geoffrey Blainey, *The Causes of War* (New York: Free Press, 1973); Michael Howard, *The Causes of Wars* (Cambridge: Harvard University Press, 1983); Arthur Stein, *Why Nations Cooperate: Circumstances and Choice in International Relations* (Ithaca, N.Y.: Cornell University Press, 1990).

[9] Organski, *World Politics*.

[10] The power preponderance school would make the opposite prediction, arguing that combatants should be less likely to negotiate settlement when a balance of power exists since both groups can still hold onto the hope that they will eventually win the war. I do not include a discussion of this theory in the text because it has never been offered as an explanation for the resolution of civil wars. Nonetheless, the same hypothesis regarding the importance of a military stalemate could be used to test this prediction.

[11] George Modelski, "International Settlement of Internal War," in *International Aspects of Civil Strife*, ed. James Rosenau (Princeton: Princeton University Press, 1964), 143. See also I. William Zartman, "The Unfinished Agenda: Negotiating Internal Conflicts," in *Stopping the Killing: How Civil Wars End*, ed. Roy Licklider (New York: New York University Press, 1993), 24; Zartman, *Ripe for Resolution*; Zartman, "Dynamics and Constraints in Negotiations in Internal Conflicts," in *Elusive Peace: Negotiating an*

the more equally matched combatants are on the battlefield, the more likely they are to pursue negotiations.

DOMESTIC POLITICAL INSTITUTIONS

A third explanation for negotiated settlements can be drawn from institutional explanations for war and peace. One could argue that the decision to negotiate depends on the domestic political constraints placed on individual leaders. According to this view, civil wars that occur in democratic countries should be more likely to end in compromise settlements, for one of three reasons.[12] First, leaders of democracies face higher domestic constraints in their use of force than leaders of authoritarian governments and are, therefore, less likely to be allowed to pursue unpopular wars.[13] Presidents Johnson and Nixon were forced to respond to a public that increasingly demanded U.S. withdrawal from Vietnam. This stands in stark contrast to Russia's pursuit of its war with Chechnya. As one noted Russian scholar has observed:

> Russia's war with Chechnya most likely would not have occurred if Russia had been a consolidated democracy. From the very beginning, roughly two-thirds of all Russians opposed the war, a figure that grew steadily over the next two years. Had their interests been represented in the state through the usual pluralist institutions found in stable, liberal democracies, the decision to attack may not have been made.[14]

Second, democratic leaders are likely to find it easier to credibly commit to peace agreements since they are more likely to be held accountable by their voting publics for promises made.[15] Abraham Lincoln's

---

End to Civil Wars, ed. Zartman (Washington, D.C.: Brookings Institute, 1995), 11; and Robert Harrison Wagner, "The Causes of Peace," in Licklider, *Stopping the Killing*, 260.

[12] Ted Gurr, however, has found that most democratic regimes have been able to avoid communal conflicts through various types of reform. Nonetheless, we should still observe a relationship between the degree of democracy in a country and the likelihood of settlement if this theory holds. See Ted Robert Gurr, *Minorities at Risk: A Global View of Ethnopolitical Conflicts* (Washington D.C.: United States Institute of Peace Press, 1993).

[13] Bueno de Mesquita and Lalman, *War and Reason*; T. Clifton Morgan and Sally H. Campbell, "Domestic Structure, Decisional Constraints, and War: So Why Can't Democracies Fight?" *Journal of Conflict Resolution* 35, no. 2 (1991): 187–211. For a related argument see H. E. Goemans, *War and Punishment: The Causes of War Termination and the First World War* (Princeton: Princeton University Press, 2000).

[14] Michael McFaul, "A Precarious Peace: Domestic Politics in the Making of Russian Foreign Policy," *International Security* 22, no 3 (1997–98): 5–35.

[15] For discussions of how democratic institutions can help leaders reveal information about their intentions and thus overcome informational asymmetries see James D. Fearon, "Domestic Political Audiences and the Escalation of International Disputes," *American Political Science Review* 88 (1994): 577–92; and Kenneth A. Schultz, "Domestic Opposi-

signature on a peace agreement between the North and the South was a credible signal of the North's intent because of the full force of the democratic institutions that accorded him his power to sign. It was improbable that he would try to renege on a treaty. By contrast, General Anastasio Somoza's word to the Sandinistas during Nicaragua's war in 1978–79 was less credible because public penalties would not have followed any renouncement of peace.

Finally, democratic leaders accustomed to sharing political power have less to lose by opening the government than authoritarian leaders who stand to forfeit monopoly control of government.[16] The Conservative Party in Colombia, for example, gave up far less when it signed a peace treaty with the Liberal Party than did the absolutist government of Chiang Kai-shek when it agreed to a coalition government with the Chinese Communist Party. A focus on democratic political institutions, therefore, leads to the prediction that the more democratic a state, the more likely the government will be to negotiate a settlement to war.

Conditions That Encourage Combatants to Strike a Bargain

Scholars in the second camp shift the focus of attention away from the conditions that encourage combatants to initiate negotiations toward the conditions that encourage combatants to make real concessions to their enemy.[17] These scholars do not ignore the importance of preexisting military, economic, or political conditions that favor settlement. They simply stress that negotiations have no chance to succeed unless combatants are able to resolve the issues driving the war and reach a mutually agreeable deal. Three factors in particular are likely to affect the chances of a settlement: the identity of the combatants, the divisibility of the stakes over which they are fighting, and the presence of an outside mediator. If identities are malleable, if stakes are easy to divide, or if mediators are present, negotiations are more likely to

---

tion and Signaling in International Crises," *American Political Science Review* 92 (1998): 829–44.

[16] Although this depends on the goals of the rebels. Governments who are accustomed to power sharing are likely to be equally intransigent if rebels aim to overthrow their leader or secede. In these cases, even the most democratic leaders would have equally much to lose.

[17] See especially Robert Randle, "The Domestic Origins of Peace," *Annals of the Academy of Political and Social Science* 392 (November 1970): 76–85; Fred C. Ikle, *Every War Must End* (New York Columbia University Press, 1971); Glenn Snyder and Paul Diesing, *Conflict among Nations* (Princeton: Princeton University Press, 1977); and James D. Fearon, "Rationalist Explanations for War," *International Organization* 49, no. 3 (1995): 379–414.

succeed. If not, combatants are unlikely to resolve their differences, and war is likely to resume.

ETHNIC IDENTITY

It is widely assumed in both journalistic and scholarly accounts of civil wars that the identity of the combatants plays a large role in their willingness to compromise.[18] Civil wars between different ethnic groups are frequently depicted as intense value conflicts fought over issues close to the heart. Such wars are thus thought to be less amenable to rational calculations of costs and benefits than conflicts between combatants drawn from similar identity groups. Ethnic conflicts are viewed as the result of kinship turned bad, of "feuds" and "bitter rivalries," not power politics. "I have six sons," a Bosnian Croat farmer told a reporter when asked whether he would implement the Dayton peace accords of 1994, "and if we are told to share our government with Muslims, all of them will join me in the war that will come."[19] By this theory, once violence erupts, identities become cemented in ways that keep combatants from working together. This theory predicts that combatants fighting over issues tied to their identities will have greater difficulty reaching a compromise settlement than those fighting over more negotiable political or economic issues.[20]

THE DIVISIBILITY OF STAKES

Others argue that the success or failure of peace negotiations depends on how easy it is for the combatants to divide the stakes over which they are fighting. "If," Paul Pillar has written, "the stakes are chiefly

[18] See Chaim Kaufmann, "Possible and Impossible Solutions to Ethnic Civil Wars," *International Security* 20, no. 4 (1996): 136–75; Patrick M. Regan, *Civil Wars and Foreign Powers: Outside Intervention in Intrastate Conflict* (Ann Arbor: University of Michigan Press, 2000); Ibrahim A. Elbadawi and Nicholas Sambanis, "External Interventions and the Duration of Civil Wars," World Bank Policy Research Paper, July 25, 2000; Francis, *Mediating Deadly Conflict*; John W. Burton, *Resolving Deep-Rooted Conflict: A Handbook* (Lanham, Md.: University Press of America, 1987); Cvijeto Job, "Yugoslavia's Ethnic Furies," *Foreign Policy* 92 (fall 1993): 52–74; Anthony D. Smith, "The Ethnic Sources of Nationalism," in *Ethnic Conflict and International Security*, ed. Michael E. Brown (Princeton: Princeton University Press, 1993), 27–41.

[19] Mike O'Connor, "Bosnia Croats Resist Peace Accord," *New York Times*, February 13, 1996, A8.

[20] See Robert Randle, *The Origins of Peace: A Study of Peacemaking and the Structure of Peace Settlements* (New York: Free Press, 1973), especially p. 430; Donald Horowitz, *Ethnic Groups in Conflict* (Berkeley and Los Angeles: University of California Press, 1985), especially chap. 14; and Burton, *Resolving Deep-Rooted Conflict*.

indivisible, so that neither side can get most of what it wants without depriving the other of most of what it wants, negotiations are less apt to be successful."[21] Many civil wars may end in decisive military victories precisely because the goals combatants are pursuing tend to be absolute, "with nothing in between to contribute to the give and take of negotiation and bargaining."[22]

Two arguments regarding divisibility can be made. One could argue that rebels fighting for total goals such as the complete control of a country, the elimination of a rival, or the revolutionary overthrow of a hated political, economic, or social system are less likely to reach a negotiated settlement than rebels fighting for limited aims such as land reform or democratic adjustment.[23] In these cases, it is possible that a middle ground exists in which to draw a compromise settlement. This theory predicts that total wars are less likely to end in negotiated settlement than limited wars.

One could also argue, however, that rebels fighting over territory may make it easier for the central government to accommodate their demands because incumbent elites can part with territory and still retain power. If this is true, one would predict that secessionist conflicts and conflicts fought for greater territorial autonomy are more likely to find negotiated settlements because these conflicts do not threaten the very existence (or livelihood) of the incumbent elite.[24] This theory predicts that territorial wars will be more likely to reach negotiated settlement than nonterritorial conflicts.

MEDIATION

Finally, many scholars and practitioners champion the ability of a mediator to surmount difficult bargaining problems and help combatants reach an agreement.[25] Mediators serve at least three important roles.

---

[21] Paul Pillar, *Negotiating Peace: War Termination as a Bargaining Process* (Princeton: Princeton University Press, 1983), 24. For similar arguments see Ikle, *Every War Must End*, 95; Modelski, "International Settlement"; and Wagner, "The Causes of Peace."

[22] Zartman, "The Unfinished Agenda," 25–26.

[23] See Stephen John Stedman, "Negotiation and Mediation in Internal Conflict," in *The International Dimensions of Internal Conflict*, ed. Michael E. Brown (Cambridge: MIT Press, 1996); and Charles King, "Devolution of Power and Negotiated Settlements in Civil Wars," paper presented at the Second Annual Convention of the Association for the Study of Nationalities, New York, April 1997.

[24] See especially, Stephen Stedman, "Spoiler Problems in Peace Processes," *International Security* 22, no. 2 (1997): 5–53.

[25] See Jacob Bercovitch and Jeffrey Z. Rubin, eds., *Mediation in International Relations: Multiple Approaches to Conflict Management* (New York: St. Martin's Press, 1992);

The first is informational. Mediators can supply missing information, transmit messages, highlight common interests, and encourage meaningful communication so that combatants can better locate a common middle ground. They can also play an important procedural role. Mediators can arrange for interactions between the parties, control the pace and formality of the meetings, and structure the agenda in order to keep the process focused on the issues. The third role is in some ways more coercive. Mediators can reward concessions made by the parties and punish intransigence in order to make disagreement costly.[26] Each of these functions is likely to help the combatants to break through bargaining impasses and locate terms agreeable to both parties. "The ability of the would-be mediator," Stephen Stedman argues, "is an independent variable that affects the success or failure of negotiation."[27] Given this theory, one expects the success of civil war negotiations to vary directly with the presence or absence of an outside mediator.

The preceding discussion reveals a range of alternative explanations for why some civil wars end peacefully while others do not. Table 1.1 lists these competing hypotheses.

What Is Missing

Current theories of the resolution of civil wars tell us much about the conditions likely to bring combatants to the negotiating table and about the conditions then likely to encourage them to reach and sign compromise bargains. The theories do not explain, however, why even signed bargains fail to bring peace, and thus do not provide a comprehensive explanation for why some negotiations end in peace while others do not. As figure 1.2 showed, a signed peace settlement does not guarantee

---

Jacob Bercovitch, *Social Conflicts and Third Parties: Strategies of Conflict Resolution* (Boulder: Westview Press, 1984); Francis, *Mediating Deadly Conflict*; C. R. Mitchell and K. Webb, eds., *New Approaches to International Mediation* (Westport, Conn.: Greenwood Press, 1988); Cyrus Vance, *Hard Choices: Critical Years in America's Foreign Policy* (New York: Simon and Schuster, 1983); David Owen, *Balkan Odyssey* (New York: Harcourt, Brace, 1995); and Chester A. Crocker, *High Noon in Southern Africa: Making Peace in a Rough Neighborhood* (New York: W. W. Norton, 1992).

[26] This typology was developed by Saadia Touval and I. William Zartman, eds., *International Mediation in Theory and Practice* (Boulder: Westview Press, 1985). For a good overview see Jacob Bercovitch, "Mediation in International Conflict: An Overview of Theory, a Review of Practice," in *Peacemaking in International Conflict: Methods and Techniques*, ed. I. William Zartman and J. Lewis Rasmussen (Washington, D.C.: U.S. Institute of Peace, 1997).

[27] Stedman, *Peacemaking in Civil War*, 23.

TABLE 1.1
The Competing Hypotheses

Theory	Associated Hypothesis	
Costs of war	Hypothesis 1	The more costly a war, the more likely combatants are to negotiate a settlement.
Balance of power	Hypothesis 2	The more equally matched combatants are on the battlefield, the more likely they are to end their war in a negotiated settlement.
Domestic political institutions	Hypothesis 3	The more democratic a state, the more likely its government is to negotiate a settlement.
Ethnic identity	Hypothesis 4	Combatants fighting over issues tied to their identity are less likely to end their war in a negotiated settlement than combatants whose identity is the same.
Divisibility of stakes	Hypothesis 5	The more divisible the stakes over which the combatants are fighting, the more likely the war is to end in a negotiated settlement.
Mediation	Hypothesis 6	The success of civil war negotiations varies directly with the presence or absence of an outside mediator.

that a civil war will end. Almost half of all combatants who signed comprehensive peace agreements during the period from 1940 to 1992 chose to return to war rather than implement the terms of the agreement. To understand why some civil wars end by negotiated settlement and others do not, we must understand how the parties' expectations about compliance with the terms of the agreement affect decisions to negotiate or fight at each step on the road to peace.

Research Methods

Two different methodologies, quantitative analysis and comparative case studies, are used in this study. Statistical analysis allows comparison of many cases at once and uncovers patterns that would not be revealed by examination of a small number of cases. It also ensures that the conclusions drawn are pertinent to a wide range of cases, not just one or two that caught the researcher's eye.

Statistical analysis, however, has its limitations. First, it is not particularly helpful in building causal theories of civil wars' resolution. The ideas in this book originated from reading detailed historical accounts of particular conflicts, not from regression analysis. Second, although patterns do emerge, important cultural and historical differences cause individuals, governments, and rebel factions to act in ways not predicted by the theory. A contextual comparison of individual cases ensures that the generalizations made here are not too sweeping and should help to reveal the limitations of the theory.[28] Finally, statistical analysis cannot confirm or disconfirm the causal mechanisms purported to link third-party intervention and power-sharing guarantees to the peaceful resolution of civil wars. It can only reveal the correlation, if any, between each of these variables and peace. A careful study of individual cases, therefore, is needed to build, refine, and test the theory.

How the Book Is Organized

The next seven chapters examine the conditions under which combatants choose to end their civil war through a negotiated settlement rather than a military victory. Chapter 2 develops the credible commitment theory highlighted above. This theory suggests that incentives to cheat on the agreement discourage combatants from cooperating and convince them to continue a war even if they would prefer to settle. The chapter presents three simple game-theoretic models to show that fears of post-treaty exploitation pervade the peace process and factor into decisions to cooperate or fight at each step along the way.[29]

Chapter 3 introduces the data set used to test the theories summarized above and explains how each of the variables specified in previous chapters is measured. This chapter may be of particular interest to scholars seeking a data set with which to test theories of civil war, intervention, and war termination.

Chapter 4 tests the competing hypotheses against all civil wars that began between 1940 and 1992. The results show that two factors have

---

[28] For an excellent discussion on the strengths of qualitative analysis see Colin Elman and Miriam Fendius Elman, "Diplomatic History and International Relations Theory: Respecting Difference and Crossing Boundaries," *International Security* 22, no. 1 (1997): 5–21.

[29] Readers not versed in this approach should have no difficulty following the text. All math is confined to the appendix.

a significant effect on combatants' decision to sign and implement negotiated settlements. Negotiations are unlikely to succeed unless an outside power is willing to guarantee the security of the combatants during
demobilization, and unless specific political, military, or territorial guarantees are written into the terms of the treaty. The results, however, also
reveal that other factors play important roles prior to the implementation of a peace treaty. The costs of war (measured as a function of battle
deaths and duration) and rebels' goals matter a great deal in bringing
combatants to the table, and territorial goals, a military stalemate, and
mediation are instrumental in reaching a bargain. In the end, however,
the two most important factors in convincing combatants to both sign
and implement peace settlements are third-party security guarantees and
power-sharing pacts. Only then do we get peace.

The links among third-party security guarantees, power-sharing
pacts, and successful settlement, however, could be spurious. This possibility is the subject of chapter 5. Here I am particularly interested in
answering three questions. First, are third-party intervention and
power-sharing guarantees necessary to obtain negotiated peace, or can
one be substituted for the other? Second, does the strength of an outside
guarantee—for example, the identity of the guarantor or the size of the
peacekeeping force—or the extent of power-sharing guarantees affect
the outcome of civil wars? Third, do third-party and power-sharing
guarantees have a direct causal effect on the outcome of civil wars, or
are they offered only in cases in which the parties would have ended the
war on their own? I find that third-party guarantees and power-sharing
pacts are both highly correlated with settlement, and that the strength
of outside security guarantees and the strength of power-sharing pacts
tend to be inversely related to each other. Some evidence indicates that
combatants are more willing to extend treaty pacts in long civil wars
and those in which a third party steps in to guarantee demobilization.
There is also some evidence that third-party security guarantees tend to
be connected to the offer of power-sharing pacts. Overall, however,
there are surprisingly few significant correlations between post-treaty
guarantees and other factors that may be related to peace.

Chapters 6 and 7 supplement these tests with in-depth case studies of
negotiations to end the civil wars in Zimbabwe and Rwanda. Here,
day-to-day negotiations are scrutinized to see if fears over post-treaty
security really do drive decisions to sign and implement peace treaties, if
combatants seek third-party security guarantees to allay these fears, and
if compliance with the terms of the agreement coincides with the arrival
of outside observers or peacekeepers. Case analysis confirms the strong
connection between third-party security guarantees, power-sharing
pacts, and the peaceful settlement of civil war.

Chapter 8 reviews the theory and the findings presented in the book. It ends by outlining the implications this study may have for scholars interested in questions of conflict and cooperation, especially under conditions of high risk, and for policymakers pursuing the more pressing question of how to resolve persistent and recurring civil wars.

2. Theory and Hypotheses

THE LITERATURE ON CIVIL WARS has generally assumed that negotiations fail because a conflict is not ripe for resolution or because
the combatants cannot agree on the terms for peace. It does not consider that combatants may look down the road and realize that any
terms they do accept may be unenforceable and therefore undesirable.
This chapter builds a theory of civil war settlement that focuses on the
problems combatants face enforcing and credibly committing to the
terms of a peace agreement. I argue that two specific factors—third-
party guarantees to protect combatants as they demobilize and power-
sharing guarantees in the first postwar government—ultimately determine whether groups will sign and implement settlements.

The first part of this chapter lays out a theory of the resolution of
civil wars and explains why third-party security guarantees and power-
sharing pacts are critical to the successful implementation of peace settlements. The second part develops three simple game-theoretic models
of the resolution process that illustrate more precisely how fears of
post-treaty exploitation influence combatants' decisions to cooperate or
fight at each stage in the peace process. These models help generate
specific hypotheses about the conditions under which combatants will
choose to sign and implement peace treaties. These hypotheses will then
be tested in chapters 4 through 8.

Implementation and Its Hazards

To understand why some civil wars end in successfully implemented
settlements and others do not, cooperation must be viewed as a three-
phase process: a negotiation phase during which combatants choose
whether to initiate peace talks, a bargaining phase during which they
choose whether to reach and sign a peace settlement, and an implementation phase during which they choose whether to execute the agreed-
upon terms.[1] In what follows, I argue that the implementation phase of

[1] I am not the first person to distinguish between different phases of cooperation. See
especially James D. Fearon, "Bargaining, Enforcement, and International Cooperation,"
International Organization 52, no. 2 (1998): 269–305; David A. Lake, *Entangling Relations: American Foreign Policy in Its Century* (Princeton: Princeton University Press,
1999); and Fen Osler Hampson, *Nurturing Peace: Why Peace Settlements Succeed or Fail*
(Washington, D.C.: U.S. Institute of Peace Press, 1996).

a peace settlement, often ignored by scholars, is the most difficult to navigate and the reason why so many civil war negotiations have failed.

The chapter begins by highlighting the unique and unavoidable process of military and political integration that combatants face if they wish to end their war in a compromise settlement. It then discusses the period of intense vulnerability this process creates—a time when the government and the rebels become increasingly less able to protect themselves from attack and enforce any additional treaty terms. It shows that the prospect of post-treaty exploitation factors into their decision to negotiate or fight throughout the peace process, and that a specific type of third-party intervention and specific types of institutional guarantees can enhance credibility and convince combatants to sign and implement settlements.

The Critical Barrier to Civil War Settlement

Implementing the terms of a compromise agreement can be difficult, but implementation is likely to be *the* critical barrier to successful cooperation whenever an agreement creates potentially devastating opportunities for post-treaty exploitation. If defendants negotiating a plea bargain or labor unions negotiating new contracts believe they could be made worse off implementing the terms of a new agreement, they will walk away from it even if they would prefer reconciliation to continued strife. In fact, the more damage each of the parties believes it could suffer as a result of a cheating opponent, the less willing each will be to sign and implement a treaty.

The structural requirements of settling civil wars create an implementation period that is both dangerous and difficult to enforce. Two requirements in particular are likely to make combatants anxious. Over the short term, the government and rebels will be obligated to demobilize, disengage, and disarm their separate militaries in order to eliminate competing armies and rebuild a national military force.[2] This process can take many forms. Mozambique's Rome accord of 1992, Cambodia's Paris peace accord of 1991, and Laos's agreement in Geneva in 1962 called for government and rebel armies to demobilize equally in order to integrate the same number of soldiers into a new national army. Somalia's Addis Ababa agreement of 1993 called for the simultaneous disarmament (but not integration) of rival factions so that a new national army could be recruited from young Somalis. In El Salvador

---

[2] Civil war adversaries could choose to partition their country into two or more independent states and thus circumvent this problem of military consolidation. As I discuss later, however, governments rarely agree to negotiate a separation of territory, leaving power sharing as the only negotiable alternative.

and Guatemala, the rebel forces were required to disband in exchange for extensive military reforms from the government.

Over the longer term, combatants will be required to hand over conquered territory to a new central government, a government they may not control. Thus, at the same time competing factions are breaking apart their separate armies and giving up territory, they are simultaneously concentrating political, military, and territorial power back toward the central government and into the hands of whoever controls the first postwar administration.

This dual process creates two opportunities for exploitation, and this is the reason so many civil wars fail to end with successful settlements. As groups send their soldiers home, hand in their weapons, and surrender occupied territory, they become increasingly vulnerable to a surprise attack.[3] And once they surrender arms and cede control of territory, their rival can more easily seize control of the state and permanently exclude them from power. Settlements of civil wars, therefore, have the unintended and unfortunate effect of forcing factions through a highly risky implementation period that may leave them significantly worse off than they would have been had they kept their armies and continued to fight.

How Does Vulnerability Affect Cooperation?

The fact that a settlement can leave groups in far worse circumstances than they would have been had they continued to fight has two potentially devastating effects on cooperation. First, combatants who wish to end their war in a negotiated settlement will look down the road, anticipate the opportunities for abuse after a treaty is signed, and shy away from seeking peace unless they are certain their opponent will comply with the terms of an agreement. Second, combatants who attempt to implement a peace agreement on their own are likely to become so sensitive to violations of the treaty that they eventually force themselves back to war.

The fact that implementation is potentially hazardous, however, does not mean that negotiations should automatically fail. If it is true that treaties create dangerous periods of implementation, it is also true that these dangers are clear to everyone involved. Hazards that are so clearly predictable should also be manageable through better, more enforceable treaties.

[3] For a more detailed discussion of the potential hazards that may arise with demobilization see Paul Collier, "Demobilization and Insecurity: A Study in the Economics of the Transition from War to Peace," *Journal of International Development* 6, no. 3 (1994): 343–51.

In what follows, I go beyond the observation that the implementation of civil war peace treaties is uncertain and treacherous to reveal why combatants are unable to circumvent these dangers without third-party assistance. Combatants can design better, more enforceable treaties to end civil wars, but they require the participation of an outside state or international organization willing to verify or enforce implementation, something outsiders are often loath to do.

Cooperation Strategies and the Resolution of Civil Wars

In theory, combatants should be able to apply at least three strategies of cooperation to the problem of demobilization. They should be able to (1) restructure demobilization in a way that makes it self-enforcing, (2) increase transparency so that cheating can be detected and punished, and (3) design costly signals that communicate their honorable intentions in order to build an atmosphere of trust.[4] What we will see, however, is that none of these strategies fully eliminates the possibility of being double-crossed and as long as cheating can cause enormous suffering, as it can in the wake of a civil war, even the most extensive measures are insufficient to produce a stable peace.[5]

RECIPROCAL DEMOBILIZATION PLANS

In his seminal book *The Evolution of Cooperation* Robert Axelrod demonstrated that given certain discount rates, individuals faced with short-term incentives to cheat consistently chose to cooperate if implementation was set up in a reciprocal, or tit-for-tat, way.[6] This strategy should apply equally well to settlements of civil wars. If demobilization

[4] A large body of literature attempts to show that cooperation can be encouraged even when no central authority exists to enforce the terms of settlement and even when there are short-term incentives to cheat. See especially Michael Taylor, *Anarchy and Cooperation* (New York: John Wiley and Sons, 1976); Robert Axelrod, *The Evolution of Cooperation* (New York: Basic Books, 1984); Robert O. Keohane, *After Hegemony: Cooperation and Discord in the World Political Economy* (Princeton: Princeton University Press, 1984); Kenneth Oye, ed., *Cooperation under Anarchy* (Princeton: Princeton University Press, 1986), and David A. Baldwin, ed., *Neorealism and Neoliberalism: The Contemporary Debate* (New York: Columbia University Press, 1993).

[5] Barry Weingast offers an excellent analysis of the problem of extreme vulnerability in "Constructing Trust: The Political and Economic Roots of Ethnic and Regional Conflict," Hoover Institution, 1994.

[6] For discussions on how an iterated prisoner's dilemma can make it rational to cooperate see Thomas Schelling, *The Strategy of Conflict* (Cambridge: Harvard University Press, 1960), 43–46; Russell Hardin, *Collective Action* (Baltimore: Johns Hopkins University Press, 1982), 145; Charles Lipson, "International Cooperation in Economic and Security Affairs," *World Politics* 37, no. 1 (1984): 1–23; and Duncan Snidal, "The Game Theory of International Politics," in Oye, *Cooperation under Anarchy*.

could be broken down into a series of small, incremental steps, governments and rebels could observe the degree to which their rival was disbanding its army and meet it soldier for soldier, gun for gun.[7] This
would allow both sides to safely weather the military transition and
reap the long-term rewards of peace. Governments and rebels, for example, could choose to demobilize at the same time, at the same rate, so
that neither side could obtain a debilitating one-step advantage. Rebels
could allow the government to incrementally extend its administration
over rebel territory in exchange for a series of political, military, or
agrarian reforms. Sequencing the transition in this way should decrease
both the costs and benefits of cheating and make cooperation more
likely.

MONITORING AND VERIFICATION

The literature on arms control and denuclearization suggests a second
possible strategy for cooperation.[8] If the government and rebels could
faithfully monitor and verify demobilization, they would increase the
likelihood that cheating would be detected and help induce compliance.
Combatants could locate observers throughout the country, set up random inspection visits, or place surveillance cameras at arms depots,
enemy bases, and assembly camps to track the movement of soldiers
and arms. A transparent process of military disengagement would make
it difficult to stockpile weapons and soldiers, warn of a possible attack,
and make combatants more confident that peace would prevail.

[7] This is similar to the notion of stability discussed in the deterrence literature. Deterrence holds when both sides understand that any attempt to escalate will be matched by
the other side. In this case, every move to demobilize is matched by an equal increment to
demobilize, every refusal to demobilize met with equal intransigence. See especially
Thomas C. Schelling, *Arms and Influence* (New Haven: Yale University Press, 1966),
chaps. 2–6; Robert Powell, "The Theoretical Foundations of Strategic Nuclear Deterrence," *Political Science Quarterly* 100, no. 1 (1985): 75–96; and Charles L. Glaser,
Analyzing Strategic Nuclear Policy (Princeton: Princeton University Press, 1990).

[8] See Steven J. Brams and Marc D. Kilgour, "Notes on Arms Control Verification: A
Game Theoretic Analysis," in *Modeling and Analysis in Arms Control*, ed. Rudolf
Avenhaus, Reiner K. Huber, and John D. Kettelle (Berlin: Springer-Verlag, 1986), 409–19;
Brams, Morton D. Davis, and Kilgour, "Optimal Cheating and Inspection Strategies under
INF," in *Defense Decision Making: Analytical Support and Crisis Management*, ed. Ru-
dolf Avenhaus, Hassame Karker, and Michele Rudnianski (Berlin: Springer-Verlag, 1991),
318–35; Kilgour and Brams, "Putting the Other Side 'On Notice' Can Induce Compliance
in Arms Control," *Journal of Conflict Resolution* 36, no. 3 (1992): 395–414; Donald
Wittman, "Arms Control Verification and Other Games Involving Imperfect Detection,"
American Political Science Review 83 (1989): 923–45; Jianzhong Wu and Robert
Axelrod, "How to Cope with Noise in the Iterated Prisoner's Dilemma," *Journal of Conflict Resolution* 39, no. 1 (1995): 183–89.

COSTLY SIGNALS

A growing literature also argues that combatants should be able to induce compliance through the use of credible and costly signals of intent.[9] Governments and rebels who desire the long-run benefits of settlements but have short-term incentives to cheat can tie their hands in ways that demonstrate their true desire for peace. The government, for example, could offer to demobilize first without requiring the rebels to do the same. It could bomb railway lines that deliver oil and other war supplies, or locate rebel assembly camps in areas surrounded by land mines, making these camps difficult to storm. The rebels in turn could allow the government to block important retreat routes to neighboring countries, or garrison government forces on rebel territory in order to hold home bases hostage. Both sides could place huge sums of money in trust in a version of a bail bond. Each of these actions should help to build an atmosphere of confidence and prevent an unwanted return to war.

In practice, however, none of these strategies is likely to work in the high-risk, high-uncertainty environment that exists immediately after a settlement is signed. Three problems in particular are likely to discourage combatants from relying too heavily on any one of these strategies. First, a tit-for-tat demobilization plan only works if combatants can reliably identify noncompliance and then consistently sanction behavior.[10] Combatants in a civil war, however, can do neither. The immediate aftermath of a civil war is filled with "noise"—bad information, conflicting signals, and inadvertent mistakes—that make it difficult to determine whether a violation has occurred and, if it has, whether it

---

[9] The literature on signaling has a long history. Some prominent examples are Robert Jervis, *The Logic of Images in International Relations* (Princeton: Princeton University Press, 1970); Robert Jervis, "Cooperation under the Security Dilemma," *World Politics* 30 (January 1978): 167–214; David M. Kreps, Paul Milgrom, John Roberts, and Robert Wilson, "Rational Cooperation in the Finitely Repeated Prisoners' Dilemma," *Journal of Economic Theory* 27, no. 2 (1982): 245–52; Kreps and Wilson, "Reputation and Imperfect Information," *Journal of Economic Theory* 27, no. 2 (1982): 253–79; Oliver E. Williamson, "Credible Commitments: Using Hostages to Support Exchange," *American Economic Review* (September 1983): 519–40; John Gerard Ruggie, "International Regimes, Transactions, and Change: Embedded Liberalism in the Postwar Economic Order," in *International Regimes*, ed. Stephen D. Krasner (Ithaca, N.Y.: Cornell University Press, 1983); Fearon, "Domestic Political Audiences"; and Andy Kydd, "Game Theory and the Spiral Model," *World Politics* 49, no. 3 (1997): 371–400.

[10] See Robert Axelrod and Robert O. Keohane, "Achieving Cooperation under Anarchy: Strategies and Institutions," in Oye, *Cooperation under Anarchy*, 249. See also Catherine C. Langlois and Jean-Pierre Langlois, "Engineering Cooperation: A Game Theoretic Analysis of Phased International Agreements," Georgetown University, September 1998, 2.

was intentional.[11] Even if reliable information could be gathered, combatants would become less able to retaliate against cheating as implementation progressed. In civil wars, demobilization can be postponed, it can be implemented gradually or in a reciprocal way, but it cannot be avoided. And as long as a known threshold exists beyond which sanctioning and defense is impossible, even carefully constructed tit-for-tat plans are likely to unravel.[12]

Second, combatants will also find it difficult to sustain demobilization using their own monitoring and verification schemes. A combatant is unlikely to have the money, manpower, or technology to track all the armaments its enemy may want to hide. "They can take my weapons today, and I'll get more tomorrow," said a Croatian police chief during inspections in 1997, "then I'll hide them, it's no trouble."[13] Combatants, therefore, have great difficulty collecting the high-quality information they themselves would demand in exchange for their own obedience. Charles Lipson has noted that "the greater the perils of betrayal, the more severe the demands on gathering information."[14] Even if combatants had the ability to station observers throughout enemy territory to monitor behavior, they would do so at substantial risk to themselves. Exchanging observers and soldiers to monitor each other's behavior would only exacerbate the fear both sides had of a surprise attack and defeat the purpose of observation.

Finally, costly signaling is relevant only when groups are uncertain about an opponent's readiness to cheat on an agreement. In civil wars, it is highly unlikely that either side would choose *not* to cheat if given the chance. Since everyone's first preference is likely to be unilateral victory (and this preference is common knowledge), any attempt to signal otherwise will be disbelieved.

In short, traditional strategies that are designed to encourage cooper-

[11] A number of articles have attempted to show that cooperation can be sustained in a noisy environment if the combatants are willing to play a generous version of tit-for-tat. See especially Wu and Axelrod, "How to Cope," 183–89; J. Bendor, R. M. Kramer, and S. Stout, "When in Doubt: Cooperation in a Noisy Prisoner's Dilemma," *Journal of Conflict Resolution* 35, no. 4 (1991): 691–719; and George W. Downs and David M. Rocke, *Optimal Imperfection? Domestic Uncertainty and Institutions in International Relations* (Princeton: Princeton University Press, 1995).

[12] The fact that combatants face an implementation process with a clear last move is quite unusual and makes tit-for-tat strategies particularly ill suited for resolving civil wars. Kenneth Oye has observed that "although any series of transactions will terminate sooner or later, governments do not generally know when the last play will occur" (*Cooperation under Anarchy*, 13 n. 25).

[13] Mike O'Connor, "Bosnia's Military Threat: Rival Police," *New York Times*, January 12, 1997, A6.

[14] Lipson, "International Cooperation."

ation in other prisoner's dilemma situations do not transfer well to the high-risk conditions that exist in the wake of a civil war. Under less extreme conditions—when players can obtain reliable information about each other's actions and survive a breakdown of the agreement— these strategies may encourage groups to sign and implement coopera- tive agreements. They will not, however, encourage incumbent govern- ments and rebels to put down their guns in situations that could lead to their own defeat. Because cheating in the wake of a civil war can cause enormous suffering, even these measures will not convince groups to proceed with settlement.

Creating Credible Commitments

In what follows, I argue that combatants in civil wars will sign and implement a peace settlement only if they are confident that their mili- tary forces will be safely consolidated and that power will be shared once they relinquish their own political and military assets. Combatants are, therefore, likely to seek two types of guarantees before they sign and implement any peace settlement. The first and most critical is a third-party security guarantee to protect against a surprise attack during demobilization. The second is a strict distribution of political, military, and territorial power in the first postwar government.

THIRD-PARTY SECURITY GUARANTEES

Civil war combatants are most concerned about weathering the short, but treacherous, period of military disengagement and are likely to actively seek outside assistance to ensure compliance during this time. Unlike the combatants themselves, third parties can guarantee that groups will be protected, violations detected, and promises kept (or at least they can ensure that groups will survive until a new government and a new national military is formed).

Two types of assistance are likely to be sought depending on the level of danger combatants believe they will face. The first, third-party veri- fication, suffices when a fairly equal balance of power exists between the combatants. In this case, an outside state, international organiza- tion, or multilateral coalition of states can verify compliance and thus provide the prompt, reliable information necessary for combatants to pursue their own tit-for-tat strategy. Outside states are more likely to have sophisticated technology such as satellites and airplanes to moni- tor the agreement, can more easily distribute observers throughout the country without threatening either party, and are more likely to obtain access to sensitive military sites in order to observe behavior. The information collected under these circumstances is likely to be far more dependable than that which the combatants can collect themselves, and therefore is more likely to elicit the desired behavior.

Third-party verification, however, is unlikely to reassure combatants of their future safety when large imbalances of power exist. Where one side is militarily stronger than the other (as was the case between the Serbs and the Muslim-Croat federation in Bosnia), or where one side must demobilize to a greater extent (as was the case in Nicaragua in 1990), a stronger type of intervention is usually needed. In these situations, combatants are likely to seek the protection of an outside mission capable of using force. The ability to meet an attack with countervailing force can reassure the weaker side that it will not be crushed, and deter the stronger side from exploiting its advantages. Another third-party strategy, therefore, is to actively enforce peace during demobilization. The third party can, for example, station soldiers in areas of greatest vulnerability (cantonment camps, capital cities, rebel territory) to ensure that any short-term vulnerabilities created by military disengagement are not exploited. This reduces the chance that either side can launch a surprise attack and makes compliance more attractive.

Not all third-party security guarantees, however, are equally effective. Since combatants have time to observe whether a promised verification or enforcement mission materializes before they demobilize, a security guarantee is effective only if the third party arrives on the ground with the promised mandate. If combatants do not believe outsiders will faithfully verify or enforce compliance, or they see outsiders failing to commit sufficient resources to the task at hand, promises to monitor and protect will have no positive effect and combatants will refuse to abide by their agreements. In short, the implementation of any peace agreement depends not only on the willingness of outsiders to serve important verification or enforcement functions, but also on the confidence the opponents have in the commitment of these outsiders. The more committed and capable a third party appears to be and the better able to communicate this commitment, the more likely it is to convince groups to demobilize.

POWER-SHARING PACTS

Solving the short-term problem of demobilization, however, does not solve the long-term problem of political participation. Combatants will still walk away from the negotiating table if they believe a settlement could leave them permanently excluded from political power and expose them to continued abuse in the future. The success of negotiations, therefore, also depends on the degree to which combatants believe the entrenched elite will open up the political process even after rivals have demobilized.

Designing credible commitments at this second stage of implementation should be easier since the cost of exploitation—political exclusion—is less than the costs of military attack. Combatants, therefore, should be able to design a self-enforcing political transition without the assistance of an outside enforcer. But how do former enemies do this? Most of the literature on postconflict political transitions focuses on democratic elections as the primary mechanism by which new leaders can be selected and power redistributed.[15] Elections can open the political process to opposition groups and be the first step in the peaceful reconstruction of a new legitimate government. Although considerable debate still exists, most scholars have focused on the types of institutions that are likely to foster harmony. The deeply divided societies that experience civil wars, many argue, are more stable if power is decentralized in a federal structure,[16] dispersed in a parliamentary, not a presidential system,[17] and divided in proportion to votes received rather than winner-take-all.[18] Checks and balances should also be instituted to bind the governing party once elected.[19] The argument assumes that opposing parties should be more willing to submit to elections and then honor the results if they have a fair chance to compete in elections and if institutions exist to enforce the peaceful transfer of power thereafter.

As I will argue below, however, solutions that offer combatants only the chance to compete in elections will not convince them to sign and implement peace agreements even if backed by the appropriate institu-

[15] For a cross-section of these debates, see Larry Diamond and Marc F. Plattner, *The Global Resurgence of Democracy* (Baltimore: Johns Hopkins University Press, 1993).

[16] An extensive literature supports this view. See James Madison, "Federalist No. 10," *The Federalist Papers* (New York: Penguin, 1961); Arend Lijphart, *Democracy in Plural Societies* (New Haven: Yale University Press, 1977); Horowitz, *Ethnic Groups in Conflict*; David Lake and Donald Rothchild, "Containing Fear: The Origins and Management of Ethnic Conflict," *International Security* 21, no. 2 (1996): 41–75; and Alicia Levine, "Political Accommodation and the Prevention of Secessionist Violence," in *The International Dimensions of Internal Conflict*, ed. Michael E. Brown (Cambridge: MIT Press, 1996), 311–40.

[17] See especially Juan Linz, "The Perils of Presidentialism" and "The Virtues of Parliamentarism," in Diamond and Plattner, *Global Resurgence of Democracy*; and Sisk, *Power Sharing and International Mediation in Ethnic Conflict* (Washington D.C.: U.S. Institute of Peace, 1996), 53–54. For a dissenting view, see Donald Horowitz, "Comparing Democratic Systems," in Diamond and Plattner, *Global Resurgence of Democracy*.

[18] For criticisms of majoritarianism, see Sisk, *Power Sharing*, ix; Lijphart, *Democracy in Plural Societies*, 25–28, 114–18; Horowitz, *Ethnic Groups in Conflict*, 629–30; and Levine, "Political Accommodation," 333–34.

[19] See Robert Dahl, *Polyarchy: Participation and Opposition* (New Haven: Yale University Press, 1971), 115.

tions. First, fighting factions know that new democratic institutions will still be too weak in the immediate aftermath of a civil war to prevent a rapid grab for power and thus enforce what the demobilized opposition itself can no longer enforce itself.[20] Most of the countries included in this study (listed in appendix 1) had no history of multiparty rule prior to the outbreak of hostilities. Instead, these countries were expected to move immediately to more open and competitive systems in which the government would willingly share power and follow guidelines negotiated during the war. Once competing armies were dispersed, however, this new government could easily ignore promises to open the political system and instead create institutions that served only its narrow interests.

Second, even if truly democratic institutions are established and free and fair elections held, domestic groups understand that these institutions are not likely to be effective overnight. As Larry Diamond has observed, "Over time, citizens of a democracy become habituated to its norms and values, gradually internalizing them. The trick is for democracies to survive long enough—and function well enough—for this process to occur."[21] Opponents in a civil war, however, do not have this luxury because the first postwar administration is likely to act quickly to fortify its advantage and secure long-term monopoly control.

Third, post–civil war societies rarely enjoy a civic culture strong enough to bolster fragile institutions and serve as a secondary control on misconduct. In fact, war-weary populations are likely to prefer order and economic advancement to continued war even if they come at the price of a one-party state. In many cases residents simply want peace. "Look at Rwanda, Burundi, Zaire," said a young business manager in Burkina Faso. "If that's power-sharing, I'm not for it."[22] Faction leaders therefore cannot count on the general population to rise up and fight efforts by a single party to set up dictatorial control.[23]

In short, if factions who have recently fought a civil war fear perma-

---

[20] For discussions regarding weakness in the institutional environment see Douglass C. North and Barry R. Weingast, "Constitutions and Commitment: The Evolution of Institutions Governing Public Choice in Seventeenth-Century England," *Journal of Economic History* 49, no. 4 (1989): 803–32; and Barry R. Weingast, "The Economic Role of Political Institutions: Market-Preserving Federalism and Economic Development," *Journal of Law, Economics, and Organization* 11, no. 1 (1995): 1–31.

[21] Larry Diamond, "Three Paradoxes of Democracy," in Diamond and Plattner, *Global Resurgence of Democracy*, 104.

[22] Quoted in John Darnton, "Africa Tries Democracy, Finding Hope and Peril," *New York Times*, June 21, 1994, A1.

[23] This of course assumes that the ruling party does not enact oppressive policies. If one-party rule becomes too tyrannical, war might once again become the more attractive alternative.

nent exclusion from power and possible imprisonment, then the simple opportunity to compete in fair elections—whether based on majoritarian or proportional principles or held in presidential or parliamentary systems—will not be enough to convince combatants to give up their military option. Neither system promises strong enough restraints on the first postwar government, and certainly cannot promise that losing the election will be better than continuing the war and gambling for complete victory. Institutions and elections may be effective over the long run, after rules and practices become routine. Or they may have greater success stabilizing a less volatile situation. But if suspending democracy is relatively easy—as it would be immediately after a civil war—then groups need far more convincing guarantees that they will not be permanently excluded from power than the promise that liberal institutions will be established to help prevent this.

Civil war factions, therefore, will likely shy away from peace settlements that distribute power in a purely competitive and therefore ambiguous way, at least in the early years of the new government. Instead, they will look for ways to guarantee themselves independent control over key leadership positions in order to insulate themselves from future harm and to prevent their rival from consolidating power. This protection can take the form of a specific quota of power, a guaranteed distribution of key ministries, or shared control over executive positions, all of which would ensure the competing factions a significant say in how the postwar state is run.[24]

Groups are likely to be particularly concerned with executive power because a politically powerful and popular leader will have relatively few restraints on behavior, especially in the early, often faltering stages of a new government. Groups can choose to establish a single, shared presidency, as the Conservatives and Liberals did in Colombia in 1957. They can create a powerful coalition cabinet comprised of equal numbers of government and opposition leaders, as the Christians and Muslims did in Lebanon in 1958. Or they can decide that if one party wins the presidency, the other party or parties can assign the majority of cabinet positions, as the government and guerrillas did in Sierra Leone in 1999. This way, nervous factions guarantee themselves a role in the most influential positions and ensure that their former rival cannot capture the state.

Militarily, groups can retain some defenses as they demobilize in order to give opposition groups at least some sustained military leverage

---

[24] This is very close to Lijphart's concept of power sharing. See especially Arend Lijphart, "The Power Sharing Approach," in *Conflict and Peacemaking in Multiethnic Societies*, ed. Joseph V. Montville (New York: Lexington, 1991), 494.

over those in power. The new national army and internal security forces could be composed of equal numbers of government and rebel soldiers, making it difficult for one group to dominate the other.[25] Soldiers could be demobilized but not forced to disarm. Competing factions could set up autonomous regions that they police themselves. Or combatants could combine military officers from one faction with enlisted soldiers from another. The Zimbabwean rebels' published statement of its "essential requirements for the transition" from civil war illustrates how important these added guarantees are.

> The Security Forces during the interim period must be an army composed of a combination of the Patriotic Front's and the Regime's armies, and a police force composed of a combination of the Patriotic Front's and the Regime's police forces, operating in both cases alongside a United Nations Peace-keeping Force and a United Nations Civilian Police Force to supervise the cease-fire and ensure peaceful integration. The foregoing structure is essential to ensure that the process towards genuine majority rule and independence will be irreversible.[26]

Allowing competing factions to retain some ability to defend themselves even after their armies have been formally disbanded would offer an important sense of security and serve as insurance against future oppression should the benefits of power sharing not materialize.

Territorially, rival factions are also likely to attempt to retain some administrative control over previously occupied regions in order to preserve a political base should things go badly. Chaim Kaufmann has argued that stable solutions to ethnic civil wars are possible only if the combatants are separated into defensible enclaves.[27] To a degree this is true, since territorial autonomy is likely to further reduce transitional vulnerabilities. The peace agreement in 1970 ending the Yemeni civil war allowed the rebel royalists to continue to administer areas under their control. The 1972 peace agreement in Sudan established southern Sudan as a self-governing region. And in Bosnia, the 1995 Dayton peace accord split the Bosnian state into two separate regions: one controlled by a Muslim-Croat federation and one controlled by the Serbs. In short, the better able the factions are at preventing the full concentration of political, military, and territorial power into the hands of a single administration, the more enforceable and credible promises to share power will be.

---

[25] For an excellent discussion of the importance of an integrated security force, see Sisk, *Power Sharing*, 57.

[26] Goswin Baumhoegger, *The Struggle for Independence: Documents on the Recent Development of Zimbabwe (1975–1980)*, 6:1129.

[27] See Kaufmann, "Possible and Impossible Solutions."

A Model of Civil War Resolution

This section develops three simple game-theoretic models of the settlement process described above. The aim of this section is to see if a more formal approach to theory building validates the logic behind the verbal argument, to specify very clearly the conditions under which successful settlement is possible, and to uncover additional insights into the process of resolving civil wars that could not be obtained using the approach above.

What we will see is that beliefs about demobilization and power sharing have a profound effect on every stage of the peace process, not just on the final implementation stage. Both the government and the rebels are clearly looking down the road and factoring in the presence of third-party security guarantees when they decide to initiate negotiations, sign bargains, and implement settlements. These models, therefore, show that decisions at every stage of the peace process are based on the combatants' expectations about compliance with agreed-upon demobilization and power sharing.[28]

The models differ in the following ways. The first depicts the implementation process in its pure form, as it would occur if the combatants demobilized on their own and if the distribution of power in the first postwar government were determined strictly through competitive elections rather than guaranteed power sharing.[29] This model reveals that combatants will not only refuse to implement an agreement, but will refuse to initiate negotiations if they believe they could be permanently shut out of power in the final play of the game. This model makes clear how important longer-term concerns about political participation are to the entire peace process.

The second model illustrates what would happen if combatants were guaranteed an important role in the first postwar administration but were still forced to demobilize without third-party assistance. The model shows that guaranteed power sharing is not sufficient to bring about peace in the absence of third-party intervention. The government and rebels will still refuse to initiate negotiations or sign a peace treaty if a safe demobilization is not guaranteed, *even if they know significant political power awaits them in the end.* Thus, this model makes clear

[28] See also George W. Downs, David M. Rocke, and Peter N. Barsoom, "Is the Good News about Compliance Good News about Cooperation?" *International Organization* 50, no. 3 (1996): 379–406; Fearon, "Bargaining, Enforcement"; and Brett Ashley Leeds, "Domestic Political Institutions, Credible Commitments, and International Cooperation," *American Journal of Political Science* 43, no. 4 (1999): 979–1002.

[29] These elections can be based on majoritarian or proportional representative principles or on a presidential or parliamentary system.

how important to the entire peace process are short-term concerns about physical safety during demobilization.

The third model adds the possibility of third-party enforcement and verification to the equation. This model confirms two prior intuitions. First, third-party security guarantees are critical to the peaceful resolution of civil wars. Combatants who are certain that an outside power will enforce or verify demobilization and are guaranteed leadership in the first postwar government will voluntarily sign and implement a peace agreement; combatants who lack third-party guarantees will not. Second, a third party's commitment to the peace process matters a great deal. The more combatants believe an outside state or international organization will expose violations or actively protect them as they demobilize, the more likely negotiations are to succeed.

Taken together, these models make it clear that the fear of post-treaty exploitation, during both military and political integration, can convince factions in a civil war to retain their weapons and reject settlements even if both sides would otherwise prefer peace to armed conflict. The models reveal that this fear will dominate decisions even if groups are guaranteed meaningful control of a new government. Most important, they show the crucial role third-party security guarantees and power-sharing pacts play in moving adversaries through all three phases of the process of resolution, to the point where peace is possible.

Model 1: The Basic Model

Each of the models considers the interaction of two players, the rebels (R) and the incumbent government (G), who must choose whether to end their war through a negotiated settlement or continue to fight. In reality, there can be more than two players in a civil war, as there were in the early years of the Angolan civil war, when three nationalist groups struggled to fill the vacuum left by Portugal's hasty departure in 1975. And the war need not be fought between rebels who wish to obtain concessions or power and an incumbent government that wishes to deny them. There are cases such as Somalia in 1982 or Algeria in 1962 where a functioning government did not exist and multiple competing factions vied for control of the state. Rebels who face an entrenched incumbent government may be somewhat more vulnerable to surprise attack or to permanent exclusion from government since their rival already controls the coercive instruments of state. This should not, however, affect how the game is played, as both sides still face the difficult process of demobilization and military and political reintegration.

Each of the models rests on five additional assumptions. The first is

that each faction has a single set of preferences and that leaders negotiating settlements represent these preferences. In truth, rebel and government leaders almost always preside over a disparate group of
members who have a range of different policy preferences; some members want to pursue a compromise settlement and others do not. It is
reasonable to assume, however, that leaders represent majority interests
within their group.[30] A second assumption is that leaders are rational
actors who wish to maximize their group's position relative to their
enemy and, therefore, would prefer complete control of government to
shared control. Third, I assume that both the rebels and the government
know that their rival, with whom they had so recently fought a war,
will act opportunistically if given the chance; they do not think their
rival will be generous or forgo the opportunity to conquer them if given
the chance. Another assumption is that once the government and rebels
initiate negotiations, both sides would prefer peace to continued war
and both sides have voluntarily entered into negotiations. This fourth
assumption allows me to consider negotiations that have the best
chance to succeed and thus isolate factors that may prevent settlement
even under the best conditions. The final assumption is that the combatants do not pay any costs to negotiate. In the real world, both the government and the rebels are likely to pay at least some costs for publicly
meeting their enemy or making concessions on stated goals and principles. Each side may also obtain side benefits from negotiating; for
example, negotiations may allow them to rest and resupply their armies.
These costs and benefits are not included in the model in order to simplify the analysis (and the math) and concentrate on the variables of
interest for the argument.

SEQUENCE OF MOVES

The structure of the game is illustrated in figure 2.1. There are three
parts, an initial negotiation phase during which the government and the
rebels decide whether to begin negotiations, a second bargaining phase
during which the government and the rebels decide whether to resolve
their differences and sign a settlement, and a final implementation phase
during which combatants choose whether to demobilize their armies
and share power. This is the three-stage resolution process described
earlier.

The game begins with a decision by the incumbent government to
initiate negotiations or continue to fight with the hopes of eventually

---

[30] For an analysis of how extremists might affect the pursuit of peace, see Andrew Kydd
and Barbara F. Walter, "Sabotaging the Peace: The Politics of Extremist Violence," *International Organization*, 56, no. 2 (2002).

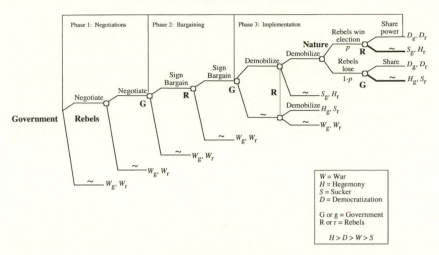

Fig. 2.1. Basic model

winning the war.[31] If the government chooses to negotiate, the rebels then have the option to negotiate or fight in the hopes that they will eventually win. If either side decides not to negotiate, the war continues and both sides receive the payoff for war (W).

If both players choose to initiate negotiations, they must then choose whether to accept compromise terms. Here the rebels and the government sequentially choose to sign or not sign a bargain.[32] Once again, if either side chooses not to sign, the war continues and both sides again receive the payoff W.

If both the government and the rebels choose to accept a bargain, the game enters the implementation phase of the resolution process. Here the rebels and the government simultaneously choose to demobilize their partisan forces or continue the war. Combatants demobilize simultaneously rather than sequentially since it is unlikely that either side would accept the security risks involved with moving first.

War continues (and implementation fails) if both sides refuse to demobilize, and the payoffs for this outcome are again denoted as W for both the rebels and the government. One side, however, can choose to hold its soldiers in reserve while its rival honorably demobilizes. The government, for example, could wait for guerrilla forces to reveal their

[31] In reality, negotiations could be initiated by the rebels, or by both parties simultaneously, either of which would produce the same results.

[32] This phase of the resolution process could also be modeled as a simultaneous choice by the government and the rebels to sign an agreement. I model it sequentially for the sake of simplicity.

positions and then launch a surprise attack. Insurgents could play a game of hide-and-seek by dispatching some soldiers to assembly areas, only to keep significant forces in reserve for a future attack. Under any of these conditions, the vanquished party would receive a far worse outcome than anything it would have received had it refused to negotiate, and the cheater would receive a far better outcome than anything it would have received had it fulfilled its side of the agreement. The payoffs for conquering one's enemy through deceit are labeled H (hegemony), while the payoffs for being conquered are appropriately labeled S (sucker).

If, however, both the rebels and the government choose to demobilize, they then distribute political power. If competitive elections are chosen, the rebels may win the election with probability p of success and $1 - p$ of failure.[33] If the rebels win control over government, they can then choose to transfer power faithfully in the next election as promised during negotiations, or they can choose to renege on this promise and establish a one-party state. Similarly, if the government wins this first election, the government can choose either to democratize or to consolidate its hold over the state. Payoffs for democratization are denoted D for both the government and rebels. A decision to set up a one-party state can be thought of as a nonviolent way of obtaining a decisive victory over an enemy and is once again denoted H for the triumphant party and S for the sucker. Thus, four outcomes are possible in this final phase of the game: the rebels win the election and faithfully democratize (D_r), the rebels win but set up a one-party state (H_r), the government wins the election and faithfully democratize (D_g), or the government wins the election and sets up its own one-party state (H_g).[34]

Given the outcomes listed above, both the rebels' and the government's preferences are straightforward: $H > D > W > S$. The preferred outcome for both the rebels and the government is a surprise military attack on their opponent during the initial stage of demobilization that would result in an easy conquest and hegemony over the state, or a victory in the first election that would allow them to set up authoritarian rule (H). Their second choice is to democratize, since this would give both players either an immediate share of power or the opportunity to compete for power in future elections (D). The players' third choice would be renewed war (W), an option that would give them some chance to ultimately beat their rival and dictate the terms of peace and would also prevent their worst possible outcome. The two worst out-

[33] In this case, "winning the election" means winning control over the executive in a presidential system or winning a ruling majority in a parliamentary system.

[34] This assumes that the loser of the first election has little effective ability to respond to any effort to achieve hegemony since opponents are then fully demobilized.

comes are being the victim of a surprise attack or being permanently excluded from the new government, both of which would deliver the dreaded sucker's payoff (S).

Using the process of backward induction, both the rebels and the government have a dominant strategy to establish a one-party state and permanently lock their rival from power should they win the first election; hegemonic control over the state is always better than democratization ($H > D$). Knowing that the winner of the first election will take full and permanent control of the state, the best choice is for both players to refuse to demobilize, a decision that leads them both back to war. When we look up the tree, we see that the only possible outcome, therefore, is renewed war. Since the final result is the same in all cases—continued war—the players are, in the first two phases of the game, indifferent between negotiating or not, and between signing a bargain or not.

These equilibrium outcomes show that civil war combatants will not implement any peace agreement if the last play of the game can deliver a devastating loss. Combatants who are likely to lose will never agree to participate in elections, and once it is in the loser's best interest to refrain from negotiating, settling, or implementing the terms of an agreement, it is in the interest of all other participants to do the same. Cooperation breaks down as a result. This basic model, therefore, shows why political, military, or territorial guarantees of power are so important in obtaining combatants' support for peace settlements.

Model 2: Guaranteed Power Sharing

But what would happen if the players could structure the game so that both parties were protected against political elimination in the final round of play? Would guaranteed power sharing affect their decision to demobilize?

In this model political power is no longer distributed exclusively through competitive elections, and both the incumbent government and the rebels know they will be guaranteed an important voice in the first postwar government. Here, power sharing (P) automatically results when both sides demobilize. What this model shows is that combatants still choose to return to war if the short-term dangers of demobilization have not been addressed.

The game is played exactly as it was in the previous model, with one important modification: in the end combatants are guaranteed a share of power (P) and need not face the uncertainty of elections. The structure of this game is illustrated in figure 2.2.

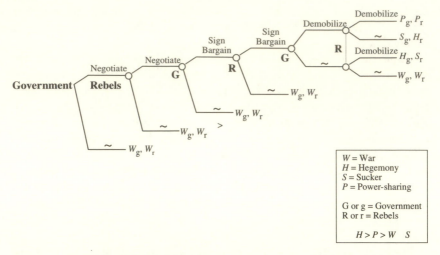

Fig. 2.2. Model with guaranteed power sharing

Groups know from the start that if both camps choose to sign an agreement and faithfully demobilize, power sharing will be their reward. This, one would expect, would propel the peace process forward and greatly encourage combatants to disengage their militaries. But the game reveals a different equilibrium outcome. Even though groups *know* they will obtain political power in the final round, their equilibrium strategy in the first two rounds remains the same: either they will refuse to negotiate or sign an agreement, or both will agree to negotiate and bargain but then refuse to demobilize.[35] Despite a long-term power-sharing pact, combatants will still choose to walk away from a negotiated settlement and return to war.

This model, therefore, depicts the destructive effects of a short-term prisoner's dilemma. Even if both factions know they would benefit more from mutual cooperation than from mutual defection, their best strategy remains to defect early in the peace process. Solving the dilemma of postwar governance, therefore, does not change the incentives combatants face to walk away from a settlement. Since neither side can afford the possibility of becoming a sucker and both sides welcome the chance to obtain hegemony, war remains the optimal strategy.

---

[35] Once again, if combatants incur costs for negotiating and costs for signing a peace agreement, they will prefer to avoid these costs and will choose to continue the war rather than talk. If, however, combatants gain certain dividends from negotiating and compromising with an enemy even if they choose not to implement terms, they will always prefer to do so rather than continue to fight.

Model 3: Adding a Third-Party Security Guarantee

In the first section of this chapter I argued that credible third-party security guarantees are critical to the peaceful resolution of civil wars. This
final model, therefore, considers how third-party verification or enforcement affects the success of negotiations in cases where power sharing is
guaranteed in the end. In this game, both the rebels and the government
choose whether to negotiate their war, to sign a bargain, and then to
demobilize, basing the choice on the likelihood of a third-party guarantor's verification or enforcement of demobilization. If both the rebels
and the government negotiate and sign, a third party either chooses to
enforce or verify demobilization or does not.

If the combatants know that a third party is committed to enforcing
or verifying compliance ($p = 1$), then cheating is costly and difficult
and combatants always choose to demobilize. Combatants can choose
to delay demobilization or attempt to cheat, but the reluctant demobilizer will pay a cost ($P - c$) for having been coerced to do so.[36] Power
sharing (P) always results, regardless of whether the combatants demobilize voluntarily or must be coerced to do so.

If the combatants know that a third party will not enforce or verify
compliance ($p = 0$), four very different outcomes result. Under these
circumstances, if both sides choose not to demobilize, cooperation ends
and combatants return to war (W). If only one of the combatants
chooses to demobilize while their rival holds onto its forces, the cooper-
ative side receives its worst outcome (S), leaving hegemony to its rival
(H). If, however, both the government and the rebels choose to demobilize in the absence of a third party, both sides obtain the mutually desirable outcome of power sharing (P). The structure and the payoffs of this
model are illustrated in figure 2.3[37]

Given the outcomes listed above, the rebels' and the government's
preferences continue to be those of the prisoner's dilemma: $H > P > P
- c > W > S$. Assuming both sides know what type of third party
they face, two equilibrium strategies are possible. If the government and
rebels are certain a third party will actively enforce or verify demobilization once a settlement is signed, both the government and rebels
always voluntarily demobilize, and both obtain power sharing (P). If on
the other hand they know that a third party will not follow through

[36] The cost of refusing to demobilize could range from targeted airstrikes by the third
party, to the resumption of hostilities when a tit-for-tat strategy breaks down.

[37] Although the third party's decision to intervene or not intervene is itself a strategic
decision, I chose not to treat the third party as strategic actor in order to focus on the
more important interactions between the government and rebels, and to resist complicat-
ing the model unnecessarily.

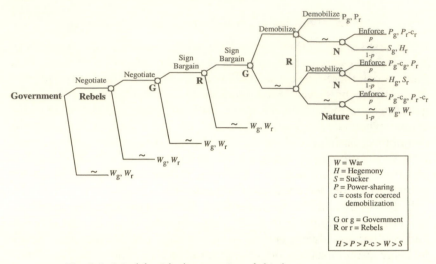

Fig. 2.3. Model with the promise of third-party guarantees

with enforcement or verification, neither side chooses to demobilize, and war (W) results.

Given this assumption, the game is easily solved through backward induction. If both the rebels and government know that the third party will actively coerce compliance or expose cheating, and both sides know they will gain a share of government in the end, the dominant strategy is *always* to demobilize.[38] Settling is a better strategy than continued war, and the equilibrium outcome for both sides is to negotiate, sign a bargain, and then faithfully demobilize. This equilibrium shows quite clearly the strong effect third-party security guarantees have on civil war settlement.

Combatants, however, are often uncertain as to a third party's actual commitment to the peace process. They may know that a third party has expressed interest in enforcing or verifying a settlement, and they can observe whether the third party arrives with the promised mandate, but they do not know how the third party will respond when tested. The model presented above, therefore, fails to include a real-world aspect of third-party intervention in civil wars. Recent history has shown that even powerful countries like the United States or relatively well-financed organizations such as NATO have failed to react when implementation has broken down. Combatants, therefore, must con-

[38] In this case, the government and rebels never find out what type of third party they faced since its commitment is never tested.

sider the possibility that a third party may not live up to its promise once demobilization begins.

To incorporate this element of uncertainty, I make both the government and the rebels unsure whether the intervening party will actually fulfill its role and protect them from a surprise attack. All combatants can do is observe certain indicators about the third party's commitment to the peace process.[39] A contingent of ten thousand soldiers, for example, signals a far greater commitment than a contingent of one thousand soldiers. Similarly, soldiers who are stationed throughout the country are more credible than soldiers confined to barracks within the capital city. The more committed a third party appears, the more likely combatants are to implement the military terms of a settlement and demobilize. Conversely, the less certain they are about a third party's commitment, the more likely they are to cheat.

This version of the game yields a number of comparative statics results based on the critical probability (p) needed to convince combatants to cooperate.[40] First, both players are more likely to negotiate, sign, and demobilize as the costs of punishment increase. In other words, Slobodan Milosevic will more likely disengage his forces from Kosovo if NATO threatens harsh punishments for refusing to do so, even if he is skeptical of NATO's commitment to the peace plan. The stronger the display of force by the third-party guarantor, therefore, the more likely combatants are to sign and implement a peace settlement.

Second, both parties are less likely to negotiate, sign, and demobilize as the benefits they obtain from complete hegemony (H) increase. The closer Milosevic and the Serbs come to a complete victory over the Bosnian Muslims, for example, the more certain they will need to be that a third party will actively enforce or verify demobilization before they will negotiate, sign and implement a settlement.

Third, both parties are more likely to negotiate, sign, and demobilize as the payoffs for power sharing increase. The Kosovo Liberation Army (KLA) will require less faith in NATO's commitment if the KLA's role in postwar governance is enhanced. The more sweeping the power-sharing pacts, the weaker a third party's commitment to the peace process need be for combatants to successfully implement peace settlements.

Fourth, combatants are also more likely to negotiate, sign, and demo-

---

[39] Observable indicators could include the size of the intervening force, its mandate, the degree of support a mission enjoys from its own citizens, the third party's reputation for resolve, its geographic distance from the bereaved state, or the resources earmarked for the mission.

[40] Due to limitations in the data, not all of these relationships were tested in the analysis that follows. Further investigation, therefore, is required to determine if these relationships actually hold.

bilize as the sucker's payoff becomes less extreme. Combatants who are protected against eradication require less certainty regarding a third party's commitment to the peace process before they voluntarily cooperate. Thus, the more the government and the rebels can protect themselves against exploitation, the less faith they need in a third party's commitment before they demobilize. Finally, combatants are also more likely to negotiate, sign, and demobilize as the costs of fighting a war increase.

This model, therefore, indicates ways in which outsiders can induce compliance even if they cannot send an unequivocal signal of resolve. Outsiders who wish to induce demobilization can threaten very explicit and costly punishments to those who consider defecting. The higher the punishment costs, the less willing the government and rebels are to cheat and the more likely they are to demobilize. Outsiders can also encourage combatants to be generous with the terms of settlement; the more generous they are to each other, the more willing they will be to demobilize without the certainty of a fully committed third party. Finally, outsiders can also attempt to reduce the benefits one faction will receive if it captures the state. A promise to withhold international recognition, to eliminate international aid, and to install economic and trade sanctions would reduce the expected benefits of conquest and encourage cooperation even in the face of a less-than-certain commitment from a third party.

One final insight can be drawn from this model. Model 3 suggests that combatants in civil wars have incentives to initiate negotiations and sign bargains even if they are not 100 percent certain a third party will step forward to help them enforce or verify demobilization. Under certain conditions specified above, combatants will attempt to negotiate a settlement in the hope that a third-party guarantor will materialize. If a third party fails to materialize, combatants will walk away from even signed settlements. Model 3, therefore, helps explain why some combatants would participate in lengthy negotiations and sign public treaties, only to return to war.

The three models, therefore, offer three hypotheses for testing in addition to the six presented in chapter 1:

> HYPOTHESIS 7. *Combatants in civil wars are more likely to sign and implement peace settlements that include a power-sharing pact in the first postwar administration than proposed settlements that do not.*
>
> HYPOTHESIS 8. *Combatants are more likely to sign and implement an agreement if they know a third party will enforce or verify demobilization.*

HYPOTHESIS 9. *The more combatants believe an outside state or international organization will expose violations or actively protect them as they demobilize, the more likely negotiations are to succeed.*

Conclusion

This chapter has laid out the logic of the credible commitment theory of civil war resolution. It argued that resolving the underlying issues over which a civil war has been fought is not enough to convince the combatants to accept and implement a peace settlement. To end a civil war through a negotiated settlement, the combatants must clear the much higher hurdle of designing credible guarantees on the terms of the agreement, something they have difficulty doing on their own. Only if a third party is willing to step forward to verify or enforce demobilization, and only if combatants are willing to disaggregate political, military, or territorial power, do promises to honor agreements become credible and negotiations succeed.

PART TWO

Data and Quantitative Analysis

3. Measuring the Variables

THIS CHAPTER EXPLAINS how each of the hypotheses presented in chapters 1 and 2 was operationalized for testing. The aim is to make as transparent as possible the process by which abstract concepts such as identity, divisibility, and guarantee were matched with concrete indicators and subjected to statistical analysis. This transparency will allow other scholars to replicate the research presented here and fill in the holes that invariably remain. Measuring variables is by nature a rough and imperfect procedure; some of the indicators described below come very close to tracking a particular variable; others are inexact approximations. I have identified potential problems with the measures, discussed attempted solutions, and pointed out remaining shortcomings. The primary and secondary sources and web sites used to collect the data are also identified.

The first section explains the data set used to test the hypotheses, how data were collected, the problems encountered, and the steps taken to correct them. In the second section I define the dependent variable—"Peace Process"—and develop ways to measure it. The third section explains how each of the independent variables specified in chapters 1 and 2 was measured for testing.

Case Selection

The competing theories on the resolution of civil wars were tested against every civil war initiated between 1940 and 1992. This fifty-two-year time period included a large enough number of cases to allow for multivariate regression analysis (seventy-two civil wars were fought between 1940 and 1992), yet was short enough to include the full universe of civil wars and not a potentially biased sample of cases. It also included civil wars fought both before and after the Cold War, helping to eliminate any bias that might result by looking only at cases that occurred in the shadow of the larger East-West confrontation.[1]

The list of cases was chosen based on the coding criteria proposed by

---

[1] Ideally, one would want to extend the data set as far back in time as possible; the more civil wars that are included, the less likely is bias in the selection of cases. However, time constraints and the availability of data forced limits.

the University of Michigan's Correlates of War (COW) project.[2] To be included as a civil war, a conflict had to (1) occur within a generally recognized state, (2) produce at least one thousand deaths per year,[3] (3) involve the national government as an active participant,[4] and (4) experience effective resistance from both the rebels and the government. The seventy-two conflicts that met these criteria are listed in appendix 1.

Since my concern is to explain how civil wars are resolved, readers may wonder why cases that had not yet ended (by December 31, 1999) are included.[5] The answer is simple. This book cannot hope to explain the resolution of civil wars by looking only at resolved conflicts and ignoring those that have been more difficult to conclude. Excluding ongoing cases from the analysis would systematically bias the results in favor of those civil wars that had already ended and were, therefore, likely to have been the easiest to resolve. In addition, I am primarily concerned with the *process* by which a civil war is settled rather than its final outcome. It is not necessary to observe how a war concludes to determine the conditions under which combatants are willing to negotiate, sign, or even implement a settlement. Ongoing cases, therefore, provide a wealth of information about resolution, even if the violence has not stopped.

Data Collection

Comprehensive data have not been collected previously on most of the variables included in this study. No existing data sets include information on the goals of combatants, their ethnic identity, the divisibility of the stakes over which they were fighting, the military situation on the ground, the terms over which they were willing or unwilling to bargain, the number of attempts at negotiation, the provisions included in any peace agreement, and the type, timing, and extent of outside intervention. This information had to be collected by researching every civil

[2] The Correlates of War Data Set is on deposit at the Inter-University Consortium for Political and Social Research, University of Michigan, and includes data on all interstate and civil wars fought between 1816 and 1992. For a detailed explanation of the rationale and procedures used in collecting and coding these data see Melvin Small and J. David Singer, *Resort to Arms: International and Civil Wars, 1816–1980* (Beverly Hills, Calif.: Sage Publications, 1982).

[3] This includes civilian as well as military deaths.

[4] This rule was relaxed in those cases where no national government existed at the time war broke out, as was the case in Angola in 1975 after the Portuguese withdrew from its colonies, and Algeria in 1962 after that country gained independence from France.

[5] Thirteen civil wars that began before 1992 had not been formally resolved by December 31, 1999. The outcome of these wars was coded according to how far along the peace process they had progressed. They were the Philippines, Angola, Afghanistan, Somalia, Burma, Sri Lanka, Sudan, Colombia, Abkhazia, South Ossetia, Nagorno Karabakh, Turkey, and Burundi.

war, using primary and secondary sources. The result is the Civil War Resolution Data Set.[6] Variables were coded using multiple sources, the most common of which were *Keesing's Contemporary Archives*; *The International Review of Peace Initiatives: Accord*; Stockholm International Peace Research Institute *Yearbooks*; Ruth R. Sivard, *World Military and Social Expenditures*; Guy Arnold, *Wars in the Third World since 1945*; the Central Intelligence Agency's *World Factbook*; Patrick Brogan, *The Fighting Never Stopped: A Comprehensive Guide to World Conflict since 1945*; Hugh Miall, *The Peacemakers: Peaceful Settlement of Disputes since 1945*; the United Nations Department of Public Information; and the Economist Intelligence Unit.[7] In addition, the coding of each variable was checked against multiple historical accounts. When existing literature was unclear or specific information was unavailable, experts on the country were consulted.

Potential Problems

Critics of the COW data set have argued that its coding criteria for civil wars are too broad and thus include many small-scale confrontations that do not merit the more momentous "civil war" status.[8] To address this criticism, two case lists were constructed for testing, one generated by COW's broad definition of civil war, and one that excluded questionable or borderline cases. Conflicts with fewer than fifteen hundred total deaths (such as Guatemala in 1954 and 1970–1971, and Indonesia in 1953) or conflicts restricted to a very small percentage of the population (power struggles within the military or a purge within the government) were dropped. The competing hypotheses were then tested against both lists. Since no significant differences were found, the broader list of cases was used in all subsequent analysis.[9] These borderline cases are marked with an asterisk (*) in appendix 1.

Others have insisted that requiring conflicts to produce at least one

[6] The full data set is available at <www-irps.ucsd.edu/irps/faculty/bfwalter>.

[7] Helpful websites include the Carter Center at <www.emory.edu/CARTER—CENTER/PUBS/SWCR9495/toc.htm>; the Initiate on Conflict Resolution and Ethnicity at <www.incore.ulst.ac.uk/cds/countries/index.html>; the United Nations Department of Peacekeeping Operations at <www.un.org/Depts/DPKO/Missions/miponuh.htm>; CIA publications and reports at <http://www.cia.gov/cia/publications/pubs.html>; and the African Centre for the Constructive Resolution of Disputes at <http://www.accord.org.za/>.

[8] See especially Pillar, *Negotiating Peace*; Stedman, *Peacemaking in Civil War*; and Licklider, *Stopping the Killing*.

[9] The only difference worth noting was in the significance and magnitude of security guarantees. When the borderline civil wars were removed from the analysis, the significance of third-party security guarantees rose from .05 to .01, but its magnitude declined by half.

thousand deaths per year is too restrictive and excludes well-known cases such as Northern Ireland, Cyprus, and South Africa that exhibit many of the characteristics of a civil war. I have chosen not to lower the one-thousand-death-per-year threshold for three reasons. First, most studies of civil war adopt COW's one-thousand-death measure, and there are good practical reasons for maintaining consistency across studies. Second, lowering the cutoff to two hundred deaths per year, as some scholars have done, would not add a significant number of cases.[10] Third, the chief theoretical interest in this study is major civil wars—wars where the need to end the violence is most pronounced. Lowering the threshold below two hundred deaths per year would incorporate many riots, coups, and skirmishes that are qualitatively different from the major civil wars under study and would likely reduce the validity of the final results.

Two modifications were made to the list of civil wars recorded in the Correlates of War Data Set. First, COW codes a civil war as having terminated once the number of deaths per year falls below one thousand in any twelve-month period. If fighting resumes in the thirteenth month and causes a thousand deaths in the next twelve-month period, COW codes this as a new civil war. The civil war in Laos, for example, experienced a nine-month lull in the fighting between June 1962 and March 1963, dropping the number of people killed below one thousand. When fighting resumed in 1963, COW recorded this as a new and separate civil war. I did not continue this coding practice in order to avoid biasing the data with multiple observations of long-standing stop-and-go wars. Instead, the Civil War Resolution Data Set records recurrent civil wars (such as the war in Laos) as a single, continuous case. Six out of the seventy-two civil wars were coded this way (China, Colombia, Laos, Guatemala, Angola, and Liberia).

One additional modification has been made. COW codes Nigeria as experiencing a civil war between 1980 and 1981. I could find no information on this conflict in any of the general reference books on civil wars, and only an occasional mention of it in detailed histories on Nigeria. This made it impossible to obtain the information necessary to code this case and include it in the analysis.

Measuring the Dependent Variable

In order to see whether the theories presented in chapters 1 and 2 predict the conditions under which civil wars are peacefully resolved, I

---

[10] See Regan, *Civil Wars and Foreign Powers*.

created a single categorical dependent variable called "Peace Process" that included four outcomes: no negotiation, active formal negotiations, a signed bargain, and a successfully implemented settlement. Breaking the dependent variable down into these four categories allows a close approximation of the three-stage resolution process outlined in chapter 1 and makes possible an assessment of the impact of each independent variable at each stage along the way.

No Negotiation versus a Formal Attempt to Negotiate

Civil wars were first distinguished based on whether combatants were willing to initiate formal negotiations to end their war. A war was coded as having experienced negotiations if three criteria were met: (1) the leaders or representatives of each of the main fighting factions met in face-to-face talks, (2) these individuals were willing to discuss both a cease-fire *and* a political solution to the war, and (3) their respective factions had the capabilities to continue the war if talks broke down.[11]

I chose these three criteria in order to distinguish negotiations designed to end a war and rebuild a country from the many negotiations during civil wars that have little to do with seeking a solution to a conflict. The first criterion ensures that leaders themselves were interested in peace and were willing to publicly pursue such an end. The second criterion eliminates meetings where no substantive issues were discussed, where delegates refused to talk to each other or were interested only in discussing the terms of a cease-fire. The third criterion separates negotiations that were attempts to cooperate between relative equals who still had the strength to return to war, from one-sided talks to dictate the terms of surrender. These latter negotiations are more aptly classified as capitulations or surrenders. Wars that did not meet these requirements were coded as having experienced "No Negotiation." Those that did were coded as having had "Active Negotiations."

Signed Bargain

A third category was constructed to determine under what conditions combatants are willing to reach and sign a peace agreement. A case was coded as having reached a "Signed Bargain" if two criteria were met.

[11] Data on negotiation attempts were obtained from *Keesing's Contemporary Archives*; Guy Arnold, *Wars in the Third World since 1945*, 2d ed. (London: Cassell, 1995); Erik Goldstein, *Wars and Peace Treaties, 1816–1991* (London: Routledge, 1992); Hugh Miall, *The Peacemakers: Peaceful Settlement of Disputes since 1945* (New York: St. Martin's Press, 1992); Patrick Brogan, *The Fighting Never Stopped: A Comprehensive Guide to World Conflict since 1945* (New York: Vintage Books, 1990); and individual case histories.

First, the combatants were able to agree on a comprehensive peace plan that included a political as well as a military solution to the conflict. The Riyadh agreement signed in October 1976 between the Palestine Liberation Organization (PLO) and the Lebanese government, for example, was not coded as a signed bargain since it dealt only with the military aspects of the civil war and made no reference to the political and religious issues that incited it. Similarly, signed agreements that included only terms for a cease-fire (even if combatants were willing to discuss larger political issues during negotiations) were not included since these were intended as temporary measures to stop the fighting and not serious attempts to resolve the underlying differences that had started the war. The fourteen-point cease-fire agreement signed between King Hussein of Jordan and the PLO in September 1970 is an example of a treaty not included in this category because it failed to address any of the political issues that instigated the war. Finally, treaties that only mandated the withdrawal of foreign troops or offered amnesty for soldiers were also not coded as signed bargains since their objective was to allow foreign states to exit gracefully, or present a coup de grace to losing parties. In this way, I distinguished comprehensive peace settlements designed to end a war from treaties that offered no long-term solution to the conflict. Not all signed treaties, therefore, that might be referred to as peace agreements, peace plans, or peace accords in historical accounts of a war were coded as such.

Second, a peace treaty had to be signed by all combatants actively fighting a war, not just a subset of actors.[12] If one of the main warring factions refused to sign a treaty or was prevented from signing by other actors, this treaty could not be considered a genuine step toward peace, and it was not recognized as a signed bargain. The settlement signed between Rhodesian president Ian Smith and Bishop Abel Muzorewa in 1978, for example, ushered in the country's first black-led government but excluded the Patriotic Front, the main rebel faction, from the plan. This was not coded as a signed bargain. Similarly, the 1973 peace agreement signed between the North Vietnamese and the United States was also not coded this way because both the South Vietnamese government and the National Liberation Front were excluded from the talks.[13]

---

[12] An exception was made in two cases (Yemen, 1970, and Lebanon, 1958) where no written agreement existed. In these rare cases, warring factions bargained for and agreed to very specific political and military arrangements without inscribing a written document.

[13] This treaty also did not meet the first criteria of a "Signed Bargain" since it was mainly an agreement about the withdrawal of U.S. forces and not a comprehensive peace plan.

Successfully Implemented Settlement

Finally, a civil war was coded as ending in a "Successful Implementation" if the signed bargain ended violence for at least five years, and if the combatants made good-faith efforts to execute the terms of the agreement during this time. A five-year time frame is the standard measure of success used in the literature.[14] If a formal peace treaty broke down within five years of being signed, it was considered a failed attempt, and the outcome in these cases was coded on the basis of the eventual military results.[15] Although peace treaties were signed in China, Laos, Philippines, Angola, Afghanistan, Chad, Uganda, Somalia, Liberia, and Rwanda, the terms were either never implemented or only partially implemented, and almost all degenerated into renewed civil war within a year. This five-year cutoff gives combatants a reasonable amount of time to attempt to implement the terms of their agreement.

A five-year measure, however, does not fully capture the progress combatants are making toward peace or whether they are willing to take the hard steps necessary to rebuild the country and bring lasting peace. It tells us whether the government and rebels were willing to stop fighting, but not whether they were willing to take the much more difficult step of disassembling their partisan armies and opening up the government in ways dictated by the peace treaty. This is the more difficult type of cooperation I hope to understand.

To distinguish those cases where the combatants are willing to implement a wide range of terms from civil wars where they are willing to stop fighting but nothing more, a second criterion for success was added. This second criterion, whether the combatants made good-faith efforts to implement the terms of the settlement, was slightly more ambiguous to code. In many civil wars the combatants implement the terms long after the scheduled timetable or never completely implement them. In El Salvador and Nicaragua, for example, the FMLN (Fara-

[14] A number of studies have coded the success or failure of a peace treaty based on how long peace lasts. The longer a settlement persists, the more successful it is considered. I do not measure successful implementation as a function of the duration of peace because I am interested in the implementation of peace settlements and not their durability, a condition that is almost certainly driven by different causal factors and dynamics. For related work on the durability of peace see Suzanne Werner, "Negotiating the Terms of Settlement: War Aims and the Bargaining Leverage," *Journal of Conflict Resolution* 42, no. 3 (1998): 321–44; and Virginia Page Fortna, "A Peace That Lasts: Agreements and the Durability of Peace," Ph.D. diss., Harvard University, 1998.

[15] Violence was considered to have ended if fewer than one thousand war deaths occurred each year for a period of five consecutive years.

bundo Marti National Liberation) and *contra* forces did not fully adhere to the demobilization timetable. In Cambodia, the Khmer Rouge signed the Paris peace agreement but then boycotted the 1993 elections and returned to war, leaving the remaining factions to implement the treaty.

The minimum requirement necessary to be classified as a "good-faith effort" was the installation of one part of the political agreement (either the installation of the transitional government or the formation of a new national government) *and* at least partial demobilization. In most cases the combatants either made no attempt to implement any of the terms (China, Laos, Afghanistan, Uganda, Somalia, Liberia) or at best implemented only parts of the military or political terms, but not both (Philippines, Chad, Rwanda, Angola). A "good faith effort," therefore, was easier to identify than I originally thought.

These four outcomes were ordered from 0 to 3, ranging from the complete absence of any attempt to negotiate a peace settlement (0), to the successful implementation of a peace treaty (3). The dependent variable—"Peace Process"—was thus coded in the following manner:

0   No Negotiation
1   Active Negotiations
2   Signed Bargain
3   Successful Implementation

By these criteria, thirty-five civil wars never experienced negotiation attempts (49 percent), fourteen civil wars had active negotiations, but the combatants failed to reach an agreement (19 percent), ten reached a signed bargain but were then never implemented (14 percent), and thirteen made it all the way through to a successfully implemented settlement (18 percent). Cases that did not end in successful implementation were coded based on highest stage the combatants had attained in the four-stage peace process.

Measuring the Independent Variables

In chapters 1 and 2 I identified nine hypotheses, one derived from each of six extant theories and three from the models presented in this book, that predict when civil war combatants are likely to resolve their wars peacefully and when they are likely to resolve them through armed battle. In what follows I describe the indicators used to measure the independent variables associated with each theory.

Costs of War: Duration of War, War-Related Deaths

Hypothesis 1 (see table 1.1) predicts that opponents are increasingly likely to negotiate a settlement as the expected costs of war increase. Two criteria were used to measure the costs of war. The first, the duration of war, was measured as a continuous variable and ranged from a low of one week (.25 months) in Bolivia, Argentina, Iraq, Uganda, Jordan, and Romania to a high of 396 months in Guatemala. The second, the number of war-related deaths, was measured as a continuous variable that ranged from a low of one thousand deaths in Indonesia in 1953 to a high of more than a million and a quarter deaths during the Chinese civil war.[16] Data for both the length of the war and total deaths were obtained from the Correlates of War Data Set through 1992, and if necessary were updated through December 1999 using the sources listed in the bibliography.[17]

There is a potential problem with measuring the costs of war as a function of the total number of war deaths rather than as a ratio of the number of deaths per capita, or as a ratio of the number of deaths per month. One could argue, for example, that a thousand war deaths in a populous country such as Indonesia is far less costly than a thousand war deaths in a smaller country such as Lebanon. Similarly, one could argue that six thousand deaths spread out over a six-year war are less painful than six thousand deaths concentrated in a single month. Measuring the costs of war by the total number of deaths, therefore, might miss the true pain a war inflicts and overestimate or underestimate its actual costs. Despite this concern, I stuck with the original measure for two reasons. First, I am interested in measuring the costs of war as perceived by the individual leaders who must decide whether to pursue a negotiated settlement to a war or continue fighting. Since total war deaths are a monotonically positive function of time, the number serves as a reasonable proxy for the information available to the decision makers when they initiate negotiations. Second, although there are good reasons to select other measures of war deaths, I use total deaths since preliminary analysis indicated that it was most closely related to the

---

[16] It should be emphasized that accurate counts of war-related deaths are notoriously difficult to obtain. Many deaths go unreported, while others are either under or over-reported for strategic reasons. For a detailed discussion of how the COW project attempted to correct this problem, see Small and Singer, *Resort to Arms*, 70–77.

[17] Dependable information on the number of deaths after 1992 could not be found for seven wars (Burma, Colombia, Georgia, Somalia, Sri Lanka, Sudan, and Turkey). In these cases, I used an average of the deaths recorded by the Correlates of War through December 1992 to estimate the number of deaths that were likely to have occurred thereafter.

outcomes of civil wars. This measure, therefore, gives the cost-of-war theory the best chance of being statistically significant in the resulting analysis.

Balance of Power: Military Stalemate

Hypothesis 2 predicts that combatants are more likely to end their war in a negotiated settlement if a fairly equal balance of power exists on the battlefield at any point during the war. Here I follow the scholarly consensus and use the presence of a military stalemate to indicate such a balance.[18] To determine whether a military stalemate existed, I sifted through reports and historical accounts of each of the wars, noting each time the battlefield situation was described as "stalemated" or at an "impasse." Although this measure is somewhat subjective, in most cases a consensus existed among historians as to whether the fighting ground to a halt. One source, for example, described the military situation in Paraguay this way: "Until the beginning of April [1947] the position was largely one of stalemate, with the insurgents holding the north of Paraguay and the Government retaining control in Asuncion and the south."[19]

This measure does have certain shortcomings. First, it ignores the fact that civil wars tend to be fought by guerrilla armies that do not engage the government in conventional military battles that could lead to a stalemate. Henry Kissinger pointed out during the Vietnam War that "the guerrilla wins if he does not lose."[20] Insurgents who can sustain a guerrilla war for decades, as FARC (Fuerzas Armadas Revolucionarias de Colombia) has in Colombia, and the MNLF (Moro National Liberation Front) has in the Philippines, have made themselves almost undefeatable even though no conventional military stalemate exists. A more accurate measure of the balance of power in these conflicts, therefore, might be the rebels' ability to occupy land from which the government is unable to dislodge them.

Second, coding a civil war as having a "Military Stalemate" regardless of how many, or when, stalemates take place may fail to pick up a connection between the onset of a stalemate and the decision to cooperate. Although this concern has merit, it does not convince me to change the coding rule, which is to count any stalemate occurring at any time. If the balance-of-power theory is valid, any stalemate that arises during a war should encourage combatants to initiate a peace process at that

---

[18] See for example Zartman, *Ripe for Resolution*; Licklider, *Stopping the Killing*.
[19] *Keesing's Contemporary Archives*, vol. 6, June 28, 1947–June 30, 1948, p. 8841.
[20] Henry Kissinger, "The Vietnam Negotiations," *Foreign Affairs* 47, no. 2 (1969): 214.

point in time. Moreover, any civil war that experiences a stalemate should be significantly more likely to end in a successfully implemented peace settlement, regardless of the timing of the stalemate. In addition, coding the presence of a stalemate only at the time of negotiations would overlook cases in which a stalemate had occurred but had not induced negotiations and would thus introduce a selection bias into the analysis.

A balance of power was coded in the following manner:

1   Military Stalemate
0   No Military Stalemate

Domestic Political Institutions: Regime Type, Executive Constraints

The third hypothesis predicts that domestic political institutions will influence combatants' willingness to sign and implement negotiated settlements. The more democratic a government, the more likely combatants are to sign and implement deals. Two measures were used to see if domestic political institutions had an effect on how a war ended: (1) an overall democracy-autocracy scale, and (2) a measure of political constraints on a government's executive branch, both of which were obtained from the Polity III Data Set.[21]

A democracy-autocracy scale is currently the most common measure of democracy in the international relations literature.[22] It assigns two scores (0–10) to every country: one based on a government's autocratic features, and one based on its democratic features.[23] The incumbent government's autocracy score is then subtracted from its democracy score to produce a net democracy number that ranges in value from very autocratic (-10) to very democratic ($+10$). Among the countries

[21] See Keith Jaggers and Ted Robert Gurr, "Tracking Democracy's Third Wave with the Polity III Data," *Journal of Peace Research* 31, no. 4 (1995): 469–82, for a full account of the scale. Note that the Polity III Data Set includes data on regime type only through 1994 and does not, therefore, provide information for the entire length of all wars included in the Civil War Resolution Data Set. If data was missing for some years of some civil wars, I coded a war based on the most democratic year listed, and the highest level of executive constraints.

[22] See, for example, David L. Rousseau, Christopher Gelpi, Dan Reiter, and Paul K. Huth, "Assessing the Dyadic Nature of the Democratic Peace, 1918–1988," *American Political Science Review* 90 (1996): 512–33; and Kenneth A. Schultz, "Do Democratic Institutions Constrain or Inform? Contrasting Two Institutional Perspectives on Democracy and War," *International Organization* 53, no. 2 (1999): 233–66.

[23] If there were a number of regime changes during the war, the case was coded based on the most democratic year, assuming that this would have been the moment at which combatants were most likely to settle.

in this study, Costa Rica received the highest net democracy score of + 10 during its war in 1948, while Iran received the lowest possible democracy score of − 10 during its 1978–79 war. Most cases fell somewhere between, with a mean score of 2.3.

A second measure of democracy was used to isolate the effect of executive constraints on a leader's decision to negotiate or fight. If democratic leaders have more incentives to negotiate because they are accountable to citizens and subgroups within society, are more credible to an opponent, or have less to lose if they agree to share power, then constraints on the executive should have a greater impact on how a civil war ends than the broader measure of type of regime. The coding for executive constraints was based on the degree of operational independence the chief executive of a country enjoyed during the civil war and was also taken from the Polity III Data Set:[24]

1   Unlimited Authority
2   Intermediate category
3   Slight to Moderate Limitations
4   Intermediate category
5   Substantial Limitations
6   Intermediate category
7   Executive Parity or Subordination

A leader was classified as having "Unlimited Authority" if he or she could easily ignore constitutional restrictions on decision making, or could revise or suspend the constitution; if no legislative assembly existed, or could be called and dismissed at the executive's whim; if the legislature could not initiate legislation or veto or suspend acts by the executive; if the executive could appoint and remove a majority of members of any accountability group at will; or if he or she repeatedly ruled by decree.[25] A leader was coded as having "Executive Parity or Subordination" if he or she had equal or less authority over most decisions than did a subgroup or legislature in society. Of the cases listed in appendix 1, leaders in Costa Rica, Greece, Uganda (1966), Zimbabwe, Burma (1948–51), the Philippines, Colombia, Sri Lanka, Sudan, Turkey, and India operated under the highest level of constraints, while leaders in Cuba, China, Yemen (1948), Iraq, Bolivia, Argentina, Guatemala (1954), Burundi (1972 and 1988), Pakistan, Nigeria, Cambodia, Nicaragua (1978–79), Iran (1978–79), Colombia, Iraq, and Rwanda

[24] If the amount of constraints changed during the war, I recorded the highest level of constraints. I once again assumed that a leader was most likely to negotiate a settlement at this point in the war.

[25] For a more detailed description of the coding criteria see the Polity II codebook (limited revised edition, December 1997).

(1963–64) had unlimited authority over decision making. Most other cases fell somewhere between, with a mean score of 3.1.

Cultural Identity: Ethnic Division

Hypothesis 4 predicts that wars involving issues of identity will be more difficult to resolve than those fought over more malleable political or economic issues. To test the effect of identity on the success or failure of negotiations, wars were classified based on whether a clear ethnic division existed between the combatants. If the combatants broke down along ethnic lines, or that faction defined itself as a separate ethnic group, its war was coded as an "Ethnic Conflict." All others were coded as nonethnic. The civil war between the Ibos and the Nigerian government (composed mostly of individuals from the Hausa and Yoruba tribes), the civil wars between the Hutus and the Tutsis in Burundi and Rwanda, and Iraq's war against the Kurds are examples of ethnic civil wars. The civil war between the Communists and the Greek government, the Chinese Communist Party and the Kuomintang, and the Conservatives and Liberals in Colombia are clear examples of nonethnic civil wars.[26]

Wars were coded in the following manner:

0 Nonethnic Conflict
1 Ethnic Conflict

Divisibility of Stakes: Total Goals, Territorial Goals, Difficulty of Division

Hypothesis 5 predicts that the more divisible are the stakes over which the combatants fight, the more likely they are to negotiate a settlement. Divisibility was measured in three ways: (1) whether the stated goals of the rebels at the beginning of the war were limited or total, (2) whether the rebels were interested in obtaining territorial control or political control, and (3) whether the population and resources within a country could be easily separated.

---

[26] Some cases, however, were difficult to classify since combatants frequently broke down along ethnic lines even if ethnic identity did not appear to be a salient issue of the war. Moreover, ethnic differences are almost always tied to broader political or economic grievances. The Angolan rebels, for example, drew their main support from the Ovimbundu ethnic group but defined themselves as fiercely anti-Communist, at least in the early stages of the war. Likewise, the civil war in Bosnia between 1992 and 1995 was fought between groups who many observers claim exhibited no clear ethnic differences. Although I was cautious not to overplay the ethnic component in any given case, Angola and Bosnia were both classified as ethnic civil wars since they fit the coding criteria described above.

If the rebels initiated the war to obtain anything less than total control over the government (i.e., political reform, regional autonomy, or territorial secession), the war was coded as involving "Nontotal Goals."[27] These conflicts were expected to have a higher rate of negotiated settlement than those fought in pursuit of more absolute goals, since the rebels did not outwardly aim to eliminate their enemy. The Sandinistas' demand for political reform in Nicaragua in 1978, and the People's Liberation Front demand that all Indian troops be withdrawn from Sri Lanka in the late 1980s are examples of civil wars fought for nontotal aims. All other wars were coded as having "Total Goals."[28] Mao Tsetung's Communist revolution in China, Greece's revolution in the 1940s, and Uganda's civil war in which the rebels aimed to overthrow President Obote's government, are examples of total conflicts.

A word of justification is in order for selecting the stated goals of the rebels as the primary basis for coding the war's aims. One could argue that the critical issue for divisibility is not the goals the rebels pursue, but how these goals are perceived by the government under attack. If incumbent elites believe that democratic reform will remove them from power, they will behave as if reform is a total goal regardless of how the rebels formulate their intent. This is especially likely when the rebels are aiming for majority rule and the government in power has only minority support. While this is a valid concern, I resisted coding goals according to the government's perception, for two reasons. First, in all but the most extreme cases (such as Zimbabwe, where the white minority government represented only 3 percent of the population), the incumbent minority could still compete for political power and have a reasonable chance for success even if political reform deposed them in the short term. This is clearly not a situation in which one side aims to eradicate the other, even if it is an outcome the incumbent government prefers to avoid. Second, it is far more difficult to reliably assess and code perceptions than it is to code statements made by rebel groups on what they aim to achieve.

I therefore coded on the basis of stated goals except in four cases in which perceptions could be unambiguously determined. Rebels in these four cases (out of seventy-two, or 6 percent) aimed for political reform that clearly threatened to throw the ruling party permanently out of power: in Paraguay, the army demanded elections that promised to depose President Higinio Morinigo; in Zimbabwe, black majority rule

---

[27] Cases were coded based on the stated aims of the rebels at the beginning of the conflict rather than the stated goals of the government since it is the rebels who almost always initiate a war and are therefore likely to define its parameters.

[28] I relied on a historical consensus rather than an operational criteria for this coding. See individual case sources in the bibliography.

would have ended white dominance in government; in Nicaragua, the Sandinistas demanded the resignation of President Somoza; and in Tajikistan, opposition groups called for the dissolution of the Supreme Soviet and the resignation of President Nabiyev. In these cases it is almost certainly true that the government perceived the rebel aims as total, and they were coded that way.

The extent of rebel goals was coded in the following manner:

0   Nontotal Goals
1   Total Goals

A second measure of divisibility was constructed to address the idea that territory is easier to divide than political control. Wars in which the rebels aimed to secede from the original territory or demanded territorial autonomy were coded as territorial wars. The widespread rebellions in Sumatra, Java, and the Moluccans in 1953 over home rule, and secession movements in Nigeria, Sudan, Congo, Pakistan, and the former Yugoslavia are examples of territorial wars. If the factions demanded control over the existing government rather than a share of territory, the conflict was coded as nonterritorial.

Whether or not a war was fought for territorial or nonterritorial objectives was denoted in the following manner:

0   Nonterritorial Goals
1   Territorial Goals

Measuring "divisibility" using the stated objectives of the belligerents, however, could be problematic since rebels frequently redefine their goals and reduce their demands as wars progress. Rebels might aim to secede from the rump state in the early, optimistic months of the war, only to demand less ambitious goals later on. They might also overstate their aims and the conditions under which they will settle in order to enhance their bargaining leverage during negotiations. The stated goals of rebels, therefore, are not necessarily the best indicators of the ease with which stakes can be divided and compromise solutions reached.

In order to address this potential coding error, I constructed a somewhat rough third measure of divisibility based on how easy it would be to divide the population and resources within a given state.[29] The logic here is that in cases where de facto territorial separation already exists and does not represent a large material loss to the government, it should be easier to settle a conflict. Division was considered "Easy" if the fighting factions occupied distinct regions of the country and the assets and

---

[29] Distribution of the population and resources was based on an analysis of CIA maps drawn at the time of war.

resources of the country were not concentrated wholly in one region or the other. The war between East and West Pakistan in 1971 and the rebellions in the Indonesian islands in the 1950s were wars where the stakes could have been easily divided. Divisibility was coded as "Moderately Difficult" if the rebels were concentrated in a distinct region but that region also possessed important resources such as oil or minerals that the central government was unlikely to easily relinquish. The Katanga province's attempted secession from the Congo in the 1960s is a case where the stakes would have been moderately difficult to divide. Division was considered "Difficult" if the populations fighting the war were intermixed throughout the country and did not occupy clear regions. Greece, Colombia, Nicaragua, Argentina, Cambodia, and Laos were some of the cases included in this group. Wars in which the population and resources was considered easy to divide were expected to be more likely to end in negotiated settlement than those coded as difficult.

Divisibility was thus coded in the following manner:

1   Easy
2   Moderately Difficult
3   Difficult

Mediation Model: Mediator

Hypothesis 6 implies that the success or failure of negotiations depends on the skill of individual mediators. This variable is somewhat tricky to operationalize since the talents that allow a mediator to succeed are often idiosyncratic and difficult to observe. Nonetheless, mediation can be partially tested by the presence of a mediator during negotiations. Given the theory, one would expect a strong relationship to emerge between the presence of such a person and the outcome of war.

Mediation was coded in the following manner:

0   No Mediator
1   Mediator

Credible Commitment: Power-Sharing Pacts, Third-Party Security Guarantee, and Strength of Third-Party Commitment

Hypothesis 7 predicts that combatants will be more likely to sign and implement treaties that offer them specific political, military, and/or territorial pacts. In order to test this hypothesis, data was collected on the terms included in each of the peace settlements proposed during negotiations. If a settlement offered the combatants guaranteed positions in the new government at the level of cabinet or above, or a specific quota of power in at least one of the main branches of government, that case was coded as having a "Political Pact."[30] Zimbabwe's Lancaster House agreement guaranteeing 20 percent of the seats in the lower house of parliament to minority whites is an example. A settlement that only included provisions for multiparty elections (as was the case in Angola in 1991), extended political participation to a larger share of the population (as was the case in El Salvador in 1992), or mandated political reforms (as occurred in Nicaragua in 1988), was not coded as having a "Political Pact" even if the resulting political changes were quite revolutionary. In such cases, warring factions would still not know the exact role they would play in the new government, and their fear of political elimination would not be addressed.

Political pacts were coded in the following manner:

0 No Political Pact
1 Political Pact

Peace settlements were also coded based on whether the main combatants were guaranteed representation in the military. If a peace settlement stipulated a quota of power in a new army, it was coded as having a "military pact."[31] Sudan's 1972 Addis Ababa agreement guaranteed southern rebels 50 percent representation in the southern army. Rebel and government leaders in Mozambique agreed on a new national army composed of fifteen thousand Frelimo soldiers and fifteen thousand Renamo soldiers. Hutu and Tutsi leaders in Rwanda agreed that government and rebel forces would merge equally to create a new twenty-thousand-person Rwandan army. And Bosnia's Dayton accord allowed each of the three ethnic groups to maintain their own armies. In contrast, Cambodia's Paris peace agreement of 1991 only mandated mutual troop and equipment reductions, and El Salvador's peace agreement in 1992, while it demanded expansive military reforms and eliminated many of the government's repressive internal security forces, did not guarantee the rebels any place in the new national military. Sudan, Mozambique, Rwanda, and Bosnia were coded as having a military pact, Cambodia and El Salvador were not.

[30] This dichotomous coding ignores variation in the content of political guarantees. A guarantee of control over the ministry of the interior is very different from a guarantee of 50 percent of the seats in parliament. A political guarantee that involves only three out of the four factions is also not equivalent to a guarantee that includes all groups. Nevertheless, a political guarantee offers groups some measure of security and sends a signal that the government is willing to share at least some of the country's political power.

[31] Again, differences in the type of military guarantees offered may have an impact on the outcome of civil war negotiations. However, given the enormous variation in the possible content of these guarantees and the fact that any guarantee signals some willingness to share military power, a dichotomous variable was deemed the best measure.

Military pacts were coded in the following manner:

0   No Military Pact
1   Military Pact

Peace agreements were also coded on the basis of territorial pacts. If a peace agreement included a provision for some form of regional autonomy, as was the case in Sudan in 1972 and Bosnia in 1995; if one or both sides was allowed to continue to administer areas under their control, as the royalist rebels were allowed to do in Yemen after their agreement in 1970; or if specific self-governing zones were established, as was the case in Nicaragua in 1990, the agreement was coded as including a "Territorial Pact."[32] All other cases were coded as including no such guarantee.

Territorial pacts were coded in the following manner:

0   No Territorial Pact
1   Territorial Pact

The credible commitment theory also predicts that the success of peace negotiations depends on the presence of third-party security guarantees (hypothesis 8). To be classified as a third-party security guarantee, outside offers had to meet two criteria.[33] First, an outside state or international organization such as the United Nations or NATO had to step in during negotiations with a verbal or written promise to verify or enforce post-treaty behavior once a settlement was signed.[34] Examples include promises "to supervise, control and verify the disengagement of forces," "to police the agreement," "to deter any violators of the agreement," "to facilitate impartially the implementation of the Agreement; to monitor and verify the ceasefire, the separation and concentration of forces, their demobilization and the collection, storage and destruction

[32] In some cases, factions were allowed to retain control over conquered territory only until elections were held or a new democratic government was formed, as was the case in the peace agreement negotiated between the Communists and Nationalists in China in 1946. Although these territorial provisions were only temporary, they were coded as a "Territorial Pact" since they offered combatants some certainty during the transition.

[33] Since guarantees had to be offered by a third party, promises of amnesty and protection offered by one combatant to another were not coded as a "Security Guarantee." During 1990 negotiations in Nicaragua, for example, the Sandinista government offered "to guarantee the personal security and civil rights of all returning rebels." I did not code this offer as a security guarantee because it did nothing to reassure the rebels that they would be protected from the Sandinistas themselves.

[34] This information was collected from specific guarantees written into peace treaties, from written mandates detailing the extent of outside involvement, and from case histories.

of weapons," and "to ensure the overall security of the country.[35] Such statements were taken to mean that the outside state or organization was willing to act as a go-between while the combatants moved forward to implement their accords.

It is important to note that this criterion does not include outside forces that are sent with the specific purpose of forcing a cease-fire on combatants who otherwise had no interest in pursuing peace. In three cases (Lebanon 1976, Iraq 1991, and Tajikistan 1990s) outsiders imposed peace using massive force in a situation of unresolved conflict. Syria's sixty thousand troops forced a truce on Lebanon's largely Christian and Muslim combatants and proceeded to occupy the country. The United Nations forced a temporary truce between the Kurds and the Iraqi government by sending seventeen thousand troops to protect Kurdish camps against attacks by Saddam Hussein. And in Tajikistan, although no peace treaty was ever signed between the Tajik government and the Islamic Revival Party, a cease-fire continues to be enforced by twenty-five thousand Russian soldiers. Syria, the United Nations, and Russia did bring peace to these three countries, but it was an imposed and artificial peace. To be coded as a "Security Guarantee" an outside force had to be offered in cases where the combatants had already decided to pursue a negotiated settlement and then only to help implement the terms the combatants themselves approved. Not all interventions, therefore, that serve to stop the fighting are by definition security guarantees.

It is also important to note that this first criterion does not include interventions designed to establish a secure environment for humanitarian assistance or for the safe departure of foreign nationals and military personnel. The United Nations' and the United States' involvement in Somalia, for example, cannot be considered a security guarantee because it was designed to facilitate the safe delivery of humanitarian aid, not to enforce or verify any agreed-upon peace treaty. Similarly, the United Nations' role in the Congo in 1960 is also not a security guarantee since it was primarily designed to ensure the safe withdrawal of Belgian forces.[36]

The second criterion was more stringent. In order for an offer to be classified as a security guarantee, an outside state or international organization had to follow through with its promise and provide the expected services. Because both the government and the rebels have time to observe whether the third party arrives and how its forces are

---

[35] These phrases were taken from third-party promises made, but not necessarily implemented, in Angola, Lebanon, Mozambique, and Rwanda respectively.

[36] There was also no peace to keep here since the combatants never signed a peace settlement.

deployed before they choose to demobilize, cases where a third party failed to arrive or came with a significantly reduced mandate were not coded as security guarantees. Here, both the government and the rebels would know that no third party existed to help enforce or verify demobilization, and implementation would be affected accordingly.

In five cases, a third party stepped forward during negotiations to offer help with implementation but failed to provide the promised assistance. None of these promises were coded as a third-party security guarantee. In Chad, the Organization of African Unity (OAU) promised to send an all-African peacekeeping force comprised of soldiers from Guinea, Benin, and the Congo to enforce a peace settlement signed in 1979, but neither the OAU nor any member state had the money to bankroll such an operation (a fact both combatants understood when the promise was made), and no such force was sent.[37] In Rwanda, Boutros Boutros-Ghali responded to a call for help during negotiations in Arusha in 1993 and promised that the United Nations would "guarantee the overall security in the county" during the implementation of the Arusha accords. The UN Security Council, however, did not authorize a mission for Rwanda until two months after the peace agreement had been signed, and then sent a force with a substantially reduced mandate and with less than half the *minimum* recommended number of peacekeepers. During negotiations in Angola in 1991, the United Nations promised "to prevent, verify, and investigate possible violations" of the Estoril accords but sent only a few hundred observers who did not have the mandate to play anything more than a symbolic role in the transition. In Nagorno-Karabakh, the Organisation for Security and Co-operation in Europe (OSCE) agreed to commit up to three thousand troops to police a cease-fire, but events in Bosnia and Chechnya reduced the willingness of members to participate, and this offer was not mentioned in subsequent negotiations. And Egypt's pledge during Jordan's 1970 civil war to lead "punitive action by other Arab countries to whomever violated the agreement" was also not coded as a security guarantee since President Nasser, the dominant figure in the pan-Arab movement, died the following day. Nasser's death undercut his pledge to organize Arab states and eliminated any credibility the promise might have had.

There are, of course, other problems with attempting to code this variable. Perhaps the most serious is this: coding "Security Guarantee" based on whether a third party follows through with its promise ignores the effect an offer of assistance might have in getting combatants to sign

---

[37] Congo eventually sent six hundred soldiers to Chad, but they arrived in the capital five months after the peace accord was signed, never left their barracks, and withdrew three months later when violence erupted.

a settlement (even if they do not then implement the terms). The Rwandan government and Tutsi rebels, for example, signed the Arusha accords in part because the UN had stepped in during negotiations, offering to protect them during implementation. The fact that the UN failed to follow through does not mean that the offer played no role in the final outcome of the peace process. While it is true that unfulfilled promises still affect the peace process (especially combatants' decision to sign bargains), such promises will almost certainly have no effect on combatants' willingness to implement any terms since parties will have ample time to observe whether the third party arrives as promised. Coding empty promises as security guarantees, therefore, would make it almost impossible to determine the effect true guarantees have on the final outcome.

A third-party security guarantee was coded in the following manner:

0 No Security Guarantee
1 Security Guarantee

As mentioned earlier, there can be substantial variation in the strength of an outside state's commitment to enforcing or verifying the peace process and its display of force. Hypothesis 9 predicts that the strength of an outside security guarantee will be related to the third party's commitment to the peace process. A third party's commitment was coded as a function of three factors. First, was the mandate precisely defined, and was it known to the combatants signing the peace treaty? This was judged based on whether the third-party guarantee was written down in the terms of the treaty itself or if it was passed as a formal resolution in the guarantor's home state or organization. The second criterion involves the type of mandate offered by the third party. Did the third party offer to send a verification mission assigned to observe and monitor demobilization, or a more robust enforcement mission? The final criterion concerned the size of the verification or enforcement force the third party offered. In this case a minimum threshold of five hundred observers was necessary for inclusion as a large verification force, and five thousand armed soldiers for inclusion as a large peacekeeping force.[38] This led to the following breakdown of cases:

0 No Security Guarantee
1 Promise to Protect but Mandate and Force Not Defined

---

[38] The primary sources consulted in the coding of this variable were United Nations peacekeeping operations (Department of Public Information, United Nations) and individual case histories. For excellent information on UN peacekeeping missions see <http://www.un.org/Depts/DPKO/Missions/miponuh.htm>.

2   Willingness to Deploy Verification Mission of under Five Hun-
     dred Observers
3   Willingness to Deploy Verification Mission of at Least Five
     Hundred Observers
4   Willingness to Deploy an Armed Peacekeeping Force of under
     Five Thousand
5   Willingness to Deploy an Armed Peacekeeping Force of at
     Least Five Thousand[39]

If the mandate and commitment were vague and ill defined, the third-
party guarantee was coded as the weakest of five possible guarantees.
Ethiopian emperor Haile Selassie's personal guarantee to the Sudanese
rebels that they would not be attacked if they signed a peace treaty in
1972 is an example of a weak security guarantee since the emperor did
not specify the number of troops he would employ, nor did he outline
their mission. All remaining guarantees were classified as either verification missions or peacekeeping missions. If the intervening soldiers did
not possess a mandate to use force, this mission was classified as a
verification mission, and this type of guarantee was deemed weaker
than a peacekeeping force. Both verification missions and peacekeeping
missions were then divided based on the size of the force promised.
Verification missions were coded as either small (fewer than five hundred observers promised) or large (more than five hundred observers
promised). Peacekeeping missions were classified as either small (fewer
than five thousand troops committed) or large (more than five thousand
troops committed).

Conclusion

In chapter 2 I argued that a critical factor determining whether a civil
war will end peacefully is the combatants' ability to obtain credible,
enforceable guarantees on the terms of the treaty. All else being equal, if
combatants are able to obtain third-party security guarantees for demobilization, and political, military, or territorial guarantees for power
sharing, they will sign and implement a negotiated settlement. If they
are unable to obtain these guarantees, they will refuse to end the war
through a negotiated settlement, and wars will terminate only after one
side has decisively won on the battlefield. Two sets of alternative
hypotheses were also presented: those that argue that the costs of war,

[39] In this case the mandate did not have to be well defined in order to classify as a large
peacekeeping force. Such a massive commitment of forces was viewed as an unambiguous
and indisputable demonstration of intent.

the military balance of power, and domestic political institutions are likely to influence combatants' willingness to negotiate and are thus more likely to determine the outcome of the war; and those that argue that the identity of the combatants, their goals, and outside mediation are likely to affect the outcome of negotiations and are thus more likely to influence success.

This chapter has laid the basis for the quantitative analysis that will follow by explaining how each of the variables was operationalized and coded (for a summary, see table 3.1). It has described the most suitable measures for both the dependent and independent variables and their limitations. The next chapter will subject each of these variables to statistical tests in order to determine which of the hypotheses best predicts when combatants will choose to end their civil war in a negotiated settlement and when they will not.

TABLE 3.1
Key Variables and Their Indicators

Source Theory	Variable	Indicator
Costs of war	Duration of war War related deaths	Length of war in months Total war deaths
Balance of power	Military stalemate	Battlefield situation described as stalemated in historical accounts
Domestic political institutions	Regime type	Autocracy-democracy scale
	Executive constraints	Operational independence of government leader
Ethnic identity	Ethnic division	Ethnic makeup of combatants
Divisibility of stakes	Total goals Territorial goals Difficulty of division	Stated goals of the rebels at start of war Stated goals of the rebels at start of war Distribution of population and resources within the country
Mediation	Mediation	Presence of a mediator during negotiations
Credible commitment	Power-sharing pacts	Treaty terms that guarantee main combatants a quota of political, military, or territorial control
	Third-party security guarantee	Promise to enforce or verify post-treaty behavior and provision of expected services
	Strength of third-party commitment	Type of mandate and size of intervening force

4. Quantitative Tests

᷒᷒ THIS BOOK ARGUES that civil wars are more likely to end peacefully if a third party enforces or verifies demobilization and if a peace treaty offers each combatant specific political, military, and/or territorial guarantees in the first postwar government. This chapter tests this theory against every civil war that began between 1940 and 1992. I am particularly interested in answering three questions. First, is it true that third-party security guarantees and power-sharing pacts substantially increase the likelihood that a war will end in a successfully implemented settlement? Second, do combatants factor the presence of third-party security guarantees and power-sharing pacts into their decision to initiate negotiations, sign bargains, and implement any resulting terms? And third, are the conditions that encourage combatants to initiate negotiations and sign agreements the same as the conditions that then bring peace?

The chapter proceeds in five parts. The first two are, respectively, a brief discussion of the methods used to analyze the data and a summary of the general findings. Each of the next three parts focuses on one of the three stages in the process of resolving civil wars. The first of these parts finds that the costs of war and a military balance of power are particularly important in getting combatants to the negotiating table. The next reveals that third-party security guarantees, certain types of power-sharing pacts, a military stalemate, territorial goals, and mediation all have a strong impact on combatants' decision to reach a bargain once negotiations have commenced. The final part shows that in the end only third-party security guarantees and power-sharing pacts encourage combatants to implement the terms of a bargain once it has been signed.

Analytic Methods

The primary method used to analyze the data is an ordered logit model with "Peace Process" as the dependent variable. (A nested logit model would also have been appropriate to use had a greater number of cases existed.) The peace process was divided into four categories to reflect the consecutive hurdles combatants must clear in order to successfully cooperate: (1) no negotiation, (2) negotiation, (3) signed bargain, and (4) successful implementation (see chapter 3). This method of analysis was chosen for three reasons. First, by looking at the resolution of civil wars as a multistage process, we can assess which of the factors plays a role in advancing the combatants toward peace and not just which factors play a dominant role in the implementation stage. This ensures that variables critical in the early stages of a peace process are not ignored, and that variables coming into play in the final stages are not over-emphasized. It also allows us to determine at what stage in the peace process expectations about compliance become a concern. Second, ordered logit analysis allows us to take into account the conditional nature of the data (i.e., you cannot influence the bargaining process unless groups first decide to negotiate). Third, ordered logit analysis is most appropriate when the dependent variable is an ordinally ranked, categorical scale in which the outcomes are fairly evenly distributed, as is the case with this three-stage peace process.[1]

A secondary method was used to analyze the conditions under which combatants will initiate negotiations. Here I used a logit analysis with "Negotiation" as the dichotomous dependent variable. I chose to run this second regression for two reasons. First, some of the hypotheses presented in chapters 1 and 2 include causal factors that materialize only after negotiations have begun and are almost certainly highly correlated with the onset of talks (i.e., mediation, third-party security guarantees, and power-sharing pacts). Including these factors in a model intended to analyze the first stage of the peace process might make it appear as if mediation, third-party guarantees, and power-sharing pacts caused combatants to initiate negotiations, when in fact the direction of causation could be the reverse. Including these factors is also likely to diminish the significance of other potentially important causal variables at this first stage and produce spurious results.[2] Second, the decision to initiate negotiations does not depend on any prior decisions, as is the case with the decision to sign and implement a settlement once negotia-

---

[1] One problem with using ordered logit is the potential for selection bias that is inherent in many ordinally ranked, categorical scales. In the case of civil wars, combatants may sign a settlement but fail to implement the terms. We cannot determine from this outcome whether one of the parties would have been willing to agree to a negotiated settlement, as we observe only the final outcome. One statistical method for dealing with this issue is selection bias probit, also known as multivariate probit, which explicitly takes into account an estimate of the effects of selection bias. However, a selection bias probit model could not be used because of the relatively small number of civil wars in the data set. I have therefore attempted to address selection bias through secondary logit analyses, reported below.

[2] In fact, when I included these three variables in an additional logit analysis with negotiation as the dependent variable (not shown), the results were overdetermined and, as a result, produced unreliable coefficients and standard errors. I interpret this as confirmation of this suspicion.

tions have begun. It is reasonable, therefore, to analyze this first stage separately from the full resolution process.[3]

Summary of General Findings

The quantitative analysis confirms that a third-party security guarantee and power-sharing pacts significantly increase the likelihood that a civil war will end in a successfully implemented settlement, but the analysis also reveals that other factors play an important role *prior* to the implementation of a peace treaty. Table 4.1 summarizes the results of the statistical analyses discussed in greater detail below, showing which factors are influential at each stage.[4]

As table 4.1 shows, the costs of a war (measured by its duration and by war-related deaths) and a military stalemate affect the decision to initiate negotiations. But once negotiations begin, factors associated with post-treaty security play a much larger role in the decision to sign and then implement a peace treaty. Mediation, a military stalemate, and nonterritorial goals help combatants obtain a signed bargain, but by far the two biggest factors in getting combatants to sign *and* implement peace settlements are third-party security guarantees and power-sharing pacts.[5] In short, beliefs about implementation *do* color decisions made in the second and third phases of the peace process.

In what follows, I investigate the substantive effect of the independent variables at stage 1, stage 2, and stage 3 of the peace process. For the negotiation phase, I present data from a simple logit model that was included to ensure that the results were not unfairly weighted in favor of variables that appear only after negotiations have commenced. For stage 2 and stage 3 (the bargaining and implementation phases) I pre-

[3] Unfortunately, this makes it impossible to test whether third-party guarantees and power-sharing pacts had an impact in the first stage of the peace process. I cannot, therefore, rule out the possibility that groups are basing their decision to negotiate at least in part on whether they believe mediators and third-party guarantees will be available during the bargaining and implementation phases. The bias introduced to the logit model by these additional variables makes it impossible to specifically test this possibility.

[4] The results reported in table 4.1 are resilient to a wide range of variations in model specification (not shown). Multicolinearity does appear to weaken the coefficients for two of the variables, total goals and military stalemate. When nonterritorial goals is removed from the equation, having total goals is positively and significantly related to the successful resolution of a civil war. Given the unintuitive nature of this finding, it is likely that the relationship that emerges is spurious. In all other cases, excluding potentially colinear variables does not produce significant changes in the remaining causal variables.

[5] This supports findings from a comparative study of five cases by Fen Hampson. In *Nurturing Peace* he found that peace settlements were more durable in cases "where there was unified and sustained third-party involvement in both the negotiation and implementation of the agreement" (207).

TABLE 4.1

Factors That Encourage Combatants to Negotiate, Sign, and Implement a
Peace Plan, by Stage of Process

Stage 1: Initiating Negotiations	Stage 2: Reaching a Bargain	Stage 3: Implementing a Peace Plan
The duration of war	A third-party security guarantee	A third-party security guarantee
The number of war-related deaths	A territorial pact	A territorial pact
A military stalemate	A political pact	A political pact
	A mediator	
	A military stalemate	
	Nonterritorial goals	

sent probabilities derived from the ordered logit analysis displayed in
table 4.3.

The Conditions under Which Combatants Negotiate

The decision to begin negotiations is the essential first step toward a
peace settlement. No settlement can ever be reached unless the parties
first agree to meet at the bargaining table. Table 4.2 presents the results
of the logit regression with "Negotiation" as the dependent variable

TABLE 4.2

Logit Analysis of Factors Affecting the Decision to Negotiate

Independent Variable	Coefficient	Standard Error
Duration of war	.02*	.01
War-related deaths	.003*	.001
Military stalemate	1.88^	1.01
Executive constraints	.26	.18
Ethnic division	.51	.84
Total goals	−.31	.76
Territorial goals	−1.73	1.18
Difficulty of division	.36	.47
Constant	−2.67^	1.59
Pseudo R^2	.36	
χ^2	23.53**	

Note: N = 72. Heteroscedasticity-consistent standard errors, clustered by country,
were employed.

^$p < .10$ *$p < .05$ **$p < .01$

and shows that the factors that bring governments and rebels to the negotiating table *are very different* from the factors that allow them to reach and sign settlements. Only two factors significantly affect whether combatants initiate peace negotiations ($p < .05$): the duration of war and the number of war-related deaths. One additional variable (military stalemate) appears to have a positive effect on the onset of negotiations, although it fails to achieve standard levels of statistical significance ($p < .10$).[6]

None of the other variables (executive constraints, regime type,[7] ethnic division, difficulty of division, territorial or total goals) had a significant effect on the decision to negotiate. Ethnic civil wars are no less likely to experience negotiations than nonethnic wars. Combatants with very different racial and tribal characteristics are just as likely to initiate negotiations as are combatants from the same ethnic group. Civil wars in Sudan, Nigeria, Yugoslavia, and Zimbabwe were driven by ethnic issues, yet the combatants in each initiated numerous formal peace negotiations. In contrast, the combatants in Costa Rica, Cuba, Paraguay, and Bolivia faced no ethnic divisions yet consistently refused to talk.

Combatants who fight in wars where the stakes are easy to divide, as was the case in Indonesia, Pakistan, and Sudan, are also no more likely to begin peace negotiations than combatants who fight for stakes that were harder to divide, as was the case in Zimbabwe, El Salvador, and China. Similarly, wars in which the rebels pursue limited goals are also no more likely to experience negotiations than wars in which the rebels have more absolute aims. Combatants appear more concerned with the immediate cost of war when they decide to initiate negotiations, and not on issues that might make bargaining easier once negotiations commence.

Finally, more democratic governments, or governments operating under a heavier burden of executive constraints, are also no more likely

---

[6] The failure of military stalemate to achieve the .05 level of significance is most likely attributable to multicolinearity between several of the independent variables. The existence of a military stalemate is moderately correlated with a war's duration and the number of war-related deaths in the war at .23 and .30, respectively. While these correlations are by no means overwhelming, when either war duration or the number of war-related deaths is excluded from the model, the military stalemate dummy becomes statistically significant at the .05 level. Moreover, the magnitude of the coefficient on the military stalemate dummy is only modestly affected by including or excluding these other two variables, suggesting that this latter causal factor does indeed meaningfully affect the outcomes of civil wars in the manner predicted by the theory.

[7] Regime type was excluded from the final model as it was highly colinear with the variable executive constraints. Additional tests that included regime type but excluded executive constraints suggest that this variable also played no significant role at any stage of the peace process.

to negotiate with rebels than less democratic governments. Civil wars fought in Costa Rica, Peru, and the Philippines were no more likely to experience negotiations than civil wars fought in far less democratic countries such as Cuba, Burma, or Iran.

Table 4.2 illuminates which variables presented in chapters 1 and 2 influence the decision to initiate negotiations. Logit results, however, are notoriously difficult to interpret. In order to make the results easier to understand, the King, Tomz, and Wittenberg simulation procedure was used to convert the logit coefficients to expected probabilities. The strong relationship between each of these variables and the decision to initiate negotiations is more readily apparent using this procedure, the results of which are shown in table 4.3.[8]

The Costs of War

Consistent with theories that emphasize the costs of war, both the duration of war and the number of war-related deaths have a sizable and significant effect on combatants' decision to initiate negotiations. As wars get longer, the probability of having active negotiations increases.[9] Holding other variables at their mean values, combatants in the longest wars are 70 percent more likely to pursue a negotiated settlement than combatants in the shortest wars. Similarly, combatants fighting the most deadly civil wars are 39 percent more likely to pursue negotiations than combatants in the least deadly wars. As war-related deaths increase, so too does the likelihood of negotiations.[10]

These findings offer strong support for rationalist accounts of war termination that view combatants, whether civil or interstate, as driven

[8] This technique involves conducting repeated simulations of a given model to estimate expected values for each β coefficient, as well as expected probabilities derived from transforming these coefficients. The "difference" in the expected probabilities for each variable is derived by setting all of the other variables to their mean value and then separately calculating the change in the probability that combatants would reach each level of the settlement process when a given causal variable moves from its lowest to its highest value. If the 99 or 95 percent confidence intervals surrounding these predicted differences *exclude* the possibility of zero effect (i.e., they *do not* run from negative to positive), we may conclude that variations in a given causal variable *do* produce statistically significant differences in the probability of reaching a given stage of the settlement process.

[9] Mason and Fett had similar findings using a somewhat different list of cases. Although their analysis did not distinguish at what phase in the peace process the duration of war was likely to have the greatest effect, they did find that the longer a war lasted, the more likely it was to end in a negotiated settlement. As we will see, however, the duration of war only had a significant effect in the first phase of the peace process, a fact that Mason and Fett's analysis could not tease out.

[10] This stands in contrast to Mason and Fett's findings. They found some support for the possibility that higher casualty rates were less likely to lead to negotiated settlements.

TABLE 4.3
Predicted Probability That Combatants Will Initiate Negotiations

Variable	Probability Estimate	Probability Difference
Duration of war		
Less than 1 month	.27	
396 months	.97	
		.70*
War deaths per year		
1,000	.55	
1,275,000	.92	
		.37*
Military stalemate		
No	.51	
Yes	.84	
		.33^

Note: Probabilities are derived from logit analysis presented in table 4.2.
^p < .10   *p < .05

by rationally motivated cost-benefit calculations. Incumbent governments and insurgents appear to be highly cost sensitive and will initiate negotiations as the cost of war rise. This finding calls into question arguments that view civil wars as uniquely emotional or irrational conflicts that are insensitive to material considerations. Civil war combatants may wish to portray themselves as more dedicated to their ideals and less willing to compromise, but their decision to pursue peace is clearly influenced by the price they pay to fight.

A Military Balance of Power

Military stalemates also appear to have a positive effect on combatants' decision to initiate negotiations. Holding all else constant, combatants who fight each other to a standstill are 33 percent more likely to pursue peace negotiations than combatants who are unable to stop their enemy from making military advances. Stalemates that occurred in Sudan, El Salvador, and Mozambique, for example, did appear to have a significant positive influence on combatants' decision to pursue peace. In each case, negotiations commenced after a military stalemate set in, indicating that the decision to prove peace was also influenced by the combatants' belief in their own ability to defeat their opponent.

Factors That Affect the Decision to Sign a Bargain

The question remains, however, whether the conditions that encourage combatants to initiate negotiations at a specific point in the war are sufficient to convince them to sign and implement settlements. A good portion of the literature on civil wars has assumed that once the military, political, and economic conditions on the ground favor negotiations, the biggest barrier to a negotiated settlement has been surmounted. To a degree this is true. Combatants have no chance to end their war in a negotiated settlement unless they are willing to meet their enemy at the bargaining table, and during the period analyzed in this study, more than half of all civil war combatants were unwilling to proceed this far. The fact that it is so difficult to convince combatants to talk to each other, however, does not mean that the conditions that prompt this important first step will enable opponents to settle their war. In fact, history shows that roughly two-thirds of all negotiations (twenty-four out of thirty-seven cases) broke down into renewed war. This high failure rate strongly suggests that other factors come into play once combatants attempt to reach, sign, and implement mutually agreeable deals.

Once combatants decide to negotiate, they face the very different and challenging task of resolving underlying conflicts of interest, something that often requires concessions and cooperation. The factors that allow combatants to navigate this phase of the resolution process, therefore, should be quite different from the conditions that bring them to the table in the first place.

Table 4.4 presents the results of the ordered logit with "Peace Process" as the dependent variable.

Although the logit coefficients show which factors significantly increase the likelihood of peaceful settlement, they do not reveal which of the factors matter in each of the three stages. A military stalemate, for example may play a large role in convincing combatants to initiate negotiations but only a minor role in the decision to implement any subsequent peace plan. The logit coefficients also do not give us much help in interpreting how important each variable is. It is not clear, for example, what a value of -2.91 for territorial goals means, given that the dependent variable is an ordered categorical variable. Territorial goals may be statistically significant; but it may also turn out to have almost no substantive affect on the probability that combatants will sign and implement a settlement. In order to rectify these two problems, I once again convert the results from table 4.4 into probability estimates, shown in table 4.5. This allows me to calculate the degree to

TABLE 4.4

Ordered Logit Analysis of Factors Affecting the Outcome of Civil Wars

Independent Variable	Coefficient	Standard Error
Third-party security guarantee	4.68**	1.62
Territorial pact	3.48*	1.80
Political pact	3.66^	2.16
Military pact	−1.69	1.86
Duration of war	.01	.01
War-related deaths	−.0005	.001
Military stalemate	1.81^	.94
Executive constraints	.11	.16
Ethnic division	.66	.78
Total goals	−.40	.81
Territorial goals	−2.91*	1.38
Difficulty of division	.23	.38
Mediator	3.62***	1.02
Constant 1	2.62	1.29
Constant 2	6.33	1.58
Constant 3	9.50	1.81
Pseudo R^2	.60	
χ^2	67.10***	

Note: N = 72. Heteroscedasticity-consistent standard errors, clustered by country, were employed.

^$p < .10$ *$p < .05$ **$p < .01$ ***$p < .001$

which each of the variables influences decisions at each stage in the process of resolving civil wars. Table 4.5 focuses specifically on the second stage of the resolution process—whether combatants reach and sign settlements.

Predicted probabilities presented in this table confirm that combatants choose to sign bargains for reasons that are quite different from those that first bring them to the negotiating table. Once combatants initiated negotiations, five completely different factors affect their decision to reach and sign a peace agreement. Only third-party security guarantees, territorial and political pacts, mediation, and nonterritorial goals have a sizable and significant effect on the decision to sign a peace agreement; the duration of war and the number of war-related deaths no longer exert any significant impact on combatants' ability to move forward. One additional factor, a military stalemate, continues to play a substantively important role in the decision to sign a peace treaty, but is not quite statistically significant ($p < .10$). Each of these relationships is discussed in more detail below.

TABLE 4.5
Predicted Probability That Combatants Will Sign a Bargain

Variable	Probability Estimate	Probability Difference
Third-party security guarantee		
No	.05	
Yes	.55	
		.50**
Territorial pact		
No	.09	
Yes	.49	.40*
Political pact		
No	.07	
Yes	.45	
		.38^
Military stalemate		
No	.09	
Yes	.32	
		.23^
Territorial goals		
No	.23	
Yes	.03	
		−.20*
Mediator		
No	.04	
Yes	.43	
		.39**

Note: Probabilities are derived from the ordered logit model presented in table 4.4. Please note that the King, Tomz, and Wittenberg simulation procedure allows tests of significance only to the 99 percent level.
^$p < .10$ *$p < .05$ **$p < .01$

Third-Party Security Guarantees

As table 4.5 shows, third-party security guarantees have the greatest impact on the willingness of combatants to sign peace settlements. Holding all other causal variables constant at their mean values, governments and rebels are 50 percent more likely to accept a compromise bargain if a third party offers to enforce or verify the transitional terms and then follows through with its promise. If a third party offers to verify or enforce demobilization, as the British did in Zimbabwe in

1979 and the United Nations did in Bosnia in 1994, combatants are significantly more likely to sign a peace treaty than if no such offers are made. Indeed, if a third party did not step forward to enforce or verify, combatants have only a 5 percent probability of signing a settlement.

Political and Territorial Pacts

Combatants are also significantly more likely to sign a peace treaty that includes a territorial or political pact than if their agreement does not. Holding other variables constant at their mean values, if a peace treaty includes a provision for territorial autonomy, governments and rebels are 40 percent more likely to sign than if a peace treaty includes no such terms.[11] Rival factions do appear to demand some administrative control over previously occupied regions in order to preserve a political base, should things go badly. This supports the notion that combatants in civil wars wish to prevent the full concentration of power in a single administration, at least in the first postwar government.

Similarly, the combatants are 38 percent more likely to sign a bargain if it includes guaranteed positions in the new government, although this relationship is less statistically significant ($p < .10$). Rival factions appear concerned with the postwar distribution of power and do seem to demand guaranteed representation as the price for peace. In contrast, the presence of a military pact does not appear to have any significant effect on combatants' willingness to sign peace settlements, a finding that suggests that rebels are more concerned with wresting political control from the hands of an entrenched and privileged elite than with obtaining military representation. This is understandable, since rebels are more likely to have the means to recruit new insurgents to their cause than to obtain legitimate administrative control over territory and political institutions.

Skeptics may argue that combatants *should* be more likely to sign treaties that include generous guarantees of territorial and political power. As I will show in chapter 5, however, the decision to extend political or territorial guarantees does not automatically lead to a signed settlement, and the decision to withhold these guarantees does not always prevent this result. In fact, some 30 percent of the treaties were signed without a territorial or a political pact. Moreover, only 53 percent of the treaties with a territorial or political pact eventually ended with a

[11] Three separate studies had similar findings using somewhat different sets of cases. See Charles King, "Devolution of Power and Negotiated Settlements in Civil Wars," Georgetown University, April 1997; Kaufman, "Possible and Impossible Solutions"; and Gurr, *Minorities at Risk*.

successfully negotiated settlement, a detail that enhances confidence in the finding. In short, it appears that specific political or territorial guarantees do increase combatants' confidence in an agreement and play an important role in shifting their preferences from war to peace.

These results offer strong support for the credible commitment theory of civil war resolution. Incumbent governments and rebels clearly look down the road and consider problems of enforcement and post-treaty security when deciding whether to sign a peace treaty or return to war, and they clearly hesitate to sign unless a third party exists to solve this problem for them.

Military Stalemate

A military balance of power continues to have a positive effect on resolution of civil wars despite not being quite statistically significant ($p < .10$). Holding all else constant, combatants who fight to a standstill are 39 percent more likely to sign a peace treaty than combatants who are unable to stop their enemy from making military advances. There are at least two reasons why civil war combatants may initiate negotiations and sign a bargain in the presence of fairly balanced military capabilities. First, military stalemates impart important information to combatants regarding their relative war-fighting abilities and help eliminate disagreements and informational asymmetries that might otherwise prevent agreement. It is easier to reach a bargain when each party knows the extent of its rival's military strength. Second, stalemates tend to bestow relatively equal bargaining power on each of the adversaries and thus promise a more equal distribution of power in any new government. If it is true, as the credible commitment theory claims, that combatants only implement those settlements that extend substantial power-sharing pacts, then only those combatants who are fairly equally matched on the battlefield will have the necessary leverage to obtain these terms.[12]

Territorial Goals

The most striking finding shown in table 4.5 is the effect of territorial goals on the likelihood of signed bargains. Although combatants involved in territorial wars are no more likely to initiate negotiations than combatants in nonterritorial confrontations, they are 20 percent *less*

[12] For an excellent discussion on the effects of the distribution of power on settlement see R. Harrison Wagner, "Peace, War, and the Balance of Power," *American Political Science Review* 88 (1994): 593–607.

likely to reach a mutually acceptable settlement once they do begin to talk.[13] Combatants who fought for territorial control, as the Sudanese did in the 1960s and 1970s and the Croatians did in the early 1990s, were significantly less inclined to reach and sign settlements than combatants who competed for nonterritorial goals such as control of government.

This result is quite startling. If anything, one would expect to find a positive relationship between territorial wars and combatants' willingness to sign a bargain, since it was hypothesized that the stakes of war should be easier to divide in territorial conflicts. In addition, the credible commitment theory implies that combatants fighting for territorial separation have an easier time cooperating since they need not worry about exploitation after a treaty. It is possible that territorial disputes represent situations where combatants have already failed to work together and were pursuing separation as a result. In this case, it is the combatants' failure to negotiate that causes rebels to shift their goals in favor of territorial separation, not the other way around. This might explain why territorial conflicts have such a low rate of negotiation.

Mediation

The final factor that has a sizable and significant effect on the willingness of civil war combatants to reach and sign bargains is outside mediation.[14] As table 4.5 shows, governments and rebels are 39 percent more likely to bargain successfully with the help of a mediator than on their own ($p < .01$). Richard Holbrook, George C. Marshall, and Lord Owen and Cyrus Vance probably deserve credit for peace agreements reached under their guidance in Bosnia, China, and Croatia respectively. Moreover, the fact that this relationship is so strong despite the rough measure of mediation (the presence or absence of an outside mediator, rather than a more refined measure of the mediator's ability) offers particularly clear support for mediation theories of resolution. An intermediary's ability to press one or both parties to accept a proposal, to

[13] This finding is compatible with one made by Ted Gurr. In his *Minorities at Risk* study, Gurr found that wars of secession were longer and more violent than those that did not aim for independence. This finding is supported by data on interstate conflicts. Evan Luard and Kalevi Holsti have found that competing governments are less likely to resolve disagreements over territory than almost any other issue, and territorial issues are one of the most frequent sources of war. See Evan Luard, *War in International Society* (London: I. B. Tauris, 1986); and Kalevi J. Holsti, *Peace and War: Armed Conflicts and International Order, 1648–1989* (New York: Cambridge University Press, 1991).

[14] Two other scholarly works had similar findings for interstate wars. Jacob Bercovitch and William Dixon both found that third-party mediation was consistently effective in preventing escalation and promoting peaceful settlement in conflicts between states.

manipulate the agenda, control information, and sequence offers in ways that push combatants toward agreement does appear to "grease the wheels" of the bargaining process and make settlement more likely. This finding lends support to bargaining theorists who argue that informational problems often stand in the way of negotiated settlements. Mediators do appear to help solve this problem, perhaps by teasing out private information, or simply opening up better channels of communication.

Factors Affecting the Decision to Implement an Agreement

Reaching and signing a peace treaty, however, does not guarantee that negotiations will succeed. As I discussed in chapter 1, in almost half of all civil wars where combatants signed a bargain (ten of twenty-three cases), the factions reverted to violence and the civil war continued. Comprehensive peace agreements were signed in Laos, China, the Philippines, Angola, Afghanistan, Chad, Uganda, Somalia, Liberia, and Rwanda, yet all failed to bring peace. In this section, I show why the conditions that allow combatants to reach a bargain will not convince them to end a war, and I discuss what can be done to improve the chances that a bargain, once struck, will be implemented.

Once again, table 4.6 displays changes in expected probabilities for the implementation phase of the resolution process as each of the significant independent variables varies from its lowest to its highest level. Once combatants agree on the final terms of a settlement, only third-party security guarantees and power-sharing pacts are decisive in convincing them to follow through with cooperation. Three other factors are significantly related to implementation, but all have only a negligible effect on the final outcome.

Once treaties have been signed, combatants are 20 percent more likely to implement the terms if a third party offers a security guarantee, 18 percent more likely to do so if the agreement includes a territorial pact, and 16 percent more likely to implement an agreement if it includes a political pact. By contrast, a military stalemate, territorial goals, and a mediator increase the likelihood of implementation by less than five percentage points each.

Third-Party Security Guarantees

Once combatants have signed a peace agreement, all of the other factors purported to influence the outcome of civil wars fade away except third-party security guarantees and power-sharing pacts. Combatants

TABLE 4.6
Predicted Probability That a Settlement Will Be Successfully Implemented

Variable	Probability Estimate	Probability Difference
Third-party security guarantee		
No	.004	
Yes	.20	
		.20**
Territorial pact		
No	.005	
Yes	.19	
		.18*
Political pact		
No	.004	
Yes	.16	
		.16^
Military stalemate		
No	.005	
Yes	.033	
		.03^
Territorial goals		
No	.02	
Yes	.002	
		−.02*
Mediator		
No	.002	
Yes	.05	
		.05**

Note: Probabilities are derived from the ordered logit model presented in table 4.4.
  ^$p < .10$ *$p < .05$ **$p < .01$

clearly are concerned with their short and long-term survival if they do implement a peace agreement and are unlikely to proceed without strong guarantees about their future security.

The unmistakable and powerful relationship between security guarantees and the outcome of civil wars is even more apparent when the eventual outcome is compared to the presence or absence of third-party guarantees. As table 4.7 shows, signed bargains are almost always implemented if a third party guarantees the safety of combatants as they demobilize. They are almost never implemented if a third party does not.

TABLE 4.7

Implementation of Settlements with and without Third-Party
Security Guarantees

	No Implemented Settlement	Implemented Settlement
No third-party security guarantee	9	2
Third-party security guarantee	1	11

Between 1940 and 1992, combatants in twenty-three civil wars signed formal peace settlements. Third-party security guarantees were offered in twelve of these cases, and all but one of these settlements were successfully implemented. Outside powers guaranteed Lebanon's 1958 agreement, the Dominican Republic's Act of Dominican Resolution, Sudan's Addis Ababa agreement, Zimbabwe's Lancaster House agreement, the Tela agreement in Nicaragua, the Chapultepec accords that ended El Salvador's civil war, Cambodia's 1991 Paris peace agreement, Guatemala's 1996 agreement, Mozambique's Rome accord, Croatia's Geneva peace agreement, and Bosnia's Dayton accord, and all brought peace. The only signed settlement that was not implemented even though security guarantees were offered was Angola, and in this case Jonas Savimbi appeared to have no interest in peace. In contrast, nine of eleven signed settlements failed to end their respective wars without outside guarantees.

Two civil wars did end in negotiated settlements without the assistance of an outside security guarantee (Colombia in 1958 and Yemen in 1970). Yet a closer look at these two cases confirms the predictions of the credible commitment theory. Colombia and Yemen were the only two wars where the opposing parties had no partisan armies to demobilize once a settlement was signed. In Colombia, the war was fought by small bands of armed peasants rather than the national army, which remained relatively uninvolved in the fighting. In Yemen, the royalist rebels had no regular army and procured fighters through negotiations with powerful regional sheikhs.[15] Thus, once the Conservatives and Liberals in Colombia and the Royalists and Republicans in Yemen agreed to cooperate, they simply bought the loyalty of either the powerful Colombian generals or the Yemeni tribes and in this way obtained a relatively neutral and ready-made national force. In short, these adversaries

---

[15] An excellent account of this war can be found in Robert W. Stookey, *Yemen: The Politics of the Yemen Arab Republic* (Boulder: Westview Press, 1978), especially 243–45 and 258.

could agree to cooperate because they could bypass the vulnerable demobilization and reintegration period all other combatants faced.[16]

Territorial and Political Pacts

Power-sharing pacts played almost an equally critical role in the final outcome of civil war negotiations. Fifty-five percent of peace treaties that included a political, military, or territorial guarantee were successfully implemented.[17] Power-sharing pacts, however, were not by themselves sufficient to ensure the successful implementation of a treaty. Combatants in nine cases (45 percent of the total) were willing to offer each other detailed power-sharing guarantees but were then unwilling to implement the terms when third-party security guarantees failed to materialize. Laos' agreement in Geneva in 1962 promised to create a new government consisting of seven neutralist representatives and four representatives from each of the right wing parties, and equally integrate the armies of the three political factions into a single national army. Uganda's peace accord of 1985 distributed important council seats to members of all the warring factions and called for the formation of a new national army. And Rwanda's 1994 accord included some of the most detailed consociational arrangements of any settlement in the study. Combatants in all of these cases, however, refused to implement any terms. In short, even the most detailed power-sharing arrangements were not enough to ensure a successfully negotiated settlement in the absence of third-party guarantees.

None of the other variables presented in chapter 3 appear to have a significant effect on the willingness of combatants to implement a peace agreement.

The Costs of War

In the end, neither the duration of war nor war-related deaths were sufficient to convince combatants to sign and implement a peace settlement. A high number of deaths and protracted violence might have convinced combatants to initiate negotiations, but once these negotiations

---

[16] This finding indicates that the credible commitment theory of civil war resolution may be applicable only in those cases where the groups control separate partisan armies, and does not apply to those situations where a negotiated peace treaty creates few security risks.

[17] Similar results emerged from a related study of intrastate wars. An analysis of all civil wars between 1945 and 1997 found that settlements that included military, political, or economic institutional guarantees in the terms of a settlement were most likely to be stable. See Caroline A. Hartzell, "Explaining the Stability of Negotiated Settlements to Intrastate Wars," *Journal of Conflict Resolution* 43, no. 1 (1999): 3–22.

were under way, they had no significant impact on the eventual outcome of a war.

The fact that combatants become insensitive to the costs of war once
negotiations begin indicates that other more important factors come
into play as combatants look down the road and decide whether or not
they will benefit from a peaceful solution to war. In keeping with the
logic of the credible commitment theory, once combatants begin to talk
about terms of settlement, the everyday costs of war *should* fade in
comparison to the potentially greater costs of post-treaty abuse. At this
point, civil war combatants should base their decision to sign and implement a peace settlement on the potential costs they expect to pay
for being duped, and not on the material costs they paid prior to
negotiations.

Territorial Goals

As mentioned earlier, territorial goals had an unusual effect on the
peace process. Whereas combatants who pursue territorial secession or
greater regional autonomy were no more likely to initiate negotiations,
territorial goals had a strong negative effect on their willingness to sign
a treaty, and a negative, although weaker, effect on their decision to
implement the terms.[18] As I explained earlier, the fact that civil wars
fought over territory are less likely to reach bargains than wars fought
for political control could be because these wars represent conflicts that
are so intractable that exit becomes the only option.

Military Stalemate

Although a military stalemate was statistically related to the implementation of a peace agreement, its impact on this final stage was also
largely irrelevant.[19] Consistent with expectations arising from the credible commitment theory, a balance of power should have little effect on
combatants' willingness to implement a peace settlement since whatever

---

[18] This finding is supported by a study of all civil wars and separatist revolts since 1945
by Mason and Fett. They found that separatist wars were no more likely to end in negotiated settlements than revolutions. This stands in contrast to a comparative study of
eighty-one international and civil conflicts in Africa, Europe, and the Middle East between
1945 and 1985 by Hugh Miall. When one looks only at conflicts in these three regions
and includes interstate conflicts as well, territorial goals make peaceful settlement *more*
likely. See Miall, *The Peacemakers*.

[19] As previously noted, military stalemate is moderately correlated with both the duration of war and the number of war-related deaths. However, taking military stalemate out
of the regression analysis does not increase the impact of either war duration or the
number of war-related deaths at any stage.

defensive advantage existed disappears as soon as combatants are forced to demobilize. Combatants who are nervous about their future would obtain no added sense of security knowing they have symmetrical capabilities if these capabilities disappear as implementation proceeds. The fact that government armies and rebel armies frequently did not disband equally or simultaneously made a balance of power even less important at this stage. Second, a balance of power can quickly turn into a decisive rout if one side demobilizes while the other reneges on the agreement and launches a surprise attack.

This finding offers partial support for balance-of-power theories but clearly indicates that such a balance is not sufficient to convince groups to proceed with a risky implementation period. A balance of power may make war sufficiently costly to bring combatants to the table, and it may impart the necessary information to allow them to reach a bargain, but if a peace settlement requires combatants to reduce the number of soldiers under arms and break down partisan armies, even a robust military balance will not convince them to implement the terms.

Constraints on the Executive

Once again, the degree of executive constraints continued to have no effect on leaders' decisions to sign and implement negotiated settlements. Leaders of democratic regimes appeared to be under no greater pressure to initiate negotiations, sign bargains, or implement peace settlements than their nondemocratic counterparts. Institutional constraints, therefore, were unable to facilitate cooperation in the risky post–civil war environment.

One can imagine a number of reasons why democratic leaders would be no more willing to implement a peace treaty than leaders who operated under fewer institutional restraints.[20] First, if it is true that a negotiated settlement could leave a group worse off than continued war, then citizens are unlikely to press for settlement in the absence of effective guarantees. Voters may wish to see their leader attempt to negotiate, but if a pact comes at the price of a high-risk transition, it is unlikely that they will push their leader so far. Second, citizens and subgroups will have greater difficulty influencing the outcome of negotiations as long as closed-door negotiations allow their leaders to control the amount of information they share with their public. Democratic constraints are effective only if citizens can trace the breakdown of a treaty to their leader.

---

[20] A similar finding was made in regard to economic reform. See Joel S. Hellman, "Winners Take All: The Politics of Partial Reform in Postcommunist Transitions," *World Politics* 50, no. 2 (1998): 203–34.

The fact that executive constraints seem to play no role in the peaceful resolution of civil wars challenges an assumption found in the literature. International relations scholars have debated whether democratic institutions can facilitate cooperation. What these findings seem to show is that democratic constraints do not make leaders more likely to cooperate in situations where the costs of cheating are high. When leaders face a particularly dangerous implementation period, it is third-party verification and enforcement that matters, not regime type.

Mediation

The evidence presented in this chapter also shows that mediation has very little impact on combatants' decision to implement peace plans even though mediation was consequential in pulling together the plan.[21] In the end, wars in which a mediator was present during negotiations were more apt to end in a negotiated settlement because they reached a mutually acceptable settlement more frequently, but mediation did not appear to be the final variable upon which successful implementation hung. This seems to indicate that in many civil wars the failure of negotiations is *not* a failure of bargaining but rather the inability to solve problems of post-treaty enforcement.

Identity, Goals, and Divisibility

The remaining theories based on ethnic differences, total goals, and divisibility continued to have no predictive power in determining how civil wars end. Once again, civil wars that broke down along ethnic lines were no less likely to end in a negotiated settlement than nonethnic wars. This finding challenges popular notions that ethnic wars are more resistant to compromise solution than nonethnic wars.[22] It also lends further support to the rational actor model that tends to view all combatants as driven by the same cost calculations regardless of ethnic affiliations or identity.

The actual distribution of population and resources also had no mea-

[21] One other scholarly work had a similar finding. In their study on the contribution of UN peace operations to peacebuilding, Michael Doyle and Nicholas Sambanis found that UN mediation had no significant effect on successful peacebuilding. They did not, however, break down the analysis into three phases and therefore could not say whether mediation had an effect earlier in the peace process. See Michael W. Doyle and Nicholas Sambanis, "International Peacebuilding: A Theoretical and Quantitative Analysis," *American Political Science Review* 94 (2000): 778–801.

[22] Quantitative studies by Roy Licklider, "The Consequences of Negotiated Settlement in Civil Wars, 1945–1993," *American Political Science Review* 89 (1995): 681–90, and by Mason and Fett, "How Civil Wars End," had similar findings.

surable impact on combatants' decision to pursue a negotiated settlement at any stage of the peace process. Wars where it would be relatively easy to divide the population and resources were no more or less likely to end in negotiated settlements. Finally, theories that claim that total wars should be more difficult to resolve through negotiated settlements than those fought over limited goals are also not supported in these relationships. The data clearly show that wars fought for total aims such as full control over the government or social revolution were as likely to end in negotiated settlement as those fought for less total aims such as a share of governmental control or political reform.

This finding suggests that it may be wrong to draw inferences about the likelihood of compromise based on the stated goals of the belligerents. Once violence erupts, civil wars appear to face the same difficult resolution problems, regardless of the initial aims, ideology, or demands of the participants. Once fighting begins, combatants appear to get frozen into adversarial positions, and the structure of the situation appears to determine to a large extent how long they will fight, and whether they will accept and implement the terms of a settlement.

Conclusion

The empirical results presented in this chapter are striking. Various circumstances in a civil war may encourage enemies to negotiate, and certain additional factors push groups to sign a compromise settlement, but unless groups receive a guarantee from an outside country or international organization that ensures their safety during demobilization, and unless they are willing to include specific political or territorial pacts in their peace treaties, they are apt not to implement the settlement. Once negotiations begin, the success of these negotiations really is driven by combatants' beliefs that a third party will step in to verify and enforce demobilization and political and territorial power will be shared.

This finding provides strong support for the credible commitment theory and attests to the unique role post-treaty security plays in the resolution of civil wars. The seventy-two civil wars that began between 1940 and 1992 differed from each other in many ways, yet one fact appeared interchangeable. Combatants who wished to end their war though peaceful means encountered similar implementation problems. The costs of war, the goals of the combatants, the military conditions on the battlefield, and mediation did encourage groups to pursue settlement. In the end, however, it was the structure of the postsettlement transition period that determined whether negotiations would end in war or peace.

The importance of third-party security guarantees and power-sharing pacts was not, however, the only finding to come out of this chapter. The findings presented confirm how important it is to view the termination of war as a three-stage process. Previously, academics and other observers of civil wars have failed to draw clear distinctions between different stages of the resolution process. Theorists have either emphasized the importance of the first stage (whether combatants choose to negotiate) or the second stage (whether combatants choose to reach and sign a compromise solution). My research not only demonstrates that a third stage in the process is critical to the ultimate success or failure of negotiations to end civil wars, but also reveals that very different conditions encourage cooperation at each step along the way.

Finally, one issue is not dealt with in this chapter that merits serious thought. Although the findings presented here offer strong support for the credible commitment theory of civil war resolution, they are far from a complete test of the theory. It is still possible that these findings are spurious, since outside security guarantees and power-sharing pacts may only be offered in cases that would have succeeded on their own and not in cases that were bound to fail. In the next chapter I look more critically at the interrelationships between third-party security guarantees, power-sharing pacts, and the outcome of civil wars to see if the findings presented here are truly robust.

5. A Closer Look at the Findings

☙ THE LAST CHAPTER CONFIRMED three principal features of the credible commitment theory. First, outside security guarantees and power-sharing pacts are significantly related to the peaceful resolution of civil wars. Second, civil war combatants do look down the road and consider compliance when they decide to sign and implement settlements. Third, the resolution of civil wars involves three very distinct steps, and the conditions that encourage combatants to proceed at each step are not the same.

The aim in this chapter is to look more critically at these findings. I am particularly interested in investigating three relationships more closely. First, do third-party security guarantees and extensive power-sharing agreements need to be paired with each other to be effective, or is it possible to obtain a negotiated peace with just one of these elements? Policymakers will want to know whether third-party intervention can be avoided if combatants are willing to construct powerful treaty guarantees for each other. Second, does the size and strength of third-party security guarantees and the number of power-sharing pacts make successful settlement more attainable? Since the empirical analysis in the previous chapter treated all outside guarantees and power-sharing pacts as identical regardless of their scope, there was no way to tell whether a more committed third party or a greater variety of power-sharing guarantees would improve the odds of successful settlement. Finally, do third-party security guarantees and power-sharing pacts have an independent causal effect on the decision to settle a civil war, or are they offered only in cases that would have succeeded on their own? Although the analysis in chapter 4 showed that third-party security guarantees and power-sharing pacts are linked to peaceful settlement, a counterargument could be made that both are offered only in cases where the prospects for peace are high.

Three sections follow. The first section tests whether third-party security guarantees and power-sharing pacts are necessary *in combination* to bring a peaceful solution to war. The data reveal that civil wars are significantly more likely to end in a successfully implemented settlement if both types of guarantees are present. This finding corresponds to the argument presented in chapter 2 that third-party security guarantees and power-sharing pacts serve different functions (outside guarantees reassure combatants about their short-term physical survival, power-sharing pacts reassure them of their long-term political viability). Both appear critical in the decision to cooperate.

The second section investigates the size and strength of third-party guarantees and the number of power-sharing pacts to see if stronger guarantees and more extensive pacts increase the odds of ending a war peacefully. I find that once combatants agree to negotiate, stronger third-party guarantees and a greater number of power-sharing pacts do not greatly increase the likelihood of a negotiated peace. A relationship does exist, however, between the strength of a third-party security guarantee and the number of pacts combatants are willing to offer. Weak third-party commitments tend to be offset with stronger, more extensive power-sharing pacts and vice versa.

The third section tests whether third-party guarantees and power-sharing pacts have an independent, causal effect on adversaries' decision to settle their wars. Two factors suggest that they do. First, security guarantees and power-sharing pacts are largely unrelated to any of the other causal variables. Second, combatants in the majority of cases behave in ways predicted by the credible commitment theory: they have great difficulty resolving issues of post-treaty security, they actively seek third-party help, and they wait to implement the military terms of the settlement until third parties arrive on the ground.

This chapter attempts to address potential doubts about the relationship between, on the one hand, third-party security guarantees and power-sharing pacts, and, on the other, the peaceful resolution of civil wars. Before continuing, however, a word of caution is in order. Each of the analyses that follows is based on a small number of cases. There are, for example, only twenty civil wars in which the combatants offered each other power-sharing pacts, and only thirteen civil wars in which an outside state or international organization offered a security guarantee. The reader should, therefore, view the following results as suggestive of trends, not as definitive tests of causal relationships.[1] Some useful generalizations, however, are possible.

Are Both Power-Sharing Pacts and Outside Guarantees Necessary?

This section attempts to answer two questions. Do combatants always require a third-party guarantor, or can they avoid outside intervention

---

[1] The small number of cases also made it impossible to break the analysis down into three separate stages. There were not sufficient cases, for example, to determine what the combatants would do at each stage in the peace process. All I can say is whether the combination of each of these factors is more or less likely to lead to a successfully implemented settlement.

by offering each other particularly generous power-sharing pacts? Conversely, do third-party guarantees work only if combatants are willing to offer each other some form of power-sharing guarantee, or can outsiders bring about peace without the help of pacts?

The Insufficiency of Power-Sharing Pacts

A more detailed analysis of the individual power-sharing pacts reveals that pacts are not, by themselves, sufficient to convince combatants to implement a peace settlement. As table 5.1 shows, even when combatants are willing to establish a power-sharing pact, if a third party did not intervene, 80 percent of these pacts (eight of ten) failed to bring peace.[2] In contrast, almost every peace treaty that included *both* a power-sharing pact and a third-party security guarantee was successfully implemented.

The Arusha accords between the Tutsis and Hutus in Rwanda offered the competing factions some of the most extensive political and military power-sharing guarantees of all the cases, yet this treaty disintegrated when United Nations peacekeepers failed to arrive. The Uganda government and the National Resistance Movement carefully distributed the seats in a new government and agreed to integrate their armies, but could find no third party willing to establish a peacekeeping force. These terms were also never implemented. Similarly, the Nigerian government promised the Ibos general amnesty, offered them a fair share of employment in federal public services, and promised that police units in Ibo areas would consist mostly of persons of Ibo origin, but this did little to reduce Ibo fear of postwar persecution. Without an external guarantor, this offer had little impact on negotiations, and it eventually failed to produce a settlement. In only two cases, Yemen in 1970 and Columbia in 1958, was a power-sharing pact sufficient to bring peace without third-party assistance. Yet, as I discussed in chapter 4, these factions had no partisan armies to disengage and could, therefore, circumvent the dangerous demobilization period that made implementation so difficult. In short, while it is clearly important to develop institutional safeguards to address longer-term concerns of political representation, a purely institutional solution is not enough to address the short-term security concerns that exist in the aftermath of a civil war.

But why would enemies go through the trouble to sign a peace agree-

---

[2] Even when power-sharing agreements were more extensive (i.e., combatants offered each other not just one type of pact but two or more types of pacts), the results were the same. Power-sharing agreements with two pacts failed 80 percent of the time (four of five), and agreements with three pacts failed 100 percent of the time (one of one) if they were not accompanied by a third-party guarantee.

TABLE 5.1

Implementation of Settlements with Power-Sharing Pacts, with and without
Third-Party Security Guarantees

	No Successfully Implemented Settlement	Successfully Implemented Settlement
Power-sharing pact with a third-party security guarantee	1 (10%)	9 (90%)
Power-sharing pact without a third-party security guarantee	8 (80%)	2 (20%)

ment in the absence of a third-party guarantee? As I discussed in chapter 2, combatants sometimes actively negotiate and even sign a peace settlement in the absence of a third-party security guarantee in the hope that one will materialize. Here, the combatants take a chance that a third party will step forward, knowing that a third party might not help them implement a peace agreement.

Third-Party Security Guarantees without Power-Sharing Pacts

The fact that power-sharing pacts tend to require third-party security guarantees to be implemented does not mean that the reverse is also true. Can a third-party security guarantee lead to peace on its own?

The data in table 5.2 are ambiguous. There were only four cases where a third-party guarantee was offered in the absence of any power-sharing pacts and in half of those cases—the Dominican Republic and Croatia—a third-party guarantee brought about peace without a power-sharing pact. In both of these cases, the outside guarantor used a significant display of force to ensure cooperation.

What is clear from table 5.2, however, is that combining a third-party security guarantee with a power-sharing pact substantially increases the likelihood of a successfully implemented settlement.[3] In all but one of the cases, a third-party guarantee together with a power-sharing pact brought peace. The only exception was the 1994 Lusaka accords signed in Angola. In this instance Jonas Savimbi, leader of UNITA, refused to

[3] Similar results emerged in a somewhat different data set constructed by Michael W. Doyle and Nicholas Sambanis. They found that peace enforcement operations had a positive role in ending violent conflict, but were more likely to succeed in concert with strategies aimed at transforming domestic institutions. See Doyle and Sambanis, "International Peacebuilding."

TABLE 5.2
Implementation of Settlements with Third-Party Security Guarantees, with and without Power-Sharing Pacts

	No Successfully Implemented Settlement	Successfully Implemented Settlement
Third-party security guarantee with a power-sharing pact	1 (10%)	9 (90%)
Third-party security guarantee without a power-sharing pact	2 (50%)	2 (50%)

abide by the terms of the agreement and appeared genuinely uninterested in peace. In this unusual, perhaps even unique, case, one side stubbornly refused to cooperate despite an adversary willing to make concessions and despite a third party willing to help with implementation. Most accounts attribute Savimbi's intransigence to UNITA's access to diamond reserves and the benefits of resource extraction.

Are Stronger Third-Party Guarantees More Effective?

The previous chapter treated all third-party guarantees and all power-sharing pacts identically. In this section, we will see whether variations in the size or strength of outside intervention or in the number of pacts make a difference in the outcome of civil wars. I do this for two reasons. The first motivation is theoretical. Chapter 2 predicted that under certain conditions combatants will faithfully implement the terms of a settlement even though they are unsure of a third party's commitment to peace. The degree of uncertainty combatants tolerate is purported to depend on three factors: (1) the punishment costs they would suffer if the third party faithfully cracked down on cheating, (2) the benefits combatants would receive if they cooperated, and (3) the benefits a combatant would receive if it won an outright victory. Here we see whether the cases support these suppositions.

The second motivation is practical. Policymakers will want to know if they can offer weaker, yet still effective, guarantees and thus commit fewer soldiers to places where they have little strategic or national interest. Outsiders will also want to know if they should press combatants to extend a wider variety of power-sharing guarantees to each other, or if guarantees in one area are sufficient. A narrower guarantee may allow outsiders to reduce the commitment they need to make in order to get a successful settlement.

Stronger Third-Party Guarantees No More Effective Than Weak Ones

There is no clear relationship between a stronger commitment of forces by the third party and the successful implementation of a peace settlement. In the vast majority of cases, a third-party guarantee, no matter how strong or weak, led to success. Larger enforcement missions such as NATO's in Bosnia were no more likely to secure a negotiated settlement than smaller verification missions such as the UN's in Guatemala or El Salvador.

This finding stands in contrast to predictions made by the credible commitment theory in chapter 2. The theory leads one to expect that more extensive outside guarantees will create a greater sense of security, which in turn increase the likelihood of successful settlement. Two factors may account for this outcome. The first is the extremely small number of cases; two or three additions could significantly alter the results. The second factor is the coding of the cases. As noted in chapter 3, only those cases where the third party arrived on the ground with the promised mandate were coded as a "Security Guarantee" and included in this analysis. What the analysis may indicate, therefore, is that once a third-party guarantee arrives on the ground, increasing the strength of that guarantee does not greatly affect the outcome of the war.

There does, however, appear to be an inverse relationship between the strength of third-party security guarantees and the number of power-sharing pacts. As figure 5.1 illustrates, when outside security guarantees were weak, peace treaties tended to include more extensive internal power-sharing arrangements. Conversely, when outside security guarantees were strong, internal guarantees tended to be more limited.

This inverse relationship is more evident when treaties are compared. The settlement to end the Sudanese civil war was underwritten by the weakest guarantee of this study. Yet in this case, Ethiopian emperor Haile Selassie's fairly thin promise to the Sudanese's rebels that "his government was committed to their security" and his personal guarantee that Anya Nya returnees would not suffer reprisals were supplemented by some of the most detailed federal provisions of any settlement.[4] Zimbabwe's weak guarantee from Britain was balanced by extensive internal security arrangements. Black Zimbabweans were offered one-man, one-vote elections in a country where they represented

---

[4] Hiskias Assefa, *Mediation in Civil Wars: Approaches and Strategies: The Sudan Conflict* (Boulder: Westview Press, 1987), 140–41.

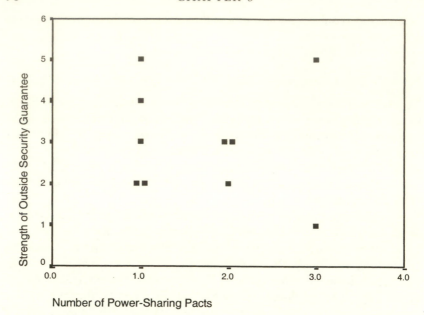

Fig. 5.1. The relationship between the strength of outside security guarantees and the number of power-sharing pacts

97 percent of the population; white civilians were required to surrender their vast private armory of weapons; certain Rhodesian military and paramilitary units were to be disbanded; and a new civil police was formed. In return, white Rhodesians were guaranteed 20 percent of the seats in the lower house of parliament, allowed to retain control over the Rhodesian air force, and permitted to keep South African forces on Zimbabwean soil. White settlers were also permitted to retain dual citizenship with Britain, a condition that promised a quick escape should things go wrong. Ultimately, the combination of internal guarantees and outside intervention convinced combatants to accept and implement a long-term solution to the war.

These very extensive arrangements can be contrasted to the strong third-party guarantee, but weak political and military guarantees, included in the agreement in 1958 to end the civil war in Lebanon, and Nicaragua's Election Agreement of 1989. In Lebanon, the treaty mentioned only that a coalition cabinet would be composed of two Muslim leaders and two Christian leaders. No other pacts were included. This treaty, however, was backed by fourteen thousand U.S. troops. In Nicaragua, eight hundred armed Venezuelan paratroopers and 260 unarmed UN peacekeepers oversaw the implementation of an agreement that included only a territorial pact.[5] In short, outsiders who were willing to send a large contingent of enforcement forces appeared to counterbalance fairly weak power-sharing arrangements.

Four of the remaining cases fell somewhere between these two extremes. Cambodia (1991), Mozambique (1992), El Salvador (1992), and Guatemala (1996) all had moderately strong outside security guarantees together with one or two power-sharing pacts. Bosnia appears to be the only exception to the rule; here the peace treaty included extensive political, military, and territorial guarantees, *and* was backed by an exceptionally large armed NATO peacekeeping force of sixty thousand. This strong third-party guarantee in the face of equally strong power-sharing pacts could be due to the great imbalance of power between Serb and Bosnian Muslim forces, to Slobodan Milosevic's lack of enthusiasm for the Dayton peace negotiations, and to the Clinton administration's determination to ensure a success after embarrassing failures in Somalia and Haiti. In short, combatants seem to be able to forge a fairly high level of security through some *combination* of third-party intervention and power-sharing pacts.

The Question of Causality

My main concern until now has been with the relationship between third-party security guarantees and power-sharing pacts, on the one hand, and the peaceful settlement of civil wars on the other. While the evidence suggests that both third-party intervention and power-sharing pacts play critical roles in getting combatants through the peace process, it is still unclear whether third-party guarantees and power-sharing pacts *cause* groups to sign and implement negotiated settlements. Skeptics could justifiably argue that these guarantees are derived from other more important causal variables.

Two tests were designed to check whether power-sharing pacts and security guarantees had an independent effect on adversaries' decision to sign and implement treaties. First, third-party guarantees and power-sharing pacts were treated as dependent variables, and a logit analysis was performed to see if any of the other factors relevant to the resolution of civil wars predicted the presence of either variable. In the second test, each of the individual cases in which signed bargains were reached was examined in greater detail. If security guarantees and power-sharing pacts were simply offered in cases that would have succeeded

[5] Nicaragua's 1989 agreement promised to create twenty-three self-governing development zones, representing 20 percent of the country, which the Contras could occupy and police on their own.

on their own, adversaries should sign and implement agreements as
soon as the issues driving the war were resolved, they should not
request outside assistance with implementation, and they should not
wait to implement the terms until third-party forces arrive on the
ground.

Are Power-Sharing Pacts Offered Only in Cases That Are Ripe for Peace?

To see if power-sharing pacts were offered only in negotiations that
were likely to succeed anyway, a logit regression was run with "power-
sharing pact" as the dependent variable. All of the other factors included in the empirical analysis in chapter 4 were included as independent variables. If power-sharing pacts are only offered in cases that are
ripe for peace, the presence of a pact should be explained by one or
more of these other factors.

Table 5.3 suggests that power-sharing pacts are not epiphenomenal.
Most of the factors associated with the peaceful resolution of civil wars
did not significantly predict the presence of power-sharing guarantees.
Factors such as war-related deaths, a military stalemate, territorial
goals, constraints on the executive, and mediation—all important at

TABLE 5.3
Logit Analysis of Factors Associated with Power-Sharing Pacts

Independent Variable	Coefficient	Standard Error
Duration of war	.01**	.006
War-related deaths	.00	.002
Military stalemate	.08	.99
Executive constraints	.19	.20
Ethnic division	−.94	1.09
Total goals	.71	1.60
Territorial goals	−1.44	1.90
Difficulty of division	.91	.53
Mediator	1.26	.90
Security guarantee	2.60**	.99
Constant	−5.74**	2.16
Pseudo R^2	.48	
χ^2	40.70	

Note: N = 72. Heteroscedasticity-consistent standard errors, clustered by country,
were employed.
**$p < .01$

one point in the resolution process—do not predict when combatants will offer binding power-sharing arrangements.

Two variables, however, did appear to be related to power-sharing pacts. Combatants seemed more apt to extend pacts to each other if they had fought long wars and if a third party stepped in to guarantee demobilization. It is not surprising that longer wars are likely to induce civil war combatants to offer each other power-sharing pacts. Lengthy wars wear the combatants down to the point where they are likely to offer generous terms. Still, the fact that groups are willing to absorb the costs involved with extending guarantees even in cases where battles were long indicates that combatants understand it as an important step in attaining peace.

The only other variable that significantly predicts the presence of power-sharing pacts is the existence of a third-party security guarantee. This relationship is more difficult to disentangle since the direction of causation is unclear. It could be that the two sides wait until a third-party guarantee is offered before they are willing to extend a pact. In practice, however, political and territorial pacts are usually decided before third-party guarantees are sought, a pattern that will become clearer in the more detailed case studies that follow. More likely, the relationship between the two factors is spurious, since both pacts and security guarantees come into play only after negotiations are under way and are therefore likely to be correlated.

In order to see if third-party security guarantees and power-sharing pacts are causally related, I repeated the analysis using only the thirty-seven civil wars in which combatants held formal negotiations (analysis not shown). Here, variables that were present in all seventy-two civil wars would have the same opportunity to affect power-sharing pacts as those present only after negotiations commenced (such as third-party guarantees). In this analysis, the relationship between security guarantees and pacts and that between duration of war and pacts fail to obtain the standard level of significance. The fact that the relationship between both of these factors and power-sharing pacts diminishes suggests that power-sharing pacts cannot be easily explained by looking at the conditions on the ground.[6]

Are Third-Party Guarantees a Rubber Stamp?

The same test was conducted using "third-party security guarantee" as the dependent variable. If it is true that third parties offer security guar-

---

[6] As an alternate test, I used all of the independent variables with the exception of power-sharing pacts to predict negotiated settlement and then showed that power-sharing pacts significantly predicted the residual from the previous regression.

TABLE 5.4
Logit Analysis of Factors Associated with Third-Party Guarantees

Independent Variable	Coefficient	Standard Error
Duration of war	.000	.005
War-related deaths	−.003	.003
Military stalemate	.79	1.02
Executive constraints	−.18	.24
Ethnic division	−.02	1.12
Total goals	−1.97	1.63
Territorial goals	−.58	1.81
Difficulty of division	−.17	.50
Mediator	2.22*	1.08
Power-sharing pact	2.50**	1.00
Constant	−1.52	1.86
Pseudo R^2	.36	
χ^2	25.58	

Note: N = 72. Heteroscedasticity-consistent standard errors, clustered by country, were employed.
*$p < .05$ **$p < .01$

antees only after other conditions point to peace, then guarantees should be largely explained by the other independent variables discussed in chapter 3. However, as table 5.4 shows, this is largely not the case. Of all the factors shown to be important at any stage in the process of resolving civil wars, only mediation and a power-sharing pact were significantly related to a third party's offer to enforce or verify a treaty. None of the other factors highlighted in chapter 3 (such as the duration of war, war deaths, territorial goals, or a military stalemate) predicts when outsiders will choose to offer assistance. Third parties are not more inclined to offer security guarantees in wars that are especially long or bloody, where the combatants have fought to a military stalemate, where they are fighting for more limited goals, or where the government operates under executive constraints. In short, outsiders did not choose to intervene only in those wars that appeared ripe for resolution.

What happens when the analysis is repeated using only the thirty-seven civil wars in which combatants held formal negotiations? In this more select set of observations the link between mediation and third-party security guarantees disappears, and power-sharing pacts and security guarantees no longer obtain standard levels of significance, although it remains sufficiently strong to warrant mention ($p < .08$). There are a number of possible reasons why third-party security guarantees and power-sharing pacts may be related. A third party willing to enforce or verify an agreement could strongly encourage combatants to offer each other such guarantees. Second, combatants might be more willing to offer such pacts after a third-party security guarantee has been acquired and the chance of successful implementation has increased. Finally, third parties might use the offer of power-sharing pacts as an indicator of how sincere combatants are about peace.

What then explains when outside states and international organizations choose to verify or enforce a peace settlement? While the statistical analysis offers few clues as to what motivates third parties to play a guarantor role, a closer look at the individual case histories offers some hints.[7] It appears that third parties intervene for a variety of case-specific reasons. Britain, for example, mediated and then intervened in Zimbabwe because it feared continued war would destabilize black-white relations in neighboring South Africa, a country of great strategic and economic interest to London. Britain also appeared to feel a sense of responsibility to its former colony. Similarly, the United States and Western Europe intervened in Bosnia, not because they believed a successful compromise settlement was inevitable, but because they feared violence might spread throughout southeastern Europe. And the United Nations has played a more active peacekeeping role since the early 1990s in part due to the philosophies of two secretaries-general—Boutros Boutros-Ghali and Kofi Annan. Most of these reasons are unrelated to the conditions on the ground at the time of settlement.[8]

As a second test of the importance of third-party security guarantees, I looked more systematically at the sequence of negotiations and the timing of third-party intervention. This second test scrutinized each of the individual negotiations to see whether combatants' ability to overcome difficult enforcement problems really did determine the success or failure of negotiations. If the credible commitment theory is valid, three patterns should emerge: (1) security issues should be the last and most difficult issue to resolve at the negotiating table, (2) the combatants—

[7] In a large-scale study of third-party interventions in civil wars, Patrick Regan found that humanitarian crises were more likely to attract outside involvement, but that very intense conflicts (those with high casualties) were considerably less likely to attract any form of outside intervention. See Regan, *Civil Wars and Foreign Powers*.

[8] For a more detailed discussion on the motivations behind third-party intervention in civil wars see Frederick S. Pearson, "Foreign Military Interventions and Domestic Disputes," *International Studies Quarterly* 18, no. 3 (1974): 259–89; Robert Cooper and Mats Berdal, "Outside Interventions in Ethnic Conflicts," *Survival* 35, no. 1 (1993): 118–42; and David Carment, Dane Rowlands, and Patrick James, "Ethnic Conflict and Third Party Intervention: Riskiness, Rationality, and Commitment," Occasional Paper Series, Norman Paterson School of International Affairs, Carleton University, Ottawa, 1995; and Regan, *Civil Wars and Foreign Powers*.

especially the rebels—should actively seek outside guarantors as they negotiate, (3) implementation should not begin until a third party actively arrives on the ground, and implementation should break down if a third party withdraws prematurely. If third-party enforcement or verification does not exert this effect, then the causal relationship between third-party security guarantees and peaceful settlement posited in chapter 2 would be questioned. A closer examination of the individual cases affirms the strong connection between third-party security guarantees and the signing and implementation of a peace treaty.

SECURITY ISSUES ARE THE MOST DIFFICULT TO RESOLVE

Questions of post-treaty internal security dominated the majority of peace talks. In 57 percent of negotiations in which the combatants eventually signed a bargain, the issue of post-treaty security dominated negotiations, and in almost all of these cases, security was the last issue on the table before a treaty was signed. In Zimbabwe, the leader of the white incumbent government, Ian Smith, accepted black majority rule two years before a settlement was signed. All subsequent negotiations were devoted almost exclusively to the question of how to demobilize and disengage the rival militaries. In Mozambique, the incumbent government acquiesced to the rebels' main demand—power sharing—ten months before a settlement was signed. The twenty subsequent rounds of negotiations were dominated by a search for what Renamo and Frelimo both called "guarantees"; guarantees that the United Nations would send peacekeeping troops, and guarantees that the government would create a multiparty government once Renamo laid down its arms. In Laos, a political settlement was reached in June 1962 but agreement on the integration of the three armed factions into a single military was not reached until five months later. In El Salvador, the difficult issues of human rights and electoral and judicial reform were resolved by April 1991, but negotiations dragged on for an additional eight months. During that time, the FMLN rebels consistently refused to agree to a cease-fire without "a prior final agreement on military reform or sufficient guarantees for its safety."[9] And in Angola, the supposedly make-or-break issue of multiparty rule was settled in the first two months of negotiations. The government and rebels then spent eleven months working out the details of three specific issues: a cease-fire, the integration of both armies, and a system of internal security during the transition. In short, security issues did appear to be the most

[9] Terry Lynn Karl, "El Salvador's Negotiated Revolution," *Foreign Affairs* 71, no. 2 (1992): 158.

difficult to resolve and were almost always the last issue on the table before a settlement was signed.

COMBATANTS' SEARCH FOR THIRD-PARTY SECURITY GUARANTEES

A closer examination of the cases also reveals that combatants in a majority of negotiations actively sought outside security guarantees and often made this a key demand to settlement. In 70 percent of civil wars in which the combatants eventually signed a bargain, either the rebels, the government, or both requested a third party to help implement the agreement. In Zimbabwe the rebels requested that the United Nations send an army composed of several thousand soldiers to oversee the transition, and every attempt to negotiate failed except the one where Britain promised direct military and political involvement during this time. In Mozambique, Renamo demanded extensive United Nations involvement in "monitoring and guaranteeing implementation." In Angola, the rebels insisted that they would not start demobilizing until a twelve-thousand-person armed United Nations peacekeeping force was in place.[10] In Rwanda, the government and the Rwandese Patriotic Front (RPF) rebels sent a joint letter to the United Nations asking it to station a neutral international force in Rwanda to help implement the agreement. In Chad, the combatants asked for "the dispatch of a neutral force there, to protect important persons; supervise the cease-fire, the demilitarization of the capital, and the disarming of civilians; and assist in the integration of various forces into a national army."[11] And in Bosnia, UN peacekeepers had been requested by Bosnian president Izetbegovic as early as 1991, and this request continued through the 1995 Dayton negotiations.

THE TIMING OF TREATY IMPLEMENTATION AND
THE ARRIVAL OF THIRD PARTIES

A closer scrutiny of the individual cases also indicates a causal connection between the timing of third-party intervention and treaty implementation. The Uganda peace accord of December 1985 created a new national army, divided leadership positions in the military council between the government and the rebels, and called for further political power-sharing. One would expect this pact to flourish without the need

[10] This demand was made after the disastrous 1991 Estoril peace accords; the UN sent only 440 unarmed international military officers and 175 civilians with no mandate to enforce demobilization.

[11] Sam C. Nolutshungu, *Limits of Anarchy: Intervention and State Formation in Chad* (Charlottesville: University Press of Virginia, 1996), 157–58.

for additional security guarantees; all the tricky military and political issues had been resolved. But security guarantees were crucial to both the acceptance and the subsequent failure of the treaty. Kenya, Tanzania, Britain, and Canada were asked to establish a peacekeeping force to monitor the cease-fire, but Britain and Canada declined to participate, and peacekeepers from Kenya and Tanzania failed to show up. The treaty broke down soon thereafter. Chad's Reconciliation Accord followed a similar pattern. Signed in August 1979, it called for the demilitarization of the capital, a general amnesty, a broad-based transitional government, and the dissolution of all armed forces. A neutral peacekeeping force from Guinea, Benin, and Congo was promised to enforce the cease-fire. In this case the combatants fulfilled the political terms of the treaty and established a coalition government, but when the neutral African force failed to arrive on schedule, no other terms were implemented. And in Nicaragua, the first contingent of armed Venezuelan soldiers did not arrive until eight months after a peace agreement was signed. Only then did Contra soldiers begin to demobilize.[12]

Similarly, individual cases also suggested a causal connection between the withdrawal of third-party monitors or enforcers and the halting of demobilization. In the end, the success of negotiated settlements seems to rest on a third-party's desire to become involved *and* remain involved until a new national government is established.

Conclusion

The quantitative analysis presented in chapter 4 showed a strong relationship between third-party security guarantees, power-sharing pacts, and the peaceful resolution of civil wars. It did not, however, tell us if these guarantees were interchangeable, if the strength of these guarantees was central to the outcome of a war, or if third-party security guarantees or power-sharing pacts had a direct causal effect on the outcome of civil wars. This chapter has addressed these issues.

Although the number of cases analyzed is small, the data permit some interesting observations about each of these relationships. First, third-party security guarantees and power-sharing pacts are not interchangeable; some combination of third-party enforcement and power-sharing pact appears critical to the peaceful resolution of civil wars. In two cases third-party enforcement, by itself, was enough to bring combatants through the difficult implementation phase, and in an even smaller percentage of cases, a power-sharing pact of one form or another was

---

[12] Jack Child, *The Central American Peace Process, 1983–1991: Sheathing Swords, Building Confidence* (Boulder: Lynne Rienner, 1992), 95–98.

enough on its own to bring about a negotiated settlement. But in most cases, a successful negotiated settlement required the presence of both a power-sharing pact and a third-party security guarantee.

Second, this chapter suggested an inverse relationship between the strength of third-party guarantees and the extensiveness of power-sharing pacts. If a third-party guarantee or a power-sharing pact was relatively weak, it tended to be counterbalanced by a greater number of pacts or a stronger security guarantee. In short, combatants seemed to be able to eliminate the uncertainty surrounding the implementation phase through a balance of external and internal guarantees.

Finally, there is some evidence that combatants are more willing to extend power-sharing pacts in long civil wars and in cases where third-party enforcement or verification is likely, and some evidence that third parties are more willing to intervene if adversaries include pacts in their treaty. Overall, however, there are surprisingly few correlations between post-treaty guarantees and other factors that might be related to peace. Third-party security guarantees and power-sharing pacts do appear to have a significant, independent effect on the outcome of civil wars.

PART THREE

❧

Case Studies

The quantitative analysis presented in chapters 4 and 5 found that third-party security guarantees and power-sharing pacts significantly increase the likelihood that a civil war will end in a successfully implemented peace settlement. Statistical analysis, however, only confirms that these factors are consistently associated with the outcome of civil wars. It says nothing about why third-party security guarantees and power-sharing pacts tend to cause combatants to sign and implement such treaties, or if the fear of post-treaty exploitation really drives behavior. A more detailed historical analysis of individual cases is needed to uncover whether the desire to make credible commitments to a peace treaty is the mechanism causing combatants to seek outside guarantees and power-sharing pacts.

The following two chapters trace the day-to-day negotiating processes in Zimbabwe and Rwanda. I chose these two cases from the seventy-two civil wars listed in Appendix 1 because they were as similar as possible on all the key independent variables except third-party security guarantees. Zimbabwe's and Rwanda's wars were neither particularly long nor short conflicts. The median duration of wars listed in appendix 1 was seventy-four months; in Zimbabwe and Rwanda they lasted eighty-four and fifty-one months respectively. Both wars produced less than the median number of battle deaths (ninety-two thousand per war).[1] Neither war experienced a military stalemate. In fact, at the time of negotiations, the rebels in both cases were advancing on the battlefield and were expected to win the war given additional time. The rebels in both cases fought for limited rather than total goals and were not interested in obtaining territorial autonomy. In Zimbabwe, the Patriotic Front demanded one-man, one-vote majority rule for the coun-

---

[1] The war in Rwanda did produce an exceptionally large number of deaths in 1994, but this was after the Arusha peace accords were signed.

try's predominantly black population, while the Rwandan rebels demanded multiparty rule and the repatriation of Tutsi refugees. Both wars had a clear ethnic component, with Zimbabwe's war fought between blacks and whites, and Rwanda's fought between Tutsis and Hutus. Combatants in both wars initiated numerous formal attempts to negotiate during which mediators were present, and both signed comprehensive peace plans that included specific quotas of power. The only causal factor that differed between the two cases was the presence of a third-party security guarantee. Zimbabwe's Lancaster House agreement was underwritten by a third-party security guarantee; Rwanda's Arusha accords were not.

Seven other civil wars were considered for case study analysis but were passed over in favor of the two cases mentioned above. Tajikistan, Liberia, Uganda, Chad, and Burundi met the selection criteria and would have worked equally well. I chose to investigate Zimbabwe and Rwanda, however, for three reasons. First, the peace processes in Zimbabwe and Rwanda have been documented to a much greater extent than any of the four alternate cases, allowing for richer and more comprehensive analyses. Second, the civil wars in Zimbabwe and Rwanda have both ended, allowing me to analyze the peace process in its entirety. Finally, there is a pressing desire among policymakers and the public to understand how a peace settlement signed in Rwanda could have ended in genocide. Rwandans paid a far higher price for the failure of the Arusha accords than citizens in any of the other civil wars under consideration. Two additional wars (Angola and Guatemala) would have worked well as a pair but were discounted because negotiations in both those wars occurred too recently to collect sufficient historical data.

I analyzed these cases with two goals in mind. The first was to tease out the causal links between third-party security guarantees, power-sharing pacts, and the resolution of civil wars, as discussed above. The second and perhaps more important goal was to ensure that other factors equally critical to our understanding of settlements not be overlooked. Have any essential variables been omitted from the analysis?

I used three strategies to meet these goals. First, I paid careful attention to any condition or event that appeared to play an important role in any stage of the peace process even if this factor had not been considered previously. It is quite likely, for example, that combatants are sensitive to a variety of costs in a war beyond its duration or battle deaths, or that other economic, political, or international variables better explain observed behavior.[2] A closer look at individual cases, therefore,

---

[2] Elisabeth Wood, for example, argues that El Salvador ended in a negotiated settlement because the conflict was fought between groups that were economically interdependent, a

serves to inform both the author and the reader of other potentially significant factors.

The second strategy was to carefully track when and how decisions to cooperate were made. If the success of negotiations really does rest on resolving difficult issues of post-treaty security, then one expects to observe the same three patterns discussed in chapter 4. First, combatants should have the greatest difficulty resolving the issue of post-treaty security, and this issue should be the last on the table before combatants sign or reject an agreement. In fact, since it will be easier for combatants to resolve the causes of war than to credibly commit to these solutions, successful negotiations should experience a lag time between the point at which a deal is reached on these issues and a settlement is signed. This is the period when combatants are likely to seek reassurance and attempt to design credible commitments to the terms. Second, the combatants should foresee the risks and dangers of implementation and actively seek outside security guarantees to neutralize their negative effects. Third, the timing of implementation should correspond to the arrival and departure of outside monitors or enforcers, thus revealing a direct connection between safety guarantees and the decision to cooperate.

The credible commitment theory would be disconfirmed if (1) security issues (such as the disposition of forces, army reorganization, and military integration and training) did not dominate negotiations, (2) combatants were willing to sign and implement peace settlement without an outside guarantor, or (3) treaty implementation was unrelated to the arrival or departure of a third party. Any one of these patterns would suggest that security fears and enforcement were not the greatest barriers to successful cooperation and would indicate that other more important mechanisms drove behavior.

We will see in chapters 6 and 7 how much of the negotiations are dominated by attempts by both sides to protect themselves against post-treaty exploitation. Combatants in both wars voiced the same fears and insecurity for any upcoming transition period. They either hesitated or refused to sign a peace treaty until sufficient arrangements were made to guarantee their safety during the transition, and implementation of the terms of each agreement coincided exactly with the arrival (or absence) of the third party. In short, a direct causal link does appear to exist between combatants' fear of post-treaty exploitation and their demand for outside guarantees and power-sharing pacts.

---

variable not included in the quantitative analysis in chapter 4. See Elisabeth Jean Wood, *Forging Democracy from Below: Insurgent Transitions in South Africa and El Salvador* (Cambridge: Cambridge University Press, 2000).

6. Negotiating for Security Guarantees: The Civil War in Zimbabwe

THE NEGOTIATED SETTLEMENT to the civil war in what was then Rhodesia, signed in London on December 21, 1979, defied most predictions of how the war would end. Despite a prime minister who vowed, "I don't believe in majority rule, black majority rule, ever in Rhodesia, not in a thousand years,"[1] despite impassioned racial, tribal, and ideological differences, despite large economic injustices and imbalances in military power, this conflict ended peacefully.[2] Why did Zimbabwe's civil war, which most observers considered intractable, end in a successfully implemented settlement?

Informed observers have attributed Zimbabwe's success to economic pressures from outside countries and to the particularly adept mediators who handled the negotiations in 1979. An examination of the process of negotiation, however, reveals that these conditions were neither new in 1979 nor sufficient to obtain a final peace agreement. Although international pressure did encourage Prime Minister Ian Smith and the nationalist rebels to participate in lengthy negotiations, the rebels did not agree to a cease-fire—the third and final element of the settlement—until Britain promised to station Commonwealth monitors, peacekeepers, and observers on Zimbabwean soil and to run the transition after the treaty. Throughout the negotiations, the Patriotic Front displayed extreme concern for its relative strength and safety during the transition period and consistently demanded assurances that it would not be attacked or permanently shut out of power if it signed an agreement. Every attempt to negotiate failed *except* when Britain promised

---

[1] Quote taken from Martin Meredith, *The Past Is Another Country: Rhodesia, 1890–1979* (London: Andre Deutsch, 1979), 212.

[2] Zimbabwe is one of the most frequently chosen cases to study in the literature. See Stephen Stedman's *Peacemaking in Civil War*; Jeffrey Davidow, *A Peace in Southern Africa: The Lancaster House Conference on Rhodesia, 1979* (Boulder: Westview Press, 1984); William H. Moore III, "Why Internal Wars End: The Decision to Fight, Negotiate, or Surrender," Ph.D. diss., University of Colorado at Boulder, which uses the Zimbabwean civil war as its crucial case study; and Stephen Low's "The Zimbabwe Settlement, 1976–1979," in Saadia Touval and I. William Zartman's *International Mediation in Theory and Practice* (Boulder: Westview Press, 1985).

direct military and political involvement. In short, Britain's ability to mollify these fears by sending peacekeepers, cease-fire observers, and election monitors to Zimbabwe was the crucial variable for success.

Current Explanations of the Settlement

Most accounts of Zimbabwe's civil war claim that the conflict was ripe for resolution by 1979, at which point skillful mediation allowed the combatants to reach a deal.[3] Accounts differ on whether costs of the war,[4] a military stalemate,[5] or international pressure[6] played a larger role in convincing the antagonists to negotiate. All agree, however, that "changed conditions would not, in themselves, have been sufficient to bring about success. The other element was the negotiating dexterity of Carrington and the British team."[7]

Both the Rhodesian government and the Patriotic Front rebels had strong economic incentives to pursue a peaceful solution in 1979, a fact that supports chapter 4's finding that rising costs are likely to convince combatants to initiate negotiations. In Zimbabwe's case, however, it

[3] A few books give full credit to individuals involved in the negotiations. For example, Cyrus Vance in his memoir *Hard Choices: Critical Years in America's Foreign Policy* (New York: Simon and Schuster, 1983) asserts, "The credit for the final negotiation of Zimbabwe's independence properly belongs to the British, principally to the skillful diplomacy of Peter Carrington" (297). Similarly, Peter Carrington, British foreign secretary and chairman of the Lancaster House Conference, believed that success was due to "my determination to take matters step by step. . . . I was sure that previous attempts had failed through attempting overprecision too early, through framing complex plans of ultimate order instead of coaxing minds towards the resolution of the next practical, intermediate step in debate." See Peter Carrington, *Reflecting on Things Past: The Memoirs of Peter Lord Carrington* (London: William Collins, 1988), 301. Most discussions of the Lancaster House conference, however, accept the dual importance of ripeness and mediation. For example, Susskind and Babbit claim, "It is hard to predict when all the preconditions for mediation will be met, yet an acceptable mediator must be 'on the scene' precisely when the opportunity for intervention presents itself. Otherwise, the opportunity may be lost." Lawrence Susskind and Eileen Babbit, "Overcoming the Obstacles to Effective Mediation of International Disputes," in *Mediation in International Relations: Multiple Approaches to Conflict Management*, ed. Jacob Bercovitch and Jeffrey Z. Rubin (Boulder: Westview Press, 1984), 42.

[4] For "costs of war" or "ripeness" arguments, see Stedman, *Peacemaking in Civil War*; Davidow, *Peace in Southern Africa*; and Susskind and Babbit, "Overcoming the Obstacles."

[5] For an exposition of the "stalemate" argument see Stephen Low's "The Zimbabwe Settlement."

[6] For the arguments on "international pressure" see Baumhoegger, *The Struggle for Independence*, vol. 1; Mariyawanda NzUwah, "Conflict Resolution in Zimbabwe: Superpower Determinants to the Peace Settlement," *Journal of Southern African Affairs* 4, no. 4 (1979): 389–400; and Low, "The Zimbabwe Settlement."

[7] See especially Davidow, *Peace in Southern Africa*, 101.

was the potential end of foreign aid and the burden of economic sanctions rather than the duration of the war or war-related deaths that pushed the two parties to the table.

By 1979, the neighboring governments of Zambia, Tanzania, and Mozambique were putting increasing pressure on the rebels to end a war that threatened stability in the region, and they threatened to cut off foreign assistance if this did not occur. The government of Rhodesia faced its own financial reasons to negotiate. Eleven years of war, worldwide economic recession, and high prices for imported oil had left Rhodesia's economy on the verge of collapse, and by 1979 whites were leaving the country at a rate of one thousand per month.[8] The government did not have money or manpower to fight indefinitely.

Outside pressure and the costs of war were thus decisive in getting the Rhodesian government and the Patriotic Front to initiate each of these peace talks. It is also true that Peter Carrington's mediation helped the two sides reach and sign the Lancaster House bargain. But the cost of war and skillful mediation were not sufficient to obtain peace. Fighting had been costly for many years and had encouraged Ian Smith and the Patriotic Front to pursue negotiations in 1974, 1976, and 1977, during which time highly skilled mediators (Henry Kissinger, David Owen, Cyrus Vance) intervened, to no avail. In fact, it was during Kissinger's intervention in 1976 and not Carrington's in 1979 that Ian Smith agreed to hand power over to the black majority. If Smith's government had conceded the issue of majority rule in 1976 and the Patriotic Front had signed a comprehensive bargain in 1978, why was it not until December 1979 that peace prevailed? That, I argue, is where third-party security guarantees come in.

The Negotiations

Zimbabwe's civil war began in 1972 as guerrilla forces rose up to challenge increasingly oppressive discrimination by the white government of Ian Smith and to force the government to discuss the issue of majority rule.[9] Negotiations to end the conflict were attempted every year from 1973 to 1979. Four of these negotiations met the coding criteria outlined in chapter 4 and are thus considered serious attempts to negotiate. The detente scenario, the Kissinger plan, the Anglo-American initiatives,

---

[8] The total white population at the time was approximately two hundred thousand.

[9] Guerilla uprisings began in 1965 when Smith, the newly elected prime minister of Rhodesia, refused to transfer political power to the black majority against the wishes of Britain. Violence did not reach one thousand battle deaths per year, the threshold in this study, until 1972.

and the Lancaster House conference were all formal negotiations in which the main warring factions held face-to-face talks, had agreed to discuss a political solution to the war, and were sufficiently strong militarily to continue the war if talks broke down.[10]

If the credible commitment theory is valid—if civil wars are more likely to end in negotiated settlements when the short- and long-term survival of both sides is guaranteed—we would expect *all* attempts to negotiate a settlement to the Zimbabwean civil war to fail except those that were underwritten by an outside guarantor and that contained specific political, military, or territorial guarantees of power. We would also expect post-treaty protection to be the issue most difficult to resolve and the issue over which negotiations were most likely to break down. However, the theory would be disproved if Ian Smith and the Patriotic Front rebels made no attempt to obtain third-party guarantees during negotiations, if both sides were willing to sign and implement a peace settlement as soon as the issues directly related to the cause of the war (in this case land reform, economic reform, and majority rule) were resolved, and if implementation did not depend on the deployment of outside observers.

The following sections explore each of the four negotiations in detail, considering features that conform to or diverge from the theory.

First Negotiations: The Detente Scenario

The first serious attempt to resolve Rhodesia's civil war began in 1974, fourteen months after its beginning, and continued intermittently through August 1975. The historical details of this first attempt reveal the important role outside pressure played in getting negotiations off the ground. The talks centered around the question of majority rule; no issue appeared more difficult to resolve at this early stage in the peace process. I emphasize this point because this issue was eventually settled long before a peace treaty was signed.

By 1974 the guerrilla war had not yet disrupted Rhodesian life seriously and did not threaten the continued dominance of Prime Minister Smith and his white Rhodesian Front government. Neighboring South Africa and Zambia, however, had much to lose from an unstable neighbor and put pressure on Smith and the rebels to end the violence. South Africa's economic and political survival depended on a peaceful

[10] Other negotiations did take place between Ian Smith and the British Government (the "Tiger," "Fearless" and "Douglas-Home" talks), and between Smith and black nationalists not in control of any armed forces. These negotiations are not included in the analysis since ZANU (the main rebel faction fighting the war) was not invited to participate.

southern Africa, and landlocked Zambia needed safe and open transportation routes through Rhodesia to the Indian Ocean.[11] Both countries insisted that the combatants initiate peace talks, and the government (supported by South Africa) and the rebels (supported by Zambia) agreed.

The fact that both Ian Smith and the rebels were willing to initiate peace negotiations at a time when battle deaths were low, the war was young, and violence failed to threaten Zimbabwe's main urban centers suggests that international pressure, a factor not discussed in the previous chapters, can play an important role in bringing combatants to the bargaining table. In this case, outsiders' ability to cut economic aid, block important escape routes, and establish embargoes directly affected the costs each of the combatants was forced to pay and appeared to factor into their decision to fight or bargain. Outside economic assistance, therefore, seems to better capture how costly the war was to fight, at this stage in the conflict, than either the duration of war or war-related deaths.

Informal negotiations began in October 1974. South African prime minister John Vorster believed his country could induce Smith to accept a peace plan that called for a three- to five-year transitional period to majority rule if given enough encouragement. In return, President Kaunda of Zambia believed he could convince the rebels to accept a cease-fire. After secret discussions with Ian Smith in November and December, Vorster promised the rebels that the Rhodesian government would release all political prisoners, lift the ban on the two main black nationalist military groups, ZAPU (Zimbabwe African People's Union) and ZANU (Zimbabwe African National Union), that made up the Patriotic Front, suspend political trials and revoke death sentences for political offenders, and suspend all politically discriminatory legislation.[12] In return, the black leaders of Zambia, Mozambique, Botswana, and Tanzania (also known as the frontline presidents for their geographical proximity to Rhodesia) promised Smith that they would attempt to convince ZANU and ZAPU to "desist from the armed struggle."[13]

Smith did not accept any transition to majority rule, but he did release the first group of nationalist leaders. Among them were Robert Mugabe, Joshua Nkomo, Edson Sithole, and Abel Muzorewa, black

---

[11] All of Zambia's exports and 95 percent of its imports traveled through the Portuguese colonies of Angola and Mozambique or through Rhodesia and South Africa. An unstable Rhodesia also posed a significant military threat to its neighbors since the Rhodesian government controlled the most powerful air force on the African continent at the time, a gift from Britain during the late 1960s.

[12] David Martin and Phyllis Johnson, *The Struggle for Zimbabwe: The Chimurenga War* (London: Faber and Faber, 1981), 140.

[13] Martin and Johnson, *The Struggle for Zimbabwe*, 141.

leaders who would later play decisive roles in the settlement of the war. Smith then demanded an immediate cease-fire during which the guerrillas would surrender arms and withdraw from Rhodesia.[14] The rebels refused. Instead, ZANU and ZAPU insisted that they would observe a cease-fire only when a date for a constitutional conference had been fixed and "meaningful discussions" toward majority rule had begun.[15]

The government and the rebels did not meet again until January 20, 1975, by which time the military and economic situation on the ground had not changed. The rebels reiterated their demands. They wanted the government to accept a parliamentary majority, to open the civil service and other areas of employment that were presently denied to black Africans, and to make appointments on merit rather than race. They understood that white Rhodesians had skills necessary for a stable and efficient government and economy and were willing to moderate their demands as a result. If Smith was willing to consider majority rule in three to five years rather than immediately, the rebels were ready to proceed with serious settlement talks. But Smith remained intransigent. There would be "no handover to a black majority government," he assured white Rhodesians.[16]

South Africa attempted to break this deadlock by increasing constraints on the Smith regime. On February 11, South Africa announced that it would withdraw the two-thousand-man police force it had provided for the Rhodesian government since 1967. Zambia in turn promised that guerrillas would no longer be allowed to infiltrate Rhodesia over the Zambezi River, their main attack line.

The withdrawal of South African forces convinced Smith to convene the constitutional conference the rebels demanded, but he remained obstinate on almost all issues. Smith, for example, refused to travel outside Rhodesia to negotiate. The rebels responded that they would not (and could not) meet in Rhodesia, since Smith refused to grant immunity to their exiled and imprisoned leaders.[17]

On August 9, 1975, a compromise was reached in the form of the Pretoria agreement. The parties agreed to meet on the Victoria Falls Bridge, which spanned the border between Rhodesia and Zambia, in coaches supplied by the South African government. There would be no preconditions to the talks, which meant that Smith would not be obliged to discuss majority rule. The object of the formal meeting was "to give the parties the opportunity to publicly express their genuine desire to negotiate an acceptable settlement." The parties would then

[14] Meredith, *The Past Is Another Country*, 167.
[15] Martin and Johnson, *The Struggle for Zimbabwe*, 172.
[16] Meredith, *The Past Is Another Country*, 172.
[17] Meredith, *The Past Is Another Country*, 186.

meet at a formal conference during which they would ratify the agreed-upon proposals.[18]

The Failure of the Victoria Falls Conference

Smith and the rebel delegation (which included Muzorewa, Nkomo, and Sithole) met at Victoria Falls on August 25, 1975. The conference floundered immediately. Muzorewa demanded a constitutional settlement "based on the transfer of power from the minority to the majority people of the country."[19] "Black majority rule," he declared, "is the only basis for success."[20] Smith responded that this was "completely and utterly unacceptable to us."[21] Muzorewa then insisted that African National Congress representatives presently in exile should be given immunity to attend future meetings.[22] Smith again refused, and the meeting broke up the next day. Neither side had yielded on any issue, and each side blamed the other for the breakdown of the talks.

Observers have argued that the Victoria Falls conference failed because it was poorly planned and executed: the "mediation framework . . . proved to be totally unconducive to serious negotiations between the parties."[23] True, Vorster's and Kaunda's attempt to mediate the war in Rhodesia was ill-defined and disorganized. South Africa and Zambia allowed Smith to haggle over cease-fire terms, locations for talks, release of prisoners, and preconditions for a constitutional conference, deflecting attention from the basic issue, majority rule. It is clear, however, that neither side was willing to compromise on the issue, and there was little that outside mediation could have done about it.

But why were the combatants, especially Smith, unwilling to discuss solutions that fell between these two extremes? The prime minister, for example, could have discussed an arrangement that gave blacks a majority in only one of the houses of parliament. Or he could have proposed a transfer of power to the black majority twenty-five years down the road. Both of these solutions would probably have been accepted by the rebels at this stage of the war, and were far better deals than the one white Rhodesians accepted four years later.

Smith refused to compromise on majority rule because his govern-

[18] "The Pretoria Agreement between the Prime Ministers of South Africa (Vorster) and Rhodesia (Smith), August 9, 1975," in Baumhoegger, *The Struggle for Independence*, 2:7.
[19] "Victoria Falls Conference: Draft Memorandum by the ANC, August 25, 1975," in Baumhoegger, *The Struggle for Independence*, 2:9.
[20] Meredith, *The Past Is Another Country*, 192.
[21] "I. Smith's Statement to the House of Assembly on the Victoria Falls Conference, August 26, 1975," in Baumhoegger, *The Struggle for Independence*, 2:9–10.
[22] "Victoria Falls Conference: Draft Memorandum," 2:9.
[23] Stedman, *Peacemaking in Civil War*, 48–50.

ment was under no military pressure to do so. Government forces still appeared far stronger than the guerrilla army, and the rebels had certainly not fought whites to a military stalemate. In fact, the government was enjoying a series of military successes. Rhodesian military intelligence boasted that "in October and November 1974 we killed more terrorists than we had killed in the total period from 1972 to October 1974."[24] Guerrilla attacks were confined to isolated farms along the Rhodesian border and did not threaten urban areas, where most whites lived. Whites "believed that they could continue indefinitely; neither sanctions nor the war yet endangered white survival. Christmas festivities in 1974 continued undisturbed by the possible approach of major changes."[25]

At this point, only South Africa could apply the economic pressure necessary to break Smith's resolve, and Vorster was not willing to push him that far.[26] Smith's haggling over details was only a smokescreen to conceal the important fact: he was under no military pressure from the rebels or economic pressure from his main patron to compromise on the issue of majority rule. As long as his army continued to advance militarily and South Africa remained sympathetic to Smith's desire to maintain white rule, there was little reason to give in.

The Kissinger Plan

By June 1975, it had become clear to both the rebels and the frontline presidents that Smith had no intention of agreeing to majority rule. When the August negotiations at Victoria Falls failed, President Machel of Mozambique, President Nyerere of Tanzania, and rebel leaders Muzorewa, Nkomo, Sithole, and Chikerema pledged to intensify the armed struggle. There was a growing feeling within the rebel organization that a resumed guerrilla war was the only way to win concessions from Smith and achieve black majority rule.[27] In February 1976, the rebels renewed their military crusade, and a new and more violent phase of the war began.

The same month, the British foreign secretary James Callaghan sent officials to Rhodesia's capital to gauge Smith's situation and to renew

[24] Martin and Johnson, *The Struggle for Zimbabwe*, 161.

[25] Meredith, *The Past Is Another Country*, 169.

[26] "Throughout the detente exercise, Vorster always had at his disposal the means to force Smith to come to terms, but he was constantly hamstrung by the need to avoid antagonizing his own electorate and provoking an outcry in Rhodesia." Martin and Johnson, *The Struggle for Zimbabwe*, 130.

[27] From the *Financial Times* of London, in Baumhoegger, *The Struggle for Independence*, 2:17.

the possibility of a peace settlement. Britain's interest in settling the conflict had increased after Fidel Castro dispatched thousands of combat troops to Angola in late 1975. The United States, led by Secretary of State Henry Kissinger, also decided that peace in Rhodesia was necessary to halt the "radicalization" of southern Africa. Kissinger feared that continued war would usher in a radical black nationalist government in Rhodesia, instigate racial unrest in neighboring states, and allow the Soviets and Cubans to gain an additional foothold in the region.[28] On April 27 Kissinger pledged American support for majority rule in Rhodesia and promised to solicit South Africa's help to ensure a rapid negotiated settlement. He emphasized that the Smith regime would face America's unrelenting opposition until a negotiated settlement was achieved.[29]

While Kissinger and Vorster plotted how and when to induce majority rule to Rhodesia, violence escalated. By June 1976 the guerrillas were attacking from three sides—Mozambique, Zambia, and Botswana—and had infiltrated far past the border region. In response, the Rhodesian government extended military service, increased taxes, cut travel and emigration, and initiated its own offensive strikes at guerrilla and refugee camps in neighboring Mozambique.[30]

Smith's raids into Mozambique were a resounding military success but disastrous politically. The attack on adjoining states and against helpless refugees convinced Vorster that the Rhodesian prime minister would never accept majority rule unless his war effort collapsed.[31] Moreover, South Africa feared that Rhodesian attacks into neighboring countries would "bring every Cuban in sight to Rhodesia's borders."[32] Immediately after the raid, Vorster blocked Smith's access to critical trade routes through South Africa, cut oil shipments, and curtailed arms and ammunition deliveries. South Africa had finally decided to make continued war very costly for the white minority regime.[33]

Despite increased economic pressure, the outlook for successful negotiations remained grim. Smith's raids into Mozambique had hurt the rebels and forced them to ease their guerrilla offensives. Smith's *military* position, therefore, was improving, and his willingness to compromise correspondingly declined.[34]

---

[28] Martin and Johnson, *The Struggle for Zimbabwe*, 232.
[29] Meredith, *The Past Is Another Country*, 222.
[30] Meredith, *The Past Is Another Country*, 230 and 237.
[31] Meredith, *The Past Is Another Country*, 241.
[32] Meredith, *The Past Is Another Country*, 238
[33] Meredith, *The Past Is Another Country*, 242.
[34] On August 25, in an interview published in the *Washington Post*, Smith insisted, "This question of quick majority rule is a facile, superficial argument to our own plan. I

For their own reasons the rebels were equally unenthusiastic about negotiations at this time. They were splintered into rival factions and did not agree that negotiations with Smith were the best strategy to obtain majority rule. Robert Mugabe, in particular, saw Kissinger's mission as a ploy to end the violence and establish a black puppet government sympathetic to white interests. His arm of the Patriotic Front, the Zimbabwe African National Union, intended to fight any settlement.[35]

South Africa, however, responded by increasing economic pressure on Smith. Vorster now blocked the flow of goods between the two countries, cut off money and equipment needed to support the war effort, and withdrew twenty-six helicopters and all helicopter pilots, cutting Rhodesia's air force in half.[36] On September 16, Rhodesia's minister of finance, David Smith, warned Ian Smith that unless Rhodesia received a large injection of money, it could not continue to pay for the war.[37]

On September 19, 1976, Kissinger handed Smith a list of five points that would be the basis of a Rhodesian settlement. Its conditions were these:

1. Rhodesia would agree to majority rule within two years.

2. Rhodesian representatives would meet immediately at a mutually agreed place with black leaders to work out an interim government until majority rule was implemented.

3. The interim government would consist of a Council of State, half of whose members would be black and half white, with a white, nonvoting chairman.

4. All members would take an oath to work for rapid progress to majority rule.

5. The United Kingdom would enact enabling legislation for progress to majority rule. Rhodesia would also enact such legislation as would be necessary.[38]

Kissinger informed Smith that he must either accept or reject the package as a whole. Kissinger believed that if Smith rejected the terms, his regime could not survive for more than three months. If Smith accepted the terms, Western powers would set up a financial trust to help Rhodesia economically and to guarantee the rights of whites.[39]

South African sanctions had the desired effect. Smith agreed to dis-

---

want to assure you that not only the whites in Rhodesia but the majority of the black people in Rhodesia oppose that sort of thing." Martin and Johnson, *The Struggle for Zimbabwe*, 247.

[35] Meredith, *The Past Is Another Country*, 251.

[36] Stedman, *Peacemaking in Civil War*, 95.

[37] Martin and Johnson, *The Struggle for Zimbabwe*, 248.

[38] Proposals as presented in Stedman, *Peacemaking in Civil War*, 166–67.

[39] Meredith, *The Past Is Another Country*, 254.

cuss a peace settlement, showing once again that outside pressure and the costs of war can induce even a highly intransigent leader to compromise. Now, however, Smith's concerns for the security of white settlers surfaced. Smith informed Kissinger that his party could not survive if it relinquished majority rule to an enemy that outnumbered whites twenty-four to one. Smith believed the survival of the white settlers could be assured only if whites retained command of important security posts. Smith insisted, therefore, that the chairman of the executive council and two key cabinet ministers, the minister of defense and the minister of law and order, be white.[40] If Kissinger approved these amendments, Smith would accept majority rule.[41]

Kissinger accepted Smith's demands, and on Friday, September 24, Smith announced via radio and television that white rule would end in two years if the rebels accepted the Kissinger plan.[42] Four years after the war began and two months after South Africa cut essential war supplies, the white minority government accepted majority rule—an issue most observers believed could never be resolved through negotiation.

The Nationalists' Rejection of the Proposal

With the main political issue driving the war resolved, negotiations immediately turned to the question of security. The rebels and frontline presidents met on September 25 in Lusaka to discuss Smith's announcement. Smith had surrendered minority rule, and for that they rejoiced. The rebels stated quite clearly, however, that they would not accept the proposals if Smith retained control of the security positions.[43] Mugabe insisted that "it does not matter what type of parliament is put up during or after the transitional government—if it does not control the army it is a sham—it's hollow because there is no guarantee that it will not topple the administration anytime."[44] If Smith controlled the ministries of defense and of law and order during the transition, rebels believed, he would manipulate or overturn upcoming elections and constitutional

[40] Martin and Johnson, *The Struggle for Zimbabwe*, 250–51.

[41] Although Smith would concede much by accepting these terms, the five points still gave him considerable space to maneuver. Smith had two years to preserve as much white influence as possible. Whites would have a major role in the drafting of the new constitution and be able to ensure that their interests were protected. They would also be in a position to play one black leader off against the others. More important, sanctions would end, the war would cease, and the exodus of white immigrants would likely end. See Meredith, *The Past Is Another Country*, 255.

[42] Meredith, *The Past Is Another Country*, 261.

[43] Meredith, *The Past Is Another Country*, 255 and 258.

[44] "Report on R. Mugabe's Comments on the Kissinger Proposals, September 27, 1976," in Baumhoegger, *The Struggle for Independence*, 2:162.

changes.[45] Therefore, Mugabe demanded that the rebels take over the Rhodesian army during the proposed transitional government.

Negotiations deadlocked over this issue. Smith refused to accept any proposal for transitional arrangements that did not give whites control of all security positions, and Mugabe rejected any such an arrangement. Vorster, satisfied with Smith's acceptance of the Kissinger plan, had already lifted sanctions, opening South African railways to Rhodesian traffic and fully restoring oil and ammunition to the white government.[46] Once South African restraints were lifted, Smith had little incentive to compromise further.

Britain, however, did not give up hope for a settlement. Between September 1976 and February 1977 the British continued to search for acceptable post-treaty security arrangements, and it was during this time that the rebels first sought third-party security guarantees. In November 1976, the Patriotic Front demanded that the transition include "a Resident Commissioner answerable to Britain" who would be "charged with the duty of ensuring full and proper implementation of the . . . Agreement."[47] Britain responded with a vague offer of a "British presence" but insisted that Britain had no intention of administering Rhodesia during a transitional period and would certainly not send troops. Smith, confident in his ability to continue the war now that South African sanctions had been lifted, rejected all counterproposals.

Why the Kissinger Plan Failed

The Kissinger talks may be viewed as two separate negotiations: those that occurred while South Africa applied severe economic sanctions, and those that took place after they were lifted. Only during the first phase did Smith have strong incentives to reach a political bargain, since he desperately needed to end the war before his government ran out of money and supplies. The second phase was simply a performance put on by Smith to pacify Washington's and Pretoria's demands for peace talks.

The first phase of the Kissinger talks, therefore, offers insights into the conditions under which seemingly intransigent leaders compromise on key issues driving a war. Until October 1976, Smith faced large costs for failing to cooperate with the Patriotic Front and could not remain stubbornly impassive at the bargaining table. He later admitted that his acceptance of majority rule

---

[45] Martin and Johnson, *The Struggle for Zimbabwe*, 255–56.

[46] Meredith, *The Past Is Another Country*, 266.

[47] "Proposal by the Patriotic Front on the Structure of the Transitional Government and on a Time Table for the Conference, November 30, 1976," in Baumhoegger, *The Struggle for Independence*, 2:224.

was not a decision that we welcomed, or that we accepted lightly, I must tell you that. We were placed in a situation where we virtually had no option. This was because of the actions of the then South African PM, John Vorster. As far as countries like Britain and America were concerned, we could defy them as we had done over the years. We could not do that to the one country which controlled our life-line. So, reluctantly—*very* reluctantly—we were forced to accept it.[48]

This first phase also offers insights into the difficult security issues that arose once the question of majority rule was resolved. As the credible commitment theory predicts, control over security institutions immediately surfaced once the main issue driving the war was settled. Statements by both Smith and Mugabe reveal the depth of their concern over this matter. Mugabe stated that "it would be ridiculous for the settlers who were murdering the Zimbabweans to be intrusted with [our] security during the crucial transitional period."[49] The rebels "would rather prefer Ian Smith having 100 per cent representation in Parliament and we having the army controlling, than having majority in Parliament with Ian Smith having the army, you see. That's not transference of power at all."[50] In short, the Patriotic Front was willing to reject Smith's offer of majority rule if it meant that Smith's party maintained control of post-treaty defense.

It is difficult to say if the deadlock over security positions would have been resolved had South Africa maintained sanctions on Rhodesia. Britain's ensuing offers to administer the transition period and integrate the army went some way to addressing these security concerns. Still, it is unlikely that negotiations would have succeeded as long as Britain continued to reject any direct involvement in the transition. Neither side would likely have proceeded toward peace as long as Britain refused to enforce or guarantee any subsequent demobilization.

The Anglo-American Initiative

The failure of the Kissinger plan did not dissuade Britain and America from trying to find a solution to Rhodesia's increasingly bloody war. The war had rapidly escalated in early 1977, and by the end of the year

---

[48] Michael Charlton, *The Last Colony in Africa: Diplomacy and the Independence of Rhodesia* (Oxford: Basil Blackwell, 1990), 2.

[49] "New UK Plot Rejected," *Daily News* (Dar es Salaam), December 25, 1976, in Baumhoegger, *The Struggle for Independence*, 2:236.

[50] "Interview with Mugabe ca. May 11/14, 1977," in Baumhoegger, *The Struggle for Independence*, 3:328. Asked if his demand for white control over the police and army during the transition was a make-or-break issue, Smith replied that it was ("Interview with Ian Smith, October 1976," in Baumhoegger, 2:176).

almost as many guerrillas and Rhodesian soldiers had been killed as in the four years from 1972 to 1976. Much of the increased violence could be attributed to guerrilla advances. After years of wavering between accommodation and rebellion, the rebels finally realized that "only through armed struggle can we achieve the right to rule ourselves."[51] By 1977, the rebels enjoyed the undivided support of a large rural population and an unlimited supply of modern weapons from the Soviet Union and China.

The Rhodesian government was not so fortunate. White emigration from Rhodesia rose to fifteen hundred a month—the highest departure figure since Smith unilaterally declared independence from Britain in 1965. The defense budget increased 44 percent, to almost a million dollars a day.[52] Call-ups for military service affected almost all white males and hurt an already beleaguered business community.

On March 9, 1977, British prime minister James Callaghan and newly elected president Jimmy Carter agreed that Britain and the United States should sponsor a new conference to end the war. The objective would be an independent Zimbabwe with majority rule by 1978.

British foreign secretary David Owen presented the first Anglo-American proposal in April 1977. It included a constitution that provided for a democratically elected government with the widest possible franchise, a bill of rights, and an independent judiciary.[53] It also included a transition period during which the Smith regime would surrender power to a neutral caretaker administration that would administer the country, organize and conduct elections, and prepare the country for the transition to independence. The proposal also established an internationally constituted and managed development fund intended to pay off whites for accepting majority rule.[54]

Mugabe and Nkomo, however, resented U.S. involvement in what they believed was a purely British-Rhodesian affair. They argued that Britain had abdicated its responsibility to the black majority in Rhodesia ever since Ian Smith illegally declared independence in 1965. The Patriotic Front insisted that before a new round of talks commenced, "Britain must prove her capability, indeed her determination, that after the successful conclusion of a constitutional conference, she will effectively and properly implement the agreement that will have

[51] "R. Mugabe's Message to the Nation," March 8, 1977, in Baumhoegger, *The Struggle for Independence*, 3:280–81.

[52] Martin and Johnson, *The Struggle for Zimbabwe*, 280.

[53] "Rhodesia. Proposals for a Settlement," published September 9, 1977 as White Paper Cmnd. 6919, Baumhoegger, *The Struggle for Independence*, 3:417.

[54] "Rhodesia. Proposals for a Settlement," 3:417.

been reached."[55] The rebels understood that without such assurances the transfer of power would never take place.

Owen refused to get involved without the United States. The British Parliament, he believed, would never agree to political or military intervention in Rhodesian affairs once an agreement was reached; London planned to use American muscle for that. In an attempt to circumvent the issue of direct British involvement, Owen changed negotiating tactics. Rather than organize a formal constitutional conference that could become bogged down in preconditions—a problem the detente scenario and the Kissinger plan faced—Owen decided to set up a series of brief meetings. He hoped that shuttle negotiations would maintain momentum, narrow the areas of disagreement, and allow him to find a settlement without further commitments from London.[56]

A Joint Anglo-American Consultative Group was established to handle the roving negotiations that began in May 1977. Led by senior British Foreign Office official John Graham and U.S. ambassador to Zambia Stephen Low, the group toured African capitals to explore possible settlement terms. They found that the principal stumbling block to peace was control of the security forces once a treaty was signed.[57]

This time, it was the Patriotic Front that demanded control of internal security. They regarded the present Rhodesian security forces as the fighting arm of the Smith regime and did not believe that these same forces would remain neutral after a settlement was signed. Smith, on the other hand, insisted that he retain control over these forces and warned that without such reassurance whites would abandon the country. Dismantling the current Rhodesian army, he insisted, "would be tantamount to signing the death warrant for a civilized nation."[58]

Graham and Low drafted a proposal to address these concerns. For the first time, Britain offered to govern Rhodesia directly. According to the new plan, a British commissioner and his team would replace Smith, supervise the existing administration, and oversee elections. Involvement would last no longer than six months.[59] During that time an international peacekeeping force would maintain a cease-fire, after which an integrated army of government forces and guerrillas would preserve the

[55] "Mugabe's Speech to the World Conference against Apartheid, June 16–19 1977," in Baumhoegger, *The Struggle for Independence*, 3:361.

[56] Martin and Johnson, *The Struggle for Zimbabwe*, 266–67.

[57] Meredith, *The Past Is Another Country*, 299.

[58] General John Hickman, the new Rhodesian army commander, quoted in Meredith, *The Past Is Another Country*, 299–300.

[59] The plan stated that they would remain no longer than six months. Six months was considered sufficient time to convert to black rule yet short enough to ensure that Britain would not become embroiled in a "Vietnam-like" quagmire.

peace.[60] The new plan seemed to contain all the necessary elements for a peaceful and secure transition: a third-party overseer, an international peacekeeping force, and an army composed of both government troops and guerrilla forces.

Both Ian Smith and the Patriotic Front hated the idea. Nkomo argued that the interim government would continue to rely on the current Rhodesian police forces, civil service, and judiciary, and that Smith, therefore, would still be in control. Nkomo revealed his fears in a speech on July 24, 1977:

> Suppose on our way to draw that constitution Smith massacres half the African delegation, what defense would that delegation have? None! Secondly, even if the constitution were successfully drawn, what guarantee is there that Ian Smith and his regime would, thereafter, be removed from power and that the constitution could then be implemented? None! . . . The forces of Smith are fighting to oppose independence. The British Government would like us to believe that these same forces can be relied upon to guarantee our independence which they are sworn to frustrate and defeat. How can they be considered reliable to guarantee the independence which it is their mission to frustrate.[61]

Nkomo and Mugabe insisted that only the Patriotic Front could take charge of an interim government and ensure the safety of all Zimbabweans.

Ian Smith also disliked the idea of British control of Rhodesia, but for different reasons. "Any suggestion of a peace-keeping force," he said, "which is going to take the place of our present forces or push them into the background, or not come under the jurisdiction of our existing command structure, this is out. It is a non-starter."[62] Smith refused to discuss an arrangement that would integrate guerrilla forces into a new army.

The two positions did not change. If Britain wanted a settlement, it would have to convince both the Patriotic Front and white Rhodesia that their opponent would not be allowed to overpower them during the transition from war to peace, and from white to black rule. David Owen, however, could not deliver this assurance. Both the Right and the Left in Parliament attacked his plan for including the possibility of British military involvement. London refused to commit "a single British troop."[63]

---

[60] Meredith, *The Past Is Another Country*, 300.

[61] "Message to Zimbabwe," July 24, 1977, in Baumhoegger, *The Struggle for Independence*, 3:387.

[62] "Ian Smith's News Conference in Salisbury, July 6, 1977," in Baumhoegger, *The Struggle for Independence*, 3:373.

[63] "Debate in the British House of Commons after D. Owen's Visit to the USA," July 25, 1977, in Baumhoegger, *The Struggle for Independence*, 3:389.

On September 1, 1977, David Owen and American representative to the United Nations Andrew Young presented a firmer, more detailed Anglo-American plan. The most difficult part remained the transition. According to the plan, the transition period would still last no longer than six months, but a United Nations force would now supervise the cease-fire, support the civil power, and act as "liaison with the existing Rhodesian armed forces and with the forces of the Liberation Armies." Responsibility for maintaining law and order during the transition period would remain with the existing Rhodesian police forces, although they would operate under a new British commissioner. Finally, a new national army would be established as soon as possible to replace the existing armed forces in Rhodesia.[64] In short, the plan called for the resignation of Prime Minister Ian Smith, the appointment of a British administrator, and the partial disbanding of the Rhodesian and black nationalist armed forces.

The Patriotic Front and the Smith regime were both dissatisfied with this solution. Smith attacked the idea of integrating "terrorists" into the Rhodesian army and called it "insane" to suggest guerrillas should form the basis of a national defense force.[65] Nkomo responded equally fervently: "We cannot accept orders to disarm, no, never. Nobody can disarm our army, nobody can tell us what the future of our country is going to be."[66] Another proposal within the plan was particularly objectionable. Britain had chosen retired British field marshal Lord Carver as resident commissioner. Carver would be given dictatorial powers to govern Rhodesia for six months during the perilous transition from white to black rule, yet he would have no effective means to ensure that whites handed over power. Except for a small personal staff, Carver would rely solely on the existing Rhodesian administration to run the country.[67]

Nkomo and Mugabe submitted their own proposal for a settlement. They asked that the armed forces of the Rhodesian regime and the police be completely dismantled. Similarly, they asked that judges, magistrates, and civil servants be subject to screening and open to reappointment in order to rid the government of any "unacceptable elements." Finally, they insisted that the rebel forces be directly involved

---

[64] "Rhodesia. Proposals for a Settlement," 3:418.

[65] Martin and Johnson, The Struggle for Zimbabwe, 269–70.

[66] "Reactions to Anglo-American Initiative by the Patriotic Front," Zambia Daily Mail (Lusaka), August 27, 1977, in Baumhoegger, The Struggle for Independence, 3:407.

[67] Meredith, The Past Is Another Country, 310–11. Carver had played a leading role against the Mau Mau movement when Kenya was still a British colony in the 1950s, and his appointment strengthened the Patriotic Front's suspicion that Britain secretly supported the Smith regime. Baumhoegger, The Struggle for Independence, 3:509.

in all transitional functions. For the Patriotic Front, "The only guarantee of the definite advent of genuine independence for Zimbabwe is the direct involvement of the patriotic liberation forces in all organs and functions of the transitional structures which secure the transition until power has been totally transferred to the people of Zimbabwe by free and fair democratic elections."[68]

By November it was clear to the British that unless substantial changes were made to the Anglo-American plan, it would never succeed. Owen tried to keep the initiative alive by proposing cease-fire talks on Malta, but Smith refused to attend.[69] In the meantime, Smith pursued his own internal settlement with Bishop Abel Muzorewa (a man who controlled no military forces and did not have the support of the Patriotic Front), and on November 24 announced that he would accept the results of the first one-man, one-vote election, which included Muzorewa as candidate for prime minister.

Muzorewa won a resounding victory in the elections, and by April 1978 the first black-led government was installed in Rhodesia. The white electorate did not panic, and there was barely a murmur of protest; they had expected majority rule since 1976 and were now resigned to the fact. In fact, if majority rule would end the devastating war, whites would welcome it. Whites were far more alarmed at the prospect of losing their land, their property, and their economic standing. As long as they could retain control of the security forces, however, they believed they could fend off raids and protect themselves against expropriation.[70]

Why the Anglo-American Initiative Failed

On the surface, the Anglo-American initiative failed because Smith refused to accept the possibility of an external police force and refused to integrate the Rhodesian army with guerrilla forces. When Smith found out that he could not retain full control of the armed forces, that he would have to share power with the Patriotic Front, he decided to pursue his own internal settlement with the militarily weak Muzorewa, hoping that a black prime minister would satisfy Britain and the United States. For their part, Britain and the United States adopted a wait-and-see attitude, hoping that Smith's plan would end the war and save them added involvement in the unstable state. But by failing to condemn

---

[68] "The Patriotic Front's Statement on the British Proposals Adopted at a Meeting of Its Co-ordinating Committee in Maputo," September 12, 1977, in Baumhoegger, *The Struggle for Independence*, 3:433.

[69] Meredith, *The Past Is Another Country*, 320–21.

[70] Meredith, *The Past Is Another Country*, 322–23.

Smith's settlement and abandoning their own Anglo-American plan, Owen and Young strengthened Smith's position. Had they condemned the internal settlement from the start, Smith would have been forced to continue the Anglo-American negotiations, and an agreement on the difficult security issues might have been reached.

Britain and the United States understood that interim arrangements would be the key to solving the war in Rhodesia. They accepted that the simple verbal promise of open elections was not sufficient to guarantee that power would be transferred to the black majority and would not assuage the fears each side had about signing a peace agreement. A neutral caretaker together with peacekeeping forces would have to be deployed. London and Washington, however, wanted to limit their involvement, not enhance it, and both countries hoped that the internal settlement would help them do so.

But the Patriotic Front considered the internal settlement a "sham agreement reached and signed by fascist and racist rebel leader Ian Smith" and his "stooges."[71] They condemned the "iniquitous deal" for leaving both political and military power in the hands of the Smith regime, for giving whites the right to veto constitutional changes, and for leaving 50 percent of the land in the hands of 3 percent of the population. They vowed to continue the war until political and military power really did rest in the hands of the black majority.[72] War continued.

The Lancaster House Negotiations

By August 1979 the Commonwealth heads of government, the United States, and newly elected prime minister, Margaret Thatcher, realized that the internal settlement between Smith and Muzorewa would not end the war and that a new constitutional conference would be needed.[73] That month, Britain sent invitations to the Patriotic Front leaders and

[71] "Statement by the Patriotic Front concerning the Internal Settlement Agreement, March 4, 1978," in Baumhoegger, *The Struggle for Independence*, 4:533.

[72] Martin and Johnson, *The Struggle for Zimbabwe*, 304.

[73] As Peter Carrington explained years later, "You couldn't leave things as they were. You had got to the end of the road with the Anglo-American proposals, and recognition of the Bishop's [Muzorewa's] regime would have led to the most appalling problems—not least the isolation of Britain by the rest of the world, including the United States. And it would have intensified the war in Rhodesia. There would have been much more blood-shed. It would have settled nothing, and, incidentally, would have brought the sorts of things that everybody has been trying to avoid in Southern Africa that much nearer—the Soviet involvement, the East German involvement, and all the rest of it." Quoted in Davidow, *Peace in Southern Africa*, 28.

to the Muzorewa-Smith delegation for a constitutional conference to be held at Lancaster House in London and chaired by British foreign secretary, Peter Carrington.[74] Both parties accepted.

Each of the delegations had different motives for attending the conference. The Muzorewa-Smith team needed to end the war and obtain international recognition for their regime. The economy teetered on the verge of disaster, and the government would continue to forfeit much-needed assistance and cash until the government was recognized and sanctions lifted. Moreover, Smith was under increasing pressure from his own white constituency to end a war it no longer understood. With a black government in power, it was unclear who or what they were fighting for.[75] Britain offered Muzorewa and Smith an added incentive for participating in talks. Britain promised that if the Patriotic Front walked out on the talks, Britain would recognize the new government; if Muzorewa and Smith refused to participate, sanctions would continue. Muzorewa's government, therefore, had much to gain from cooperation.

Nkomo and Mugabe had different reasons for attending. The Patriotic Front's biggest patrons, the frontline states Zambia, Mozambique, Botswana, and Tanzania, continued to suffer greatly from the war and made their own deal with the rebels. If the rebels attended the conference and it failed because of Britain or Muzorewa, they would unconditionally support continued conflict. If, however, Mugabe refused to go to London and explore a compromise solution, they would close down the war.[76]

Few participants or observers believed the conference would succeed. The two delegations distrusted one another profoundly, and both sides continued to demand full power during the transition period; their terms for settlement had not changed since the failed Geneva conference of 1976.[77]

The Lancaster House conference was set up to resolve three core issues in sequence: the constitution, the transition, and the cease-fire. Carrington had ordered the agenda this way to build momentum; political issues would be discussed first, since they were expected to be the

---

[74] Martin and Johnson, *The Struggle for Zimbabwe*, 315.

[75] Martin and Johnson, *The Struggle for Zimbabwe*, 298.

[76] Charlton, *Last Colony in Africa*, 68–69. According to Robert Mugabe, "The frontline states said we *had* to negotiate, we *had* to agree to go to this conference. There we were, we thought we were on top of the situation back home, we were moving forward all the time, and why *should* we be denied the ultimate joy of having militarily overthrown the regime here? . . . Nevertheless, we agreed to give the exercise a trial. But, at that time, I never felt it would succeed." Charlton, *Last Colony in Africa*, 69–70.

[77] Davidow, *Peace in Southern Africa*, 14–15.

easiest to resolve, followed by transitional governance issues. Discussions on the cease-fire and all corresponding security matters would be negotiated last, when it would be more difficult for either side to back down.

At each stage Carrington was careful to obtain early approval from Muzorewa, who offered little resistance in the hopes of forcing the rebels to be the ones who rejected the deal. Carrington and the Patriotic Front then battled back and forth—a fascinating tug-of-war between the British secretary, who used the threat of recognizing Muzorewa to obtain concessions from the guerrillas, and Robert Mugabe, who used the threat of continued war to force Britain to accept increasingly greater involvement in the transition.[78] A brief description of the discussion surrounding each of these core issues will make clear just how critical British involvement and the location of assembly points for disarming forces was to the final signing and implementation of the settlement.

The Constitution

In their opening speech on September 10, 1979, the Patriotic Front announced that they would not compromise on two key issues. First, they expected to share both political and military responsibility with Britain during the transition. Second, they wanted to discuss military issues before constitutional matters.[79] The rebels made it clear that post-treaty security was their ultimate concern. Carrington refused to change the order of the discussion but assured the Patriotic Front that the conference would seek a comprehensive agreement on transitional arrangements. Carrington then distributed a thirteen-page summary of constitutional proposals.

The Muzorewa delegation accepted Carrington's constitutional proposals on September 21 with no revisions.[80] The plan included numerous safeguards to protect white interests.[81] Eventually, the Patriotic Front agreed that 20 percent of the seats in the lower house of parliament be reserved for whites, but rejected the other guarantees that they believed left too much power in the hands of the white population.[82]

---

[78] Davidow, *Peace in Southern Africa*, 49 and 51.

[79] *Financial Times*, September 11, 1977.

[80] Smith was the only member of the delegation to vote against it.

[81] This included "an extensive bill of rights guaranteeing individual freedoms, an undetermined number of white seats in a 100 person legislature for a period of seven years, remuneration for any lands that might be distributed, and the honoring of pension rights for white public officials." See Stedman, *Peacemaking in Civil War*, 178.

[82] Davidow, *Peace in Southern Africa*, 59.

Negotiations surrounding the new constitution increasingly focused on the issue of land. The Patriotic Front believed that land should be returned to the Africans from whom it had been taken, while Britain and Muzorewa insisted that whites be compensated for their property. Nkomo and Mugabe refused to change their position until Britain, backed by the United States, offered a "land compensation package" that guaranteed reparations while also guaranteeing that land be available to distribute to the black community.[83] With these assurances, the Patriotic Front accepted a new constitution that contained all the reforms the guerrillas had been fighting for: one-man, one-vote elections, majority rule, and independence.[84] It also solved an issue of particular concern to minority whites: land redistribution. By October 5, 1979, all the main issues driving the war were formally resolved.

The Transition

With the constitution approved, the issue of post-treaty governance immediately surfaced. The Patriotic Front had already issued a plan that included a specific quota of political power in the transition and outside intervention. This plan proposed that an eight-man transitional governing council be created, composed of four Patriotic Front members and four British-Muzorewa regime representatives, with a British chairman at the helm. The army, police, public service, and judiciary would also be run by similarly integrated councils. A United Nations force would keep the peace.[85]

Britain presented its own proposal for the transitional period. Britain insisted that the Rhodesian and guerrilla armies not be integrated, and that the day-to-day running of the country continue in the hands of the existing ministries.[86] Britain did, however, offer to become more involved in the transition. This time Britain promised to take direct control of Rhodesia during the transition to majority rule, appoint a governor with executive and legislative power who would have overall control of the election, and send Commonwealth *observers* (not forces) to the area.[87] Carrington, however, continued to insist that British

---

[83] Davidow, *Peace in Southern Africa*, 63.

[84] Martin and Johnson, *The Struggle for Zimbabwe*, 318–19.

[85] Davidow, *Peace in Southern Africa*, 67.

[86] *Financial Times*, October 18, 1977.

[87] The critical military arrangements remained vague: "The commanders of the security forces will be responsible to the governor who will assume authority over the civil police." *Financial Times*, October 23, 1977.

involvement not exceed six months, and that no British troops, peace-keeping forces, or UN action be included.[88]

Once again, Britain attempted to limit outside involvement in the transition, and once again the rebels objected. The plan included no power sharing, no UN presence, and no peacekeeping force. In response, the Patriotic Front published its own "Essential Requirements for the Transition":

> The Security Forces during the interim period must be an army composed of a combination of the Patriotic Front's and the Regime's armies, and a police force composed of a combination of the Patriotic Front's and the Regime's police forces, operating in both cases alongside a United Nations Peace-keeping Force and a United Nations Civilian Police Force to supervise the cease-fire and ensure peaceful integration. The foregoing structure is essential to ensure that the process towards genuine majority rule and independence will be irreversible.[89]

The rebels continued to demand equal representation in the interim security forces and a UN force to guarantee the peace.

On November 9, Britain changed its stance and announced that it would be prepared to contribute to a Commonwealth military monitoring force of several hundred men. Carrington emphasized that these men would be "monitors," not peacekeepers—an offer that was far from the UN army composed of many thousand soldiers that Nkomo and Mugabe had demanded.[90] The Patriotic Front responded by insisting that rebel armies be treated equally by the governor during the transitional period.[91]

On November 13 Carrington announced that Britain would be willing to extend the role of the proposed Commonwealth force and the length of the interim period. Two days later he agreed that the Patriotic Front would not only "maintain the ceasefire" on an equal basis with the Salisbury government army "from day one" but would be regarded as an equal defense force during the interim period. He also promised that the monitoring force would remain in Zimbabwe until the new government was established and independence granted, not just through

---

[88] Davidow, *Peace in Southern Africa*, 68.

[89] Baumhoegger, *The Struggle for Independence*, 6:1129.

[90] Davidow, *Peace in Southern Africa*, 73.

[91] According to Jeffrey Davidow, U.S. observer to the negotiations, "This [request] was more than just matter of pride. It related to their concern that if law and order deteriorated to the point where it could not be restored by the police alone, the governor would assume their separate or joint culpability and rely solely on the Rhodesian military for help. Those forces would, in turn, use their operational freedom to the Patriotic Front's disadvantage." Davidow, *Peace in Southern Africa*, 74.

the election.[92] Carrington hoped these added security assurances would help reassure the Patriotic Front and convince them to accept the British transitional plan.[93]

The added assurances had the desired effect, and on November 15, 1979, the Patriotic Front finally accepted Britain's proposal for the transition. Once the political and transitional issues were resolved, negotiations proceeded to the most contentious issue of the conference: how to demobilize, disarm, and disengage the rival militaries.

The Cease-Fire

The final topics on the agenda were the cease-fire and the logistics surrounding the demobilization of the competing armies. Once again Carrington opened the talks by presenting a ten-point plan. It called for a cease-fire to commence within seven to ten days of the completion of a Lancaster House agreement. By that time all cross-border infiltration of Patriotic Front troops would have to stop, and those guerrillas within the country would have to gather with their arms at designated assembly points. A Commonwealth monitoring force (of several hundred) and an integrated committee of the commanders of the three armies would assist the British governor in maintaining the cease-fire.[94]

Although Muzorewa and his delegation seemed satisfied with the proposal, the Patriotic Front called the proposals "repugnant." Nkomo claimed that Britain's proposals would place Front guerrillas in what he termed "concentration camps" and leave Salisbury's forces in their own bases, strategically placed to control all the major towns with "their bombers and fighters and South Africa sitting across the river." If the Patriotic Front won the election, the regime's forces "would be ideally placed to pre-empt that victory by a coup."[95]

Nkomo and Mugabe offered their own plan. It called for

- A substantial Commonwealth "peacekeeping" (not monitoring) force of several thousand capable of enforcing the cease-fire
- A Commonwealth cease-fire supervisory commission
- Both parties being responsible to the government for observance of cease-fire and a joint cease-fire supervisory commission under a British chairman
- Demarcation of areas dominated by one side or the other
- Disbandment of certain Rhodesian military and paramilitary units

[92] *Financial Times*, November 14 and 15, 1977.
[93] *Financial Times*, October 14, 1977.
[94] Davidow, *Peace in Southern Africa*, 78.
[95] "Nkomo Fears Salisbury Plot to Eliminate Patriotic Front," *Financial Times*, November 24, 1979, in Baumhoegger, *The Struggle for Independence*, 6:1188.

- Surrender of a vast private armory of weapons held by Rhodesian civilians
- A new civil police[96]

Carrington responded by releasing a revised cease-fire proposal. In it he promised to station Commonwealth monitors wherever Patriotic Front forces and Rhodesian government forces were assembled.[97]

On the surface, Carrington's new proposal appeared to provide adequate and equal security to both the Patriotic Front and the Rhodesian government forces. In reality, the Patriotic Front forces remained far more vulnerable to attack. The plan required that Front guerrillas be moved into as many as fifteen assembly points. The government forces, however, would be permitted to remain in their original bases and airfields with their full array of arms and equipment. Moreover, all of the guerrilla assembly points would be located in the periphery of the state, leaving government forces exclusive control of the urban and industrial heartland.[98]

The Patriotic Front opposed the size and composition of the Commonwealth forces; they were too small to be effective and too Anglo-centric to be unbiased. They also resented the unequal treatment of their forces and the short length of the cease-fire period. Carrington agreed to increase the Commonwealth force to over one thousand, but he rejected any additional contributor states and refused to increase the cease-fire period. London's Conservative government insisted on keeping the transitional period as brief as possible in order to minimize their political vulnerability at home.[99]

The Patriotic Front and Britain finally agreed on all elements of the cease-fire plan except the unequal treatment of rival forces during the transition period. The issue of "reciprocal disengagement" consumed the rest of the negotiations. According to Mugabe,

> If we were weak on this point, we would find our soldiers placed in positions which would reduce them from the strong instrument we had built

[96] *Financial Times*, November 20, 1977.

[97] Davidow, *Peace in Southern Africa*, 80.

[98] *Financial Times*, November 26, 1977. According to the *Financial Times* of December 17, 1979, "It is easy to see why the Front objects. A careful look at the British map shows that there are no Patriotic Front "assembly bases" on the wide arc of 'midland' Rhodesia which stretches from Umtali in the east to Bulawayo and Plumtree in the Southwest. This is the most strategic area of the whole country: it is the prime area of white settlements and white farms, of main transport routes, or main industry and main towns. The British map, the Front argues, leaves the whole arc in the effective charge of the Salisbury forces. It disregards the presence of guerrillas there." Quoted in Baumhoegger, *The Struggle for Independence*, 6:1234.

[99] Davidow, *Peace in Southern Africa*, 81.

and developed to a much weaker instrument. They would have given up
most of their arms and they would have been in assembly areas which gave
a greater advantage to the Rhodesian forces than to us. We insisted that
they should keep their arms, at least for their own protection. Then came
the question, where would they be placed? It was in working these points
out that we faced great problems.[100]

Negotiations deadlocked on this issue, and on December 3 Carrington
told the press that he was "as close to despair as I have been in the
whole three months of negotiations.[101]

On December 4 Carrington offered the Patriotic Front two additional
assurances (although he refused to bend on the issue of equal disengagement). Carrington increased the monitoring force to twelve hundred
and promised that the South African troops currently stationed in Rhodesia would not be allowed to interfere in the transition. He also vowed
that the Rhodesian Air Force, which Britain refused to ground, would
be "monitored effectively," a concession that would prevent the government from bombing rebel assembly camps.[102]

The conference then entered eleven days of bickering as Nkomo and
Mugabe argued over additional cease-fire terms.[103] In an attempt to
break the impasse, Carrington announced that Lord Soames would
leave immediately to assume his position as governor of Rhodesia; sanctions would be lifted as soon as Soames landed in Salisbury, at which
point Carrington would pursue a final settlement with the Muzorewa
government.[104]

Carrington's threat came with a concession.

I am conscious of the concerns expressed by the PF that their assembly
places should not be in close proximity to Rhodesian bases and that they
should not be "encircled." There has never been any question of the PF
being encircled. They will be under the authority of their own commanders
and other forces will be in close proximity to them.

[100] Charlton, *Last Colony in Africa*, 130.

[101] Davidow, *Peace in Southern Africa*, 82.

[102] "Lancaster House Conference: Reports on the Conditional Agreement on the
Ceasefire Terms, December 5, 1979," *Daily Telegraph* (London), December 6, 1979, in
Baumhoegger, *The Struggle for Independence*, 6:1212.

[103] On December 15, 1979, the *London Observer* wrote, "Despite late efforts to bring
the Front into the settlement, their 'no' to Britain's final terms made the outcome of 14
months of Lancaster House negotiations look like possible collapse. The crisis came not
over the constitution and the ceasefire, but over details as to how the guerrillas would be
assembled after they emerged from the bush." "The Lancaster House Conference: Reports
on the Final Plenary Session, December 15, 1979," in Baumhoegger, *The Struggle for
Independence*, 6:1232.

[104] Davidow, *Peace in Southern Africa*, 84.

On the day Soames left for Rhodesia, Carrington assured Nkomo and Mugabe that the Patriotic Front's assembly points would be located near their operation areas and far away from the Rhodesian army bases. Moreover, the Rhodesian forces would be required to take the first step of initiating the cease-fire by "moving into the close vicinity of their bases to permit the Patriotic Front to assemble their forces."[105] The offer for the government to move first was an important compromise.

The breakthrough finally came on December 15. Carrington yielded even further on the topic of assembly points. He promised that additional assembly points would be created if the thirty thousand troops the Patriotic Front claimed would assemble did in fact show up.[106] Later that weekend, Britain formally offered a sixteenth assembly point located in the heart of Rhodesia.[107]

Carrington would go no further. At this point, Tongogara, head of the military arm of the Patriotic Front, and President Machel of Mozambique attempted to persuade Mugabe that the cease-fire terms were sufficient to ensure the protection of the guerrilla forces. As long as rebel soldiers were close to the Mozambiquean and Zambian borders, they could survive attack. Machel also reminded Mugabe that Mozambique wanted a settlement and would not continue to support the Patriotic Front if it refused this plan.[108]

On December 17, 1979, the Patriotic Front accepted the cease-fire agreement and initialed the British offer. Muzorewa signed four days later.

Implementation

The credible commitment theory expects the timing of implementation to correspond to the arrival of outside monitors or enforcers, and this is exactly what occurred. With the peacekeepers and monitors in place at the time of settlement, implementation proceeded on schedule. According to U.S. observer Jeffrey Davidow, "After some rocky first days in which the expected flow of guerrillas into the assembly points was disappointingly low, the numbers entering picked up rapidly. By January 4, the end of the two-week ceasefire period, 17,000 [rebel soldiers] had entered the camps and more straggled in later, until the numbers reached about 22,000."[109]

---

[105] Davidow, *Peace in Southern Africa*, 85.
[106] Davidow, *Peace in Southern Africa*, 86.
[107] Davidow, *Peace in Southern Africa*, 88.
[108] Charlton, *Last Colony in Africa*, 126.
[109] Nonetheless, despite this high compliance rate, the Patriotic Front did not demobilize completely. Approximately one-third of the rebels had been ordered by their commanders

Elections were held on March 4, 1980, three months after the Rhodesian government and the Patriotic Front signed the Lancaster House agreement. Mugabe won a landslide 62 percent of the vote in the British-supervised elections and set up a cabinet that included two white members, Joshua Nkomo, and three members of Nkomo's opposition party.[110] On April 15 Mugabe went a step further to alleviate whites' fear about their future and named Lieutenant-General Peter Walls, former commander of the white Rhodesian Forces, as commander of the new national army.[111] Two days after Peter Walls was named commander of the Zimbabwe army, and almost four months after his arrival, Lord Soames formally ceded political power to Robert Mugabe.[112] By November 1980, the integration of rebel and government forces was completed under British supervision, and the new Zimbabwean army was formed. The political and military transition was now complete.

Why the Lancaster House Negotiations Succeeded

International pressure and the high costs of war once again played an important role in convincing the Rhodesian government and the Patriotic Front to initiate the Lancaster House negotiations. In this case, pressure from South Africa, the United States, and the frontline states and the increasing costs of war, especially for the white minority population, were critical in convincing the two sides to meet again. But Mugabe admitted that these pressures were not enough to get him to sign a peace agreement. An interviewer remarked, "The diplomats relate the story that you were in fact determined to break on this issue [the cease-fire] and only Machel [president of Mozambique] restrained you." Mugabe responded:

> No, we defied Machel on that one completely. Machel would have wanted us to accept even before the first concession was made! On that one we said, "No. In the ultimate it is our own salvation, and we will not go." . . . Our soldiers could have been decimated by a well organized attack in the positions which they had been given.[113]

The Patriotic Front and the Rhodesian government participated in negotiations because outside pressure and the high costs of war induced them to do so, and they compromised on key issues such as majority

---

not to enter the camps and instead to "bury their arms and meld in with the local population" in case the peace treaty broke down. See Davidow, *Peace in Southern Africa*, 91.

[110] For further details see *Keesing's Contemporary Archive*, August 1980.

[111] *Africa Research Bulletin*, April 1–30, 1980, 5640.

[112] See the *Africa Research Bulletin*, April 1–30, 1980, 5639–40.

[113] Charlton, *Last Colony in Africa*, 125.

rule and the reciprocal disengagement of forces for these same reasons. But as Mugabe made clear, it was unlikely that the rebels would ever have signed and then implemented the final agreement if a third-party guarantee had not been arranged.

The preceding analysis discloses that the negotiations were dominated by the question of internal security during the transition. Give-and-take bargaining over political or economic positions did not determine the success or failure of the Anglo-American and Lancaster House talks. Instead, success hinged on resolving three critical issues. Would the rebel forces have equal authority of internal security during the transition to majority rule? Would Britain agree to monitor the transition, ensuring that the process toward majority rule was irreversible? And would the rebels have some ancillary means to protect themselves even if Smith and his South African supporters decided to return to war?

The negotiations to end the civil war in Zimbabwe reflect the Patriotic Front's effort to extract credible commitments from a government that had been strongly opposed to black rule. Ian Smith's successive concessions and Britain's increasing willingness to run the transition gradually reassured the rebels that they could not be exploited should the government choose to back out on the deal. Outside pressure and war costs did convince the Rhodesian government and the Patriotic Front to initiate negotiations, and Peter Carrington did help them locate acceptable terms. But in the end, the Patriotic Front would never have signed the final cease-fire agreement without British and Commonwealth participation in the transition.

Conclusion

This chapter has examined the process by which the Rhodesian government and the Patriotic Front ended their war during the 1970s. In this case, the combatants' fear of the transition, their determination to seek outside security guarantees, and their decision to sign and implement a peace treaty were linked. The Patriotic Front was willing to return to war and forgo the benefits of majority rule as late as December 1979 because effective guarantees for the safety of the Front's armed forces did not exist. In addition, the rebels specifically asked for outside assistance in monitoring compliance, and every attempt to negotiate failed until Britain promised extensive involvement in the transition.

The history of the negotiations in Zimbabwe, therefore, illustrates the powerful role post-treaty security fears play in the resolution of civil wars and the part outside intervention plays in convincing combatants to proceed with implementation. The combatants in this case were able to end their war peacefully because Britain, a far more powerful entity than either the white Rhodesians or the black majority, guaranteed the safety and security of both parties. Twelve hundred Commonwealth forces, numerous British observers, and a well-known British governor stationed on Zimbabwean soil would have made it significantly more difficult for either side to renege on the deal, and thus enhanced the probability that peace would prevail.[114] Additional measures, such as allowing the rebels to keep their arms, locating rebel camps near escape routes, allowing white settlers to keep British citizenship, and retaining South African forces on their border, further reassured combatants and enhanced their faith in their own survival. In the end, the Patriotic Front and the Rhodesian whites were able to move from war to peace because Britain stepped in and guaranteed the safety and survival of both sides.

[114] It is also important to note that Lord Soames had authority to request that additional British troops be sent to Zimbabwe if necessary.

7. The Breakdown of Rwanda's Peace Process

By almost all indicators, Rwanda's civil war should have ended in a successful negotiated settlement. Both the Tutsi rebels and the Rwandan government had agreed to participate in negotiations brokered by a team of Tanzanian mediators whom most people considered highly skilled. The rebels were not demanding a territorial split; instead they called President Habyarimana to reform his authoritarian regime. The two parties were able to reach and sign a highly detailed peace settlement that guaranteed both parties representation in the legislature and a set percentage of slots in the military. And most important for the purposes of the credible commitment theory, the United Nations offered to guarantee the security of the two sides during the implementation period. This promise was written into the Arusha accords and signed by the president of Rwanda and the chairman of the Rwandese Patriotic Front (RPF)—the political arm of the antigovernment guerrilla force composed mostly of former Uganda-based Tutsi refugees. In short, almost all factors purported to lead to a peaceful solution were present at the time the Arusha accords were signed in 1994.

Rwanda's civil war, however, did not end peacefully. In fact, negotiations were followed by one of the most rapid genocides in recorded history.[1] Eight months after the Arusha accords were signed Hutu hardliners began to systematically kill moderate Hutus and Tutsis, reigniting the war and setting the stage for an all-out RPF victory. Almost none of the terms of the settlement had been implemented. Within three months of the start of the genocide, the war was over. Tutsi rebels overpowered government forces to form a new Tutsi-led government, but not before an estimated three-quarters of a million of their own people had been slaughtered.

The breakdown of Rwanda's peace accord during the supposed implementation period despite the offer of power-sharing pacts and the promise of a third-party security guarantee makes Rwanda a particularly difficult test for the credible commitment theory of civil war resolution. If the RPF rebels and government were willing to travel so far along the path to peace, making real concessions and solving key differ-

[1] For details about the speed with which killings took place see Alan J. Kuperman, "Rwanda in Retrospect," *Foreign Affairs* 79, no. 1 (2000): 94–118.

ences, why were they unwilling to implement the terms of their agreement?

Some policymakers and academics argue that the post-treaty genocide was a continuation of the decades-long ethnic feud between the minority Tutsis and majority Hutus or the result of a flawed peace treaty that gave key segments of the government few incentives to implement the deal. What we will see, however, is the key role UN intervention played in final implementation and how the UN's failure to fulfill its promise allowed a small group of extremists to organize and carry out the genocide. The RPF and the Rwandan government did not refuse to implement the Arusha accords because the Hutus and Tutsis could not resolve their differences; the Rwandan government and the RPF settled all the issues driving the war and constructed one of the most comprehensive agreements to end a civil war. Nor did the Rwandan government refuse to implement the accords because the RPF obtained more generous terms; the terms of the settlement were in keeping with the RPF's stronger military position. Rather, the rebels and the government refused to implement the terms of the Arusha accords because the United Nations failed to follow through with its post-treaty security guarantee, and without this reassurance neither side was willing to proceed with settlement. The result was a stalled implementation and a spiral back to war.

What follows is divided into four parts. The chapter begins by discussing current explanations for why the peace process in Rwanda failed. This section highlights potentially important causal variables that will be tracked in the ensuing analysis. The next three sections analyze the Arusha peace process chronologically. In the first of them I look closely at the conditions that encouraged the combatants (especially the Habyarimana government) to initiate negotiations in July 1992. Here we see how the rising costs of war and a change in the president's regime brought the incumbent government to the table. The next part explores the conditions under which the Rwandan government and the RPF agreed to sign the Arusha accords, paying special attention to the sequence by which individual issues were resolved. Here we see a direct link between the UN's offer of post-treaty security and an equal division of military positions, and the final ratification of the peace deal. In the final part I analyze the implementation stage of the peace process. Here we see that the UN's unwillingness to follow through with its promise to protect both Hutus and Tutsis caused the government and the RPF to suspend implementation of this rich and detailed settlement, giving militant extremists time to sabotage the agreement.

Before continuing, a word of caution is in order. Although more has been written on Rwanda's civil war (and especially the genocide) than most civil wars in the twentieth century, data on the negotiation process itself remains limited. It is difficult, for example, to collect concrete evidence on Habyarimana's motivations for signing the Arusha accords or for refusing to implement the terms.[2] In addition, there are limitations to the case selection method used. Several potentially important causal factors (ethnicity, divisibility, goals) did not vary throughout the Rwandan civil war, making it difficult to determine what role they played in the final outcome. In short, although this case analysis is not a definitive test of the theory, it does allow for a more nuanced understanding of each of the factors at each stage of the peace process.

Current Explanations

Journalists and academics offer different explanations for the failure of the Arusha accords to bring peace. Journalists tend to describe the genocide that followed the Arusha accords as a continuation of the decades-long ethnic feud between the minority Tutsis, who had enjoyed a privileged position in society during German and Belgian colonial rule, and majority Hutus, who now dominated government. The *New York Times*, for example, described the genocide as "centuries-old tribal hatred,"[3] and *USA Today* explained the killings as "long-smoldering tribal hatred [that] boiled over."[4] Proponents of this explanation have argued that Hutus and Tutsis parties agreed to negotiate and sign a peace settlement only because outside states pressured them to do so. The result was an agreement that neither party wanted to fulfill.[5]

Academics, on the other hand, tend to blame the failed peace on the uneven terms of the settlement.[6] According to this perspective, the Arusha accords contained two fatal flaws. First, they unduly favored the

[2] The best source of information on the negotiations process are accounts by Bruce D. Jones, an expert on the Arusha negotiations. This chapter draws heavily from Jones's extensive account of the Arusha peace process in *The Best Laid Plans . . . Peace-Making in Rwanda and the Implications of Failure* (New York: Sage, 2001).

[3] Donatella Lorch, "UN in Rwanda Says It Is Powerless to Halt the Violence," *New York Times*, April 15, 1994, A3.

[4] Marilyn Greene, "Two U.S. Envoys Dispatched to Rwanda," *USA Today*, May 3, 1994, A5.

[5] Not all reporters characterized the conflict as ethnically driven. For one exception see Peter Rosenblum, "Understanding 'Tribalism'; Reporting Is Reduced to Simplistic Caricature with Phrases Like 'Ancient Tribal Conflict,'" *Weekly Review*, April 23, 1994, B1.

[6] See, for example, Arthur Jay Klinghoffer, *The International Dimension of Genocide in Rwanda* (London: Macmillan, 1998); Gerard Prunier, *The Rwanda Crisis: History of a Genocide* (New York: Columbia University Press, 1995); and Rene Lemarchand, "Managing Transition Anarchies: Rwanda, Burundi, and South Africa in Comparative Perspective," *Journal of Modern African Studies* 32, no. 4 (1994): 581–604.

RPF by giving the rebels an equal number of cabinet posts in the transitional government and an equal number of officers in the new Rwandan army despite the fact that Tutsis represented only 15 percent of the population.[7] The disproportionate representation of Tutsis in the new government gave incumbent elites and fellow Hutus few incentives to implement their side of the bargain. Second, the Arusha accords almost completely excluded the most powerful hard-line Hutu faction from any new administration. This created a deeply disaffected but heavily armed minority group, the *akazu*, with no stake in the successful implementation of the accords.[8] Proponents of this explanation have argued that President Habyarimana agreed to uneven terms because of heavy external pressure to end the war. Rene Lemarchand, a noted scholar of the Great Lakes region of Africa, calls the terms of the Arusha accords "a recipe for disaster" and questions "whether the Arusha accords would have been signed in the absence of repeated nudging from the OAU, Tanzania, France, the United States, and Belgium." It should be no surprise, therefore, that the groups who stood to lose so much from a settlement would actively seek to prevent its implementation.

Mounting evidence emerging in the aftermath of the 1994 genocide challenges these existing explanations. First, the destructive power of ethnic hatreds does not account for the delayed timing of the genocide or the choice of targets. Bruce Jones, one of the preeminent experts on the Arusha peace process, writes that the genocide "was not spontaneous, not an eruption of ancient tribal hatreds, as it was quickly portrayed by the western media. Rather, this was a planned, coordinated, directed, controlled attack by a small core."[9] It took the militant *akazu* eight months of incendiary radio broadcasts, newspaper stories, and groundwork to convince moderate Hutus that Tutsis could not be trusted. Moreover, the *akazu*'s first victims were not Tutsis, but politicians, journalists, and civil rights activists who supported a democratic transition, many of whom were Hutus.[10] The Hutus' and Tutsis' supposed mutual animosity fails to explain why these hatreds took months to surface once a peace settlement was signed and why Hutus initially targeted other Hutus.

Second, blaming the terms of the Arusha accords on external pressure ignores the strong incentives Habyarimana had to strike a bargain with an enemy that was likely to win the war. Habyarimana certainly faced considerable outside pressure to reform his government and negotiate

---

[7] Lemarchand, "Managing Transition Anarchies."

[8] The *akazu* were senior ministers in Habyarimana's party and senior military figures in the armed forces.

[9] Jones, *The Best Laid Plans*, 31.

[10] Prunier, *The Rwanda Crisis*, 242–43.

with the rebels, but he was under no similar pressure to accept specific terms in the treaty. Jones points out that "external delegations, or observers, actually tried to limit the concessions made in Arusha"; they feared that government concessions were too generous and could create a backlash.[11] What propelled negotiations forward was a strong desire by moderates on both sides of the negotiating table to find peace and the government's recognition that it was unlikely to obtain better terms against an increasingly powerful rebel army. In short, it was the strong military position of the RPF that established the terms of the Arusha accords, not outside observers.[12]

Finally, although it is clear that Hutu extremists rejected the terms of the Arusha accords and instigated their destruction, peace settlements almost always create disenfranchised parties who would prefer to see settlements fail. Extremist groups such as the "real IRA" (Irish Republican Army) and Hamas have all attempted to sabotage peace agreements that majorities on both sides favored. Treaties that succeed do so in part because they anticipate problems "spoiler" groups may cause, and they design ways to neutralize their negative effects. This is exactly what the more moderate Hutus and Tutsis negotiating the accords did when they called upon the UN to help implement the terms. Peace failed in Rwanda because this promised assistance did not materialize. The presence of a dissatisfied minority group was not, therefore, an insurmountable obstacle to peace.[13]

The following three sections trace the process by which President Habyarimana and the RPF chose to pursue peace in 1992 and then return to war in 1994. If the credible commitment theory is correct, their decision process should follow the three patterns discussed in chapters 5 and 6. First, the Rwandan government and the Rwandese Patriotic Front rebels should have the greatest difficulty resolving issues of post-treaty security. Second, both sides should foresee the dangers involved in the post-treaty transition and actively seek third-party security guarantees to guide them through this phase. Finally, both the government and the RPF should refuse to integrate their forces and demobilize excess soldiers until a third party arrives on the ground. Each of these actions would strongly suggest that credible commitments were the chief obstacle to peace once negotiations got under way, and that combatants could not resolve this problem without outside assistance. The theory would be called into question if security issues were

[11] Jones, *The Best Laid Plans*, 62.

[12] In fact, it is becoming generally accepted that President Habyarimana was assassinated in April 1994 because it appeared as if he would implement the terms of the agreement against the wishes of more hard-line elements within his party.

[13] Jones, *The Best Laid Plans*, 36.

not the most difficult to resolve, if the combatants did not actively seek third-party assistance, or if the arrival and departure of third-party forces had little effect on the final outcome of a war.

What we see confirms many of the findings presented in chapters 4 and 5. Looking first at the prenegotiation phase, then the formal bargaining phase, and finally the implementation and peacekeeping period, we will trace the influence of the costs of war, type of regime, mediation, treaty pacts, and third-party security guarantees on the government's and the RPF's decisions to cooperate or fight at each step along the way.

The Conditions Leading to Negotiations

The Rwandan government, headed by President Juvenal Habyarimana, and the Rwanda Patriotic Front, headed by Major-General Paul Kagame, initiated peace negotiations in June 1992, twenty-one months after the RPF, composed mainly of Tutsi exiles living in Uganda, invaded Rwanda. The rebels had two aims: to replace Habyarimana's dictatorship with a multiparty government, and to force the government to allow Tutsi refugees living in Burundi, Zaire, and Uganda to return to Rwanda.

Two factors appeared to heavily influence the government's decision to negotiate with the rebels. First, as the costs-of-war theory predicts, the government agreed to participate in negotiations only after a series of successful military attacks by the RPF caused the government's economic situation to deteriorate significantly. The attacks gave the RPF control over the country's wheat-producing northern territory and displaced hundreds of thousands of people who normally worked the fields. The attacks also cut the main transportation route from the country and forced the government to call up tens of thousands of new recruits for its army.[14] By 1993, war-related expenses, which had accounted for 15 percent of the budget in 1990, now took up approximately 70 percent.[15]

---

[14] The capture of valuable territory was not included as a measure of the costs of war in the quantitative analysis. I expressed concern in chapter 3 that the duration of war and the number of battle deaths did not capture the range of factors that were likely to affect war costs. Although Rwanda's civil war was neither a particularly long nor bloody conflict, the government's loss of control over this fertile agricultural region did appear to be quite costly and is thus interpreted this way in this analysis. For a discussion of the importance of the northern region to the government of Rwanda, see *The United Nations and Rwanda, 1993–1996* (New York: United Nations, Department of Public Information, 1996), 32.

[15] Human Rights Watch, "Choosing War," 14. See <http://www.igc.org/hrw/reports/1999/rwanda/Geno1-3-11.htm#P638—245631>.

Habyarimana's government was paying serious economic costs to pursue its war with the rebels, costs that encouraged it to begin negotiations.

A second, more indirect factor also affected the government's decision to negotiate. Western donor countries had pressed Habyarimana to adopt a more democratic form of government since the war began in 1990.[16] In April 1992, three months before negotiations commenced, the heavily aid-dependent Rwandan government yielded to this pressure and announced it would form a coalition government with a number of opposition parties. In keeping with predictions made by the democratic regime theory, it was this less autocratic coalition government that chose to pursue formal peace talks with the RPF, not the dictatorial Habyarimana regime.[17]

Conditions leading up to negotiations, therefore, confirm one of the results of the quantitative tests presented in chapter 4. Of all the factors purported to affect the decision to initiate negotiations, the costs of war did seem to play a significant role in Habyarimana's decision to begin talks with the RPF. The loss of important farmland in the north and the threatened loss of critical developmental assistance made the government of Rwanda reconsider its uncompromising stance toward the RPF and look for peaceful alternatives to war. The case, however, once again reveals the influential though indirect role international pressure (and type of regime) can play in bringing a recalcitrant party to the negotiating table. In this case, the threatened loss of international aid forced Habyarimana to install a more democratic government, which in turn was more open to negotiations with the RPF than the previous one-party regime. Therefore, international pressure and regime type in addition to war costs were critical to get negotiations off the ground.

The Conditions Leading to a Signed Bargain

Once negotiations commenced, a different set of factors pushed the Rwandan government and the RPF through thirteen months of stop-and-go negotiations and toward a formal peace treaty. Four factors in particular helped break key deadlocks and convince the two sides to compromise on vital issues. They were (1) the RPF's increasing military strength, (2) Tanzania's skilled mediation, (3) the United Nations' written guarantee to ensure the overall security of the country, and (4) a strict division of political and military positions in the post-treaty tran-

---

[16] Jones, *The Best Laid Plans*, 43.

[17] Rwanda went from a -7 to a -4 on the Polity III democracy scale between 1991 and 1992, indicating that the regime showed more democratic features during this time.

sition government. The type of regime in power and a balance of military strength did not appear to have a significant impact at this stage.

The following section traces the sequence by which the Rwanda government and the RPF resolved their main disagreements and reached a bargain. We will see that the main grievances were resolved fairly early in the negotiations, leaving security issues for last; that the combatants did seek the help of a third party; and that the two biggest stumbling blocks to settlement, the makeup of the new Rwandan army and the composition of the officer corps, were surmounted by a strict allotment of slots between the former government and rebel forces.

Resolving the Issues: Arusha's Timeline

Negotiations began on July 12, 1992, in Arusha, Tanzania, and were brokered by Ambassador Ami Mpungwe of Tanzania, who by all accounts was a highly skilled and experienced mediator.[18] Mpungwe and his team organized the agenda around five basic items, starting with issues they thought would be easiest to resolve and ending with the most difficult. These five items were a military cease-fire, an agreement on the principles of law, power sharing within a transitional government, the repatriation of Tutsi refugees living outside Rwanda, and the integration of the two competing armies.

As the credible commitment theory predicts, the first two issues were resolved smoothly.[19] Soon after negotiations commenced, the government and the RPF agreed on the terms of the cease-fire and on the rule of law. The first sticking point came over power sharing in the transitional government.[20] Two issues in particular dominated the discussion. The first was whether the Coalition pour la Défense de la République (CDR), an extremist and vehemently anti-Tutsi party, would be included. Habyarimana, who needed the support of this hard-line faction to retain power, insisted that the CDR be incorporated in the first postwar government. The RPF refused and, in the end, prevailed. Positions were to be conferred on the Rwandan government, the RPF, and remaining opposition parties, but not the CDR.

As the credible commitment theory predicts, the combatants insisted that political power be distributed mathematically, with each of the

---

[18] For comments lauding the skill of Tanzania's mediation team see Howard Adelman and Astri Suhrke, with Bruce D. Jones, *Early Warning and Conflict Management in Rwanda: Report of Study II of the Joint Evaluation of Emergency Assistance in Rwanda* (Copenhagen: DANIDA, 1996), 24, and Jones, *The Best Laid Plans*, 54.

[19] For a detailed description of these early negotiations see Prunier, *The Rwanda Crisis*, 166–67.

[20] Jones, *The Best Laid Plans*, 55.

major opposition parties and Habyarimana's party given control over at least one key portfolio.[21] The RPF would control the vice prime minister, the minister for the interior, and three additional portfolios; Habyarimana's party would be in command of defense–public works, the presidency, and three additional portfolios; other parties were to be assigned other ministries.[22]

The second contentious issue was the exact allocation of seats in the transitional parliament, and once again they were allocated precisely.[23] Habyarimana's party and the RPF would each hold eleven seats in the new assembly, with other parties holding an additional eleven.[24] A wide distribution of portfolios and seats would make it difficult for any one party to change the terms of the agreement or set up a one-party state. Human Rights Watch observed that "this carefully calibrated three-part division of power in the government would make it almost impossible for any one group to dominate and thus be able to disrupt the movement toward elections and real peace."[25] In short, each party knew exactly what role it would play in the government that was scheduled to rule once a peace treaty was signed, and this knowledge likely convinced each of the parties to sign.

The next issue on the agenda was the fate of Tutsi refugees living in neighboring countries, and it was settled with little problem. By June 10, 1993, the two main issues driving the war—the repatriation of refugees and political power-sharing—were resolved. The combatants now turned to the last and most difficult item on the agenda: the integration of the competing armies into a new national military.[26]

The first step taken by the Rwandan government and the RPF was a request for third-party assistance in implementing whatever security plan was constructed. In a joint letter to both the Organization of African Unity and the UN, the two enemies stated that "the implementation of the peace agreement in Rwanda requires the deployment of a neutral

[21] This transitional government would last no longer than twenty-two months, after which free elections would be held to determine the new government of Rwanda.

[22] The Mouvement Démocratique Républicain (MDR, the main opposition party) would occupy the positions of prime minister and foreign minister and two additional portfolios; the Parti Social Démocrate (PSD, the second largest opposition party) would get three posts including finance; the Parti Libéral (PL, an opposition party with many Tutsi members) would direct three portfolios including justice; and the Parti Démocrate Chrétien (PDC, a Christian Democratic party), would get one. See Prunier, *The Rwanda Crisis*, 192; and Jones, *The Best Laid Plans*, 56.

[23] Jones, *The Best Laid Plans*, 55.

[24] Two additional seats would be given to two parties that were presently not represented in the coalition government, the PCD and the CDR.

[25] Human Rights Watch, "Choosing War," 15.

[26] Jones, *The Best Laid Plans*, 57.

international force as soon as the peace agreement is signed."[27] Both the Rwandan government and the Tutsi rebels recognized that implementation of the accords would be shaky, given elements of opposition. Both parties recognized the hazards they might face as they attempted to integrate their armies and set up the transitional government, and they took clear measures to find third-party assistance.

Secretary-General of the United Nations Boutros Boutros-Ghali agreed to help, and a clause was added to the Arusha accords stating that the UN would "guarantee the overall security in the country and verify the maintenance of law and order, ensure the security of the delivery of humanitarian assistance, and assist in catering to the security of civilians."[28] The international force would also assist with disengagement, disarmament, and demobilization leading to the integration of the armed forces.

With third-party assistance assured, the parties addressed the integration of military forces. This issue took months of negotiations and on two occasions "threatened to collapse the entire process."[29] The government and RPF disagreed on two points, the percentage of officers each side would contribute to the new army, and how far down the military chain of command each side would be allowed to contribute officers. In the end, the military integration agreement called for a fifty-fifty division of the officer corps down to the level of field commander, but allowed the government to retain a 60 percent share of the troops.[30] With this issue resolved, the Arusha accords were signed.[31]

The sequence by which issues were resolved and the demands that both sides made for third-party security guarantees and a strict division of political and military positions follow the predictions made by the credible commitment theory. Outside protection during demobilization and guaranteed representation in post-treaty military and political institutions were key requirements for the signing of the accords. In fact, the last two issues on the table were the presence of a neutral security force and the exact distribution of power in the new national army. Immediately thereafter, on August 4, 1993, the peace treaty was signed.

A closer look at the negotiations, however, also reveals the important role outside mediation and the balance of power played in pushing the

[27] *United Nations and Rwanda*, Document 16, S/25951, June 15, 1993, 165.
[28] *United Nations and Rwanda*, nn. 2, 3. See also Howard Adelman and Astri Suhrke, "Early Warning and Response: Why the International Community Failed to Prevent the Genocide," *Disasters* 20, no. 4 (1996): 299.
[29] Jones, *The Best Laid Plans*, 57.
[30] The two parties would also split consecutive positions in any unit (i.e., commander and second-in-command). See Prunier, *The Rwanda Crisis*, 193.
[31] Jones, *The Best Laid Plans*, 57–58.

government forward at key impasses.[32] The Tanzanian mediation team almost certainly helped break deadlocks over CDR involvement in the transitional government and over integration of forces and allowed the combatants to reach a mutually agreeable deal.

In addition, a clear connection existed between the RPF's successful military offensive that began on February 8, 1993, and Habyarimana's willingness to tackle the final issues of post-treaty security that stood in the way of a settlement. Contrary to the predictions of balance-of-power theories, it was the rapid military *advance* of the rebels and the decisive *shift* in the balance of power that occurred in early 1993 that appeared to break the deadlock. Had the government been able to fight the rebels to a military stalemate, it is unlikely that the final issue of integration of forces would have been satisfactorily resolved. In short, although the second stage in the Rwanda peace process confirms the preeminence of post-treaty security concerns, it also brings to light the important role skilled mediation and a decisive show of military force played in allowing combatants to resolve real conflicts of interest.

The Conditions Influencing Implementation

All factors strongly favored the successful implementation of the Arusha accords at this point in the peace process. The costs of returning to war were high—especially for the government, which faced a stronger and more successful rebel army. The main issues driving the war—multi-party rule and refugees—had been resolved. Political and military power would be shared in the transitional government, and the United Nations had agreed to take responsibility for implementation. Bruce Jones remarks that "the Arusha Accords were a rich, detailed blueprint for the resolution of the underlying themes of the Rwandan conflict . . . not leaving too much out for the implementation process where such deals often break down."[33] If any settlement were to be implemented successfully, this would be the one.

Recall, however, that the credible commitment theory predicts that implementation will not automatically follow the signing of a peace set-

[32] "Ambassador Mpungwe was widely held to be critical to the success of the negotiations, forging agreements through backroom diplomacy, nursing consensus, and serving as a conduit for ideas and solutions generated by the observer teams. Both Paul Kagame, and Theogene Rudasingwa (General Secretary for the RPF and one of their delegates) have publicly commended the Tanzanian role. Diplomatic observers in Dar-es-Salaam give Ambassador Mpungwe much credit for the success—on paper—of the Arusha accords." Jones, *The Best Laid Plans*, 54. This was also the conclusion of the Joint Evaluation. See *International Response*, 2:24.

[33] Jones, *The Best Laid Plans*, 62.

tlement, no matter how detailed or popular. Instead, implementation depends on the *willingness* of the third party to fulfill its promised role. In Rwanda, the government and the RPF would demobilize only if UN forces arrived on the ground and proved capable of fulfilling their declared mission. If UN forces were slow to arrive, had a changed mandate, or were reluctant to perform their duties, neither the Rwandan government nor the RPF would demobilize, and the peace process would eventually fail.

The aftermath of the Arusha accords confirms this prediction. Despite the UN's promise, the Security Council did not authorize a mission for Rwanda until two months after the peace agreement was signed and almost a month after the transitional government was to have been established. This delay ran directly counter to pleas, made by both Habyarimana and the RPF, that "the neutral international force . . . be deployed as quickly as possible after the signing of the peace agreement in order to permit its speedy implementation . . . thereby avoiding excessively long intervals, which might be detrimental to the peace process."[34] Both parties realized that a delay in implementation would give extremists the opportunity to reverse the momentum toward peace and destroy the Arusha process.

The timing of implementation was directly tied to the arrival of UN forces. The transitional government was scheduled to be installed after a battalion of RPF soldiers arrived in Kigali to ensure the safe transfer of power. The RPF, however, would not deploy troops in the capital until French soldiers (who had supported the Rwanda government) had withdrawn.[35] The French in turn refused to leave Kigali until UN peacekeepers arrived.[36] The arrival of UN forces, therefore, held the key to the entire transition.[37]

In the end, the UN agreed to send 2,217 peacekeepers, less than half the minimum recommended contingent. They were deployed bit by bit and with a mandate greatly reduced from that described during negotiations. Boutros-Ghali had promised a force that would "guarantee overall security" and "assist in tracking of arms caches and neutralization of armed gangs throughout the country"—that is, peacekeepers with robust Chapter VII enforcement capabilities. What arrived was a much

---

[34] *United Nations and Rwanda*, 165.

[35] Fear of a possible surprise attack at this time led rebel leader Paul Kagame to call off the scheduled busing of soldiers to Kigali, saying, "I was suspicious. It was late, after 4:00 P.M. And the buses therefore were going to enter Kigali very late at night, which was risky. So I told everyone to get off the buses." Interview by Charles Onyango-Obbo, from *Monitor*, December 19, 1997. See <http://www.africanews.com/obbo/>.

[36] Klinghoffer, *International Dimension of Genocide*, 32.

[37] Adelman, Suhrke, and Jones, *Early Warning*, 35.

weaker Chapter VI mission that was allowed to operate only in the capital city. It could "contribute to," but not "guarantee," security. The use of force was allowed only in self-defense.[38]

Worse yet, UNAMIR (United Nations Assistance Mission for Rwanda) did not have the resources to perform even a limited verification role. It did not have the money or the intelligence capabilities to provide reliable information on compliance.[39] Helicopters were expected but never arrived.[40] In fact, funding was so low that between October 1993 and April 1994 the contingent in Rwanda had to operate "hand-to-mouth, at one stage borrowing from UNICEF simply to remain operational."[41]

During this time, the government and rebel forces maintained the cease-fire but refused to leave their field positions or demobilize. In the meantime, those opposed to the settlement had the opportunity to build support for their own plans to topple Arusha. Hard-liners who stood to lose from implementation of the accords broadcast incendiary propaganda about upcoming Tutsi domination, distributed weapons to extremist militias, and planned a counterattack.

These plans were not unknown. On January 11, 1994, three months before extremist militias began killing moderate Hutus and Tutsis in Kigali, a senior figure in the Rwandan government sent a letter to UN headquarters informing New York of a plot to kill large numbers of Tutsis. According to the letter, Hutu extremists were planning to assassinate politicians at the scheduled ceremony to swear in the transitional government. In the process, they planned to challenge Belgian UNAMIR soldiers, expecting that by killing some, they would convince the UN to pull its entire mission out of Rwanda.[42] A Rwandan official later explained that the attack on Belgian peacekeepers was inspired by newscasts of the UN's 1993 response to a similar ambush in Mogadishu: "We watch CNN too, you know," he said.[43]

The UN's response to the letter was telling. Despite repeated requests

---

[38] From a comparison of articles B1, B3, and B4 of the Arusha accords with articles 3a and 3h of the Security Council Resolution 872 of October 5, 1993. See the Institute for Global Communications website for a more detailed discussion of the differences at <http://www.igc.org/hrw/reports/1999/rwanda/Geno1-3-11.htm.>

[39] UNAMIR stands for the United Nations Assistance Mission for Rwanda. See Adelman, Suhrke, and Jones, *Early Warning*; and Prunier, *The Rwanda Crisis*, 231–52.

[40] Klinghoffer, *International Dimension of Genocide*, 32.

[41] Jones, *The Best Laid Plans*, 71–72.

[42] Howard Adelman and Astri Suhrke, with contributions by Bruce Jones, "Early Warning and Conflict Management," Joint Evaluation of Emergency Assistance to Rwanda, Royal Danish Ministry of Foreign Affairs, 1997, <http://www.um.dk/danida/evalueringsrapporter/1997—rwanda/>.

[43] Quoted in Jones, *The Best Laid Plans*, 80, from a confidential author interview, Kigali, June 1996.

by the UN force commander in Rwanda to bring UNAMIR up to authorized strength and to permit search and seizure of arms caches in the capital, New York did nothing.[44] The RPF and the government, therefore, had many months to observe UN inactivity, and in an environment of increasing instability and violence they could see that third-party enforcement or verification would not be forthcoming. If the two sides chose to honor the agreement and demobilize, they would have to do so on their own.

Events continued to deteriorate in Rwanda between January and April 1994. Then, on April 6, 1994, the plane carrying President Habyarimana was shot down as he returned from a meeting in Tanzania. The assassination set off the preordained slaughter, and within two weeks an estimated 250,000 Tutsis were killed, many under the eyes of UNAMIR soldiers in the capital city.[45] One of the first victims targeted was the new prime minister of the transitional government, Agathe Uwilingiyimana, and ten Belgian UNAMIR soldiers stationed to protect her. Other early targets were journalists, lawyers, human rights activists, and opposition intellectuals who supported the peace process, most of whom were Hutus.[46] These initial attacks were strategic. Eliminating moderate Hutu leaders would remove competition for leadership and make future compromises with Tutsi moderates less likely. Murdering Belgian soldiers would, the plotters hoped, instigate withdrawal.[47]

The plan initially succeeded. Within five days of the attack on its peacekeepers, Belgium announced it would withdraw entirely from Rwanda. The United Nations followed soon thereafter, and by April 20, only 470 UN soldiers remained in Rwanda. On April 8, one day after the start of the genocide, the RPF had renewed its offensive. Three days later, RPF troops reached Kigali and began a battle for control of the capital.[48] The war ended three months later, with the total defeat of Hutu forces by the RPF.

Although it is impossible to know with certainty what would have happened had the UN sent the type of military force expected by the architects of Arusha, Hutu extremists probably could not have carried out their campaign. UNAMIR commander Major General Romeo Dal-

[44] Not only would the UN not send the promised resources, but the organization stated very clearly that it believed "the responsibility for the maintenance of law and order must remain with the local authorities." *United Nations and Rwanda*, 85.

[45] Kuperman, "Rwanda in Retrospect."

[46] Jones, *The Best Laid Plans*, 31.

[47] The Belgian contingent was also the largest and most well equipped set of peace-keepers. If they withdrew from Rwanda, they would take with them vital logistics and communications equipment that was necessary for the entire UN mission. See *United Nations and Rwanda*, 113–14.

[48] For details, see Prunier, *The Rwanda Crisis*, 268.

laire maintained that if he "had had that brigade group in Rwanda, there would be hundreds of thousands of lives spared today."[49] In its final report, the Carnegie Commission on Preventing Deadly Conflict concluded that "early intervention—within two weeks of the initial violence—by a force of 5,000 could have made a significant difference in the level of violence in Rwanda."[50] Had the UN provided the mandate and the resources it promised, and the political will to accept even a small number of casualties, the terms of the Arusha accords probably would have been implemented and the killing deterred.

But why did the UN decide to withhold the resources it almost certainly knew would be necessary to implement the Arusha accords? Boutros-Ghali encountered two problems in putting his promises into operation. The first was structural. UN procedures for budgeting and deploying peacekeeping operations were slow and required a powerful supporter in New York to push a mission to the forefront of the agenda. Rwanda, however, was only of peripheral interest to the major powers on the Security Council (except France) and thus failed to garner the support or the sense of urgency necessary for decisive action.[51] The second problem was timing. The Arusha accords were signed at a time the United States was attempting to extricate itself from Somalia and limit its involvement in Yugoslavia.[52] It was also a time of increasing pessimism about the UN's ability to bring peace and an increasing sense that the United States could not and should not be the "world's policeman."[53]

The great tragedy of Rwanda, however, is how close the Arusha peace process came to succeeding. A relatively small but operational UN contingent for verification or enforcement could have made a difference. Unlike Somalia and Bosnia, where the parties to the conflict did not voluntarily agree to negotiate, the combatants in Rwanda's war willingly signed a comprehensive peace agreement and then honored a

---

[49] From the Carnegie Commission on Preventing Deadly Conflict, Final Report. P. 191. Original source: "Rwanda: U.N. Commander Says More Troops May Have Saved Lives," Inter Press Service, September 7, 1994. Others have also made this point. See Brian Urquart, "For a UN Volunteer Military Force," *New York Review of Books*, June 10, 1993; Alison L. Des Forges, "Alas, We Knew," *Foreign Affairs* 79, no. 3 (2000); and Jones, *The Best Laid Plans*. For a contrasting view see Kuperman, "Rwanda in Retrospect."

[50] Carnegie Commission on Preventing Deadly Conflict, *Preventing Deadly Conflict: Final Report* (New York: Carnegie Corporation of New York, December 1997), 6.

[51] Adelman, Suhrke, and Jones, "Early Warning and Conflict Management," 36–37.

[52] Jones, *The Best Laid Plans*, 73.

[53] In a commencement address at the U.S. Naval Academy in 1994, President Clinton stated that "we cannot solve every such outburst of civil strife or militant nationalism simply by sending in our force." Paul Lewis, "Boutros-Ghali Angrily Condemns All Sides for Not Saving Rwanda," *New York Times*, May 26, 1994, A1.

cease-fire. They refused to implement the terms only when it became clear that the UN had neither the will nor the muscle to fulfill its intended role.

Conclusion

The peace process in Rwanda is a brutal reminder of the costs of failing to implement a peace treaty. The disaster that followed the Arusha accords cannot be attributed primarily to historical enmity between the Tutsis and Hutus, or to disaffected hard-liners. Most Hutus and Tutsis supported the Arusha accords and a peaceful end to the war. This case study reveals that even if combatants in a civil war are able to resolve their underlying differences, even if they are guaranteed a significant voice in the first postwar government, and even if they are willing to honor a cease-fire, they will not implement the terms of the settlement until they are convinced that a third party can guarantee their safety as they demobilize and prepare for peace. A fair and comprehensive peace agreement is not enough to bring peace. Rwanda failed to end its civil war peacefully because neither the Rwandan government nor the RPF believed the UN would be able to ensure the peaceful transfer of power, and it was the fear of exploitation in the immediate aftermath of signing the accords that ultimately paralyzed the process and opened the door for abuse.

A close examination of the peace process shows that the Rwandan government and RPF rebels sought the UN's involvement, that they pushed for the rapid deployment of UN forces, and that they pressed for additional assistance as hard-liners gained strength. The less credible the UN became, the more empowered the extremists' forces became, and the less likely either side was to proceed with implementation.

In a number of ways, however, this case forces reevaluation of assumptions underlying the credible commitment theory. First, this case reminds us that the two "sides" negotiating an agreement are rarely as unified as I have presumed. Habyarimana's government and his supporters frequently disagreed on the type of concessions that should be made to the RPF. Intraparty disputes accounted for some of Habyarimana's hesitancy in transferring power after the Arusha accords were signed, and Habyarimana's disaffected inner circle (the *akazu*) clearly played a role in the ultimate failure of the peace process.

Second, the Rwanda case also reveals the effect a military balance of power can have on the willingness of combatants to cooperate. In Rwanda's case, a pseudo-balance of power did appear to play a partial role in bringing combatants to the negotiating table, but it was a decisive *shift* in the military balance that forced the government to make the concessions necessary to obtain a signed bargain. The government conceded on the most important issues of the negotiations only after its military position deteriorated sharply.[54] This runs counter to the balance-of-power theory presented in chapter 1, which predicted that a military stalemate is most likely to bring peace. A more nuanced look at the effect of power balances on peace is therefore warranted.

Third, the Rwanda case also indicates that the real world is more complex than a few variables can describe. Once again, outside pressure in the form of economic aid and sanctions played an important role in the first stage of the peace process by raising the price the Rwandan government would have to pay if it refused to negotiate. The war in Rwanda was costly in its own way, and it was these somewhat unusual costs that eventually drove the reluctant government to the negotiating table.

Rwanda teaches us one final lesson. Although third-party security guarantees are necessary to convince combatants to sign and implement peace agreements, a false guarantee can be worse than no guarantee at all. It is likely that neither the Rwandan government nor the RPF would have signed a peace treaty had the international community been more honest about its commitment to Rwanda. In this situation, extremists would not have had the luxury of organizing and executing their genocidal plan, and the RPF would have been in a position to protect Tutsi civilians and defend itself from attack. The result would have been a more rapid RPF victory over the incumbent government and the preservation of a quarter of a million lives. In short, a false hope of international intervention is worse than no hope at all.

[54] Adelman, Suhrke, and Jones, "Early Warning and Conflict Management," 25.

8. Explaining the Resolution of Civil Wars

⤷ THIS BOOK HAS ARGUED that the greatest problem opponents encounter in trying to resolve a civil war is not that of reaching an agreement, as so many people have assumed, but that of writing an enforceable contract under conditions of extreme risk. Combatants decide to pursue peace settlements in part because a third party is willing to verify or enforce demobilization, and because their role in the first postwar government can be safeguarded. These guarantees are necessary for the combatants to credibly commit to treaties that create enormous opportunities for post-treaty exploitation.

This book has also argued that in order to understand how civil wars end, the resolution process must be viewed as taking place in three stages, beginning with the decision to initiate negotiations, continuing with the decision to strike a mutually agreeable bargain, and ending with the decision to implement the terms of a treaty. Although I expected the conditions that influenced combatants at each stage in this process to be quite different, I maintained that the last stage—implementation—would be the most difficult to navigate and the one on which peaceful outcomes would rest. The results from both the quantitative and qualitative analysis supported these predictions. Civil war combatants tended to initiate negotiations when the costs of war were high, and their military capabilities were fairly equally balanced (two factors that indicated that combatants were sensitive to the costs involved with winning a war and their chances of achieving victory, at least in the early stages of a peace process). Once negotiations began, however, combatants became far more concerned with post-treaty security and the distribution of power than any other conditions on the ground. In the end, only third-party security guarantees and power-sharing pacts had a significant effect on combatants' willingness to implement a peace settlement.

Three tasks remain. The first is to revisit the findings and discuss any unexpected results that were revealed in the analysis. The second is to extend the findings beyond the resolution of civil wars in order to highlight the contribution this research makes to the broader field of international relations. Does this study of civil war resolution help explain cooperation in other high-risk, high-uncertainty environments? The final task of this chapter is to offer specific recommendations to policymakers who must grapple with the difficult issue of resolving persistent civil wars.

Findings

Quantitative Analysis

The quantitative analysis in chapter 4 showed that third-party security guarantees and power-sharing pacts were critical when combatants considered whether to sign and implement peace settlements. When a third party stepped in to guarantee the security of the combatants in the immediate post-treaty transition period, and political or territorial power was guaranteed to the combatants, civil wars almost invariably ended with a successful settlement. If a third party did not step in and a power-sharing pact did not exist, combatants almost inevitably walked away from the table and returned to war. Combatants were clearly looking down the road and factoring in the likelihood of compliance when deciding whether to end their war in a negotiated settlement or attempt a decisive victory. This finding strongly supports the credible commitment theory of civil war resolution. Adversaries seem unable to credibly promise to abide by the terms of a treaty that offers enormous rewards for cheating and enormous costs for being cheated upon, and they require third-party guarantees to help them through.

The quantitative analysis also revealed that other factors play a crucial role prior to the implementation of a peace treaty and are thus equally necessary for the peaceful settlement of civil wars. The duration of war and a military stalemate mattered a great deal in bringing combatants to the table. Mediation, a military stalemate, and nonterritorial goals were then instrumental in combatants' decision to reach and sign a bargain. But by far the two most important factors in convincing combatants to both sign and implement peace settlements were third-party security guarantees and power-sharing pacts. Only then were you likely to get peace.

The findings presented in chapter 4, however, told only part of the story. For the credible commitment theory to hold, third-party security guarantees and power-sharing pacts needed to have an independent effect on combatants' decision to sign and implement peace treaties. If guarantees were simply offered in cases that would have succeeded on their own, their role in the outcome of negotiations would have been undercut. The evidence in chapter 5 showed that third-party security guarantees and power-sharing pacts were largely unrelated to any of the other potentially important causal variables. There was some evidence that outside states and international organizations were *more* likely to offer security guarantees in conjunction with mediation and power-sharing pacts, but there were surprisingly few correlations between post-treaty guarantees and other factors related to peace.

Case Studies

The statistical analysis showed which variables were significantly related to the different stages of the peace process. It could not, however, demonstrate why third-party security guarantees and power-sharing pacts appeared to be so important to the final outcome. We still did not know, for example, whether government and rebel leaders actively sought these guarantees, and if they did seek them, if they did so because they anticipated problems with post-treaty compliance.

In order to show that civil war combatants chose to sign and implement negotiated peace treaties based on their ability to obtain third-party security guarantees and extract power-sharing pacts from each other, I examined the negotiating process in the Zimbabwean and Rwandan civil wars. A close analysis of these two cases confirmed the degree to which post-treaty security weighed on the minds of the combatants as they debated whether to sign and implement peace settlements. The case studies also revealed that combatants were aware of the difficult strategic situation they would face during the transition to peace and that they actively sought measures to neutralize these risks. In both Zimbabwe and Rwanda, the question of post-treaty security was far more difficult to resolve than the issue of majority rule or multiparty rule. In addition, both the Patriotic Front in Zimbabwe and the Tutsi rebels in Rwanda asked for outside security guarantees, and both waited to demobilize until the promised peacekeepers had arrived on the ground. The great tragedy in Rwanda was that the UN refused to deploy its promised mission, giving extremists time to sabotage the deal. A deeper look at individual cases, therefore, not only confirmed that guarantees were critical, decisive factors in the decision to sign and implement peace settlements, but were also sought to allay real fears of post-treaty opportunism.

Zimbabwe and Rwanda, however, also revealed interesting nuances not discussed in earlier chapters. First, in both cases outside pressure in the form of economic sanctions, economic or military assistance, and open borders appeared instrumental in combatants' decisions to participate in peace talks and in their decisions to compromise on treaty terms.[1] The outside world clearly had the means to make war harder to

---

[1] This conclusion is supported by Patrick Regan's study of successful third-party interventions. He found that a mixed strategy of military intervention and economic sanctions

pursue and thus make cooperation more or less attractive. This pattern suggests that combatants are sensitive to a variety of different costs when deciding whether to pursue a peaceful solution to their wars, many of which are controlled by outside states.[2]

Second, individual case histories also offered a window into the conditions under which third parties were likely to intervene. Britain, the United States, and the United Nations all attempted to avoid direct involvement in Zimbabwe and Rwanda. In the end, however, Britain played an extensive role in the implementation of the Lancaster House peace plan, while the UN walked away from any responsibility for Rwanda's Arusha accords. Why did Britain choose to follow through with its promise, while the United Nations did not? Part of the answer lies is the contrast between unilateral and multilateral intervention; it was easier for Britain as a single state to organize and mount a peace mission than it was for the multimember UN to coordinate a timely response. An international organization that must please multiple governments is less likely to obtain the mandate, resources, and coordinated command structure necessary to respond effectively. It is also less likely to offer a credible security guarantee as a result. Part of the answer lies in Britain's self-interest in ending Zimbabwe's war. As the former colonial power, Britain would not remain blameless if the war continued. The permanent members of the UN Security Council, on the other hand, had no economic, strategic, or political reason for intervening in Rwanda. The only incentive they had was to prevent humanitarian suffering, and this was not viewed by many members as a sufficient reason to step in.

Finally, the case studies offered new insights into the question of third-party neutrality. Although much has been written about the need for impartial mediation, Britain's part in the success of the Lancaster House agreement suggests that strict neutrality is not always necessary or desirable to obtain a successful settlement.[3] In this case, it appears

---

was most effective in bringing about a cessation of military hostilities in intrastate wars. See "Conditions of Successful Third-Party Intervention in Intrastate Conflicts," *Journal of Conflict Resolution* 40, no. 2 (1996): 336–59.

[2] A particularly interesting example can be found in Angola. In November 1999 the DeBeers Corporation announced that it would no longer trade in UNITA-mined diamonds. It has long been accepted that UNITA financed its long-standing fight against the Angolan government through diamonds, a fact that could change if the market for its good were blocked. See the *Humanitarian Times*, November 24, 1999.

[3] Although most scholars and practitioners believe that mediators will be more effective if they are unbiased and impartial, two studies dispute this claim. I. William Zartman has argued that it is more important for mediators to be able to deliver a favored side than to be unbiased (*Elusive Peace*, 21). Andrew Kydd, has argued that biased mediators can reduce the likelihood of war by providing more credible information about the resolve of

that Britain's bias in favor of the white Anglo-Saxon settlers facilitated settlement, not because it reassured the black majority, but because it greatly reassured the tiny white minority that stood to lose significantly from the transition to majority rule. The Zimbabwe case suggests that in certain circumstances a biased third party can actually enhance feelings of security and help deliver the weaker side.

The data, therefore, suggest that at least three refinements need to be made to our understanding of civil war resolution. First, the case studies reveal that outside pressure is likely to have a significant impact on combatants' decision to pursue negotiated settlements. This suggests that additional research needs to be done on the effects of different types of third-party actions on the settlement process, not just on the effects of third-party mediation and security guarantees. Second, the cases also reveal that third parties have numerous motives for offering to guarantee settlements, most of which have nothing to do with the conditions on the ground. Additional research, therefore, needs to be done on the conditions under which outside states and international organizations choose to offer their services, and on the conditions that determine the level of their commitment, issues this book does not fully address. Finally, a closer look at two outlying cases—Colombia in 1958 and Yemen in 1970—brought to light the unusual circumstances under which combatants can peacefully resolve their civil wars without outside assistance. The details of these two cases reveal that a negotiated peace is possible in the absence of third-party security guarantees, but only when organized, partisan armies do not exist and demobilization need not occur.

Implications for International Relations

The theory presented in this book differs from other theories primarily by asserting that combatants' concerns about their security after a treaty is signed dominate every decision they make during the peace process, and that if combatants fail to address complex issues of enforcement, attempts to negotiate will fail.

The ideas presented here, however, also speak to four larger debates in the field of international relations. First, this book offers insights into when cooperation may succeed even under conditions of extreme risk and uncertainty—conditions that are especially prevalent in the wake of

---

parties. See Kydd "Mediation, Preferences, and Credibility," University of California, Riverside, August 2000. Richard Betts has also argued in favor of biased intervention, but for different reasons. See "The Delusions of Impartial Intervention," *Foreign Affairs* 73, no. 6 (1994): 20–33.

a civil war. What this study suggests is that cooperation can occur even when the costs of cheating are exceptionally high, but for this to happen, parties need extremely strong guarantees against exploitation—something that almost certainly will require third-party assistance. Under these conditions groups will almost always demand direct third-party enforcement or verification and shy away from less secure institutional solutions.

Second, the findings also have relevance for the game-theoretical literature that attempts to explain why bargaining may break down despite mutual gains from cooperation. The findings suggest that if negotiating parties are asked to consolidate their assets into a single organization, they have far greater difficulty binding themselves to an agreement than groups who can remain independent or autonomous thereafter. In these cases, the greatest obstacle to success is not reaching mutually acceptable bargains, but in forging credible commitments to a highly risky implementation process.

Finally, this book also offers a counterstudy to the transitions-to-democracy literature. Adam Przeworski has argued that democracy is likely to succeed if the outcome of elections remains uncertain to those involved. "If outcomes were either predetermined or completely indeterminate," he writes, "there would be no reason for groups to organize as participants. It is the uncertainty that draws them into the democratic interplay." The research reported here, however, shows that parties will not agree to end their conflict and move to a more liberal, competitive political system if power is distributed solely through competitive *and* *uncertain* elections. Where the institutional framework is too weak to enforce election outcomes, uncertainty works against cooperation. The lessons learned from transitions to democratic rule in the former authoritarian regimes of Eastern Europe and Latin America, therefore, should not necessarily be applied to all other types of democratic transition. High-risk situations require greater guarantees against political exclusion.

Implications for Policymakers

Since the end of the Cold War, the international community has concentrated significant time and money trying to end civil wars around the globe. This study offers at least six suggestions on how this energy may best be focused to achieve greater success.

The main finding is that the implementation of settlements cannot be left to the combatants themselves. In civil wars combatants will hesitate to sign and implement settlements unless a third party actively intervenes to enforce or verify demobilization. This is an important point to emphasize because it sometimes appears as if combatants should be able to resolve their differences on their own. One of the perverse findings to be drawn from this study is that negotiated settlements that appear to have all the elements of success—a cease-fire agreement, specific arrangements for future governance, resolution of underlying issues— still fail if they lack the guarantees necessary to reassure groups to proceed with implementation.

This leads to a second, related observation. Outsiders should not be lured into the false belief that combatants who have resolved the root causes of the war and signed comprehensive peace plans will be able to implement these terms on their own. Moreover, outsiders should not make a third-party security guarantee conditional on combatants' willingness to *begin* demobilizing, as the United Nations did in Rwanda after the Arusha accords. Noncompliance is not necessarily a sign that combatants are uncommitted to peace; it is simply a sign that they are nervous about their own security.

Third, the more committed a third party appears to be in fulfilling its promise to verify or enforce, the more likely combatants are to sign and implement peace treaties. If groups do not believe that peacekeepers will effectively verify compliance or protect them as they report to assembly areas, or if they are not convinced that peacekeepers will remain involved until demobilization is complete, then their role as a reassuring device is undercut, and it is highly unlikely that implementation will proceed. This does not mean that outsiders must send massive numbers of peacekeeping troops to coerce compliance from the participants. It means only that the troops they do send must be convincing.[4]

Fourth, not all types of third-party intervention are likely to have a positive effect on conflict resolution. One of the main lessons to emerge from this book is that only a certain type of outside intervention offered at a specific time in the peace process will help negotiations succeed. Intervening in a haphazard way or before combatants have willingly initiated peace negotiations will not obtain the desired effect and could prolong a war. Studies, therefore, that track the effect of external intervention on settlement regardless of the type and timing of this intervention are likely to draw an overly pessimistic conclusion about the role outsiders can play in the peaceful resolution of civil wars. It is only a specific type of outside assistance, offered at a specific time in the peace process, that is most likely to aid successful settlement.

---

[4] As the model in chapter 2 showed, combatants will choose to disengage their armies voluntarily if they believe a third party is committed to its task. Coercion is not necessary if the threat to use force or verify compliance is credible.

Fifth, relying too heavily on the promise of free and fair elections as a means to introduce democracy to states emerging from civil war can be dangerous. If groups that have recently fought each other fear that the victor of the first postwar elections will set up an authoritarian state, outlaw the opposition, and possibly imprison them, they will refuse to participate in negotiations and will choose instead to continue the war. Outsiders, therefore, should refrain from pushing for a "quick and easy" democratization process and understand that they cannot simultaneously end a civil war and set up a fully liberal democracy without some sort of democratic transition between. Outsiders should instead encourage negotiating leaders to divvy up important political positions that insulate them from the vagaries of elections, and to design peace agreements that include provisions for regional autonomy, both of which are more likely to bring peace.

A government based on mutual guarantees, however, is not without its drawbacks. Consociational power-sharing solutions or pacts have long been criticized for being undemocratic, having no "grassroots backing," being the "ultimate form of elite manipulation," "freezing" group boundaries, and excluding important parties that were not major players in a war.[5] The government shared between Cambodia's Hun Sen and Prince Norodom Ranariddh that began in 1993, for example, was paralyzed by in-fighting between the two prime ministers, ultimately falling victim to a coup in 1997. True, pacts can be inflexible and highly inefficient. However, the fact that such regimes are likely to have difficulty obtaining a policy consensus on almost any issue is the reason why adversaries are likely to find them so attractive. A counterintuitive conclusion to draw from this book is that groups who fear political domination may actually find this paralysis quite reassuring. There is great comfort in knowing that policies detrimental to your interests can *not* be made.

Nevertheless, the fact that power-sharing guarantees can be inefficient, exclusionary, and inflexible means that this type of government will not be stable over time. Eventually, citizens will demand greater efficiency from their government, and new parties will demand more open, competitive systems. If these consociational systems do not evolve, they will eventually topple. The fact that power-sharing pacts are likely to be unstable over time, therefore, means that a second transition will almost certainly be needed to maintain peace over the long term. The ultimate challenge facing enemies in a civil war, therefore, is

---

[5] For criticisms, see Sisk, *Power Sharing*, 38–39; Brian Barry, "Political Accommodation and Consociational Democracy," *British Journal of Political Science* 5 (October 1975): 477–505; and Horowitz, *Ethnic Groups in Conflict*, 586.

how to adroitly transform the inflexible institutional structures that are necessary to convince each of them to sign a settlement in the highly tense postwar environment into the more liberal, open institutions that are necessary to bring peace and stability over time.[6]

The civil wars analyzed here suggest that at least one final lesson can be drawn from past experiences. When attempting to resolve these conflicts, enforcement does matter, but only in the short term. If outside states truly expect these settlements to last over time, they must consider how the institutional parameters of any new government shape groups' expectations about their future security and factor into decisions to fight or cooperate. Military force may be crucial for demobilization, but creative institutional design matters far more in the long run.

---

[6] For research that looks specifically at this problem see Fortna, "A Peace That Lasts."

APPENDIX 1

TABLE A.1
Civil Wars That Began between 1940 and 1992

Civil War	Active Negotiations	Signed Bargain	Outcome[a]
Greece, 1944–49	Yes	No	Decisive victory
China, 1946–50[b]	Yes	Yes	Decisive victory
Paraguay, 1947*	No	No	Decisive victory
Yemen Arab Republic, 1948*	No	No	Decisive victory
Costa Rica, 1948	No	No	Decisive victory
Colombia, 1948–62[c]	Yes	Yes	Successful settlement
Burma, 1948–51	No	No	Decisive victory
Indonesia, 1950	No	No	Decisive victory
Philippines, 1950–52	No	No	Decisive victory
Bolivia, 1952*	No	No	Decisive victory
Indonesia, 1953*	No	No	Decisive victory
Guatemala, 1954*	No	No	Decisive victory
Argentina, 1955*	No	No	Decisive victory
Indonesia, 1956–60	No	No	Decisive victory
Lebanon, 1958*	Yes	Yes	Successful settlement
Cuba, 1958–59	No	No	Decisive victory
Iraq, 1959	No	No	Decisive victory
Vietnam, 1960–65	No	No	Decisive victory
Congo, 1960–65	No	No	Decisive victory
Laos, 1960–73[d]	Yes	Yes	Decisive victory
Algeria, 1962–63*	No	No	Decisive victory
Yemen Arab Republic, 1962–69	Yes	Yes	Successful settlement
Sudan, 1963–72	Yes	Yes	Successful settlement
Rwanda, 1963–64	No	No	Decisive victory
Dominican Republic, 1965	Yes	Yes	Successful settlement
Uganda, 1966	No	No	Decisive victory
Guatemala, 1966–96[e]	Yes	Yes	Successful settlement
China, 1967–68	No	No	Decisive victory
Nigeria, 1967–70	Yes	No	Decisive victory
Burma, 1968–80	No	No	Decisive victory
Cambodia, 1970–75	No	No	Decisive victory
Jordan, 1970	No	No	Decisive victory
Pakistan, 1971	No	No	Decisive victory
Sri Lanka, 1971	No	No	Decisive victory
Burundi, 1972	No	No	Decisive victory
Philippines, 1972–	Yes	Yes	Unresolved
Zimbabwe, 1972–79	Yes	Yes	Successful settlement
Pakistan, 1973–77	No	No	Decisive victory
Lebanon, 1975–90	Yes	No	Decisive victory[f]
Angola, 1975–[g]	Yes	Yes	Unresolved
Afghanistan, 1978–	Yes	Yes	Unresolved
Iran, 1978–79	No	No	Decisive victory
Nicaragua, 1978–79	Yes	No	Decisive victory
Cambodia, 1979–91	Yes	Yes	Successful settlement
El Salvador, 1979–92	Yes	Yes	Successful settlement

TABLE A.1
Continued

Civil War	Active Negotiations	Signed Bargain	Outcome[a]
Mozambique, 1979–92	Yes	Yes	Successful settlement
Chad, 1980–88	Yes	Yes	Decisive victory
Uganda, 1980–88	Yes	Yes	Decisive victory
Iran, 1981–82	No	No	Decisive victory
Peru, 1982–	No	No	Unresolved
Nicaragua, 1982–90	Yes	Yes	Successful settlement
Somalia, 1982–	Yes	Yes	Unresolved
Burma, 1983–*	No	No	Unresolved
Sri Lanka, 1983–	Yes	No	Unresolved
Sudan, 1983–*	Yes	No	Unresolved
Colombia, 1984–	Yes	No	Unresolved
Iraq, 1985–	No	No	Unresolved
India, 1985–93	Yes	No	Decisive victory[h]
South Yemen, 1986	No	No	Decisive victory
Sri Lanka, 1987–89	No	No	Decisive victory
Burundi, 1988	No	No	Decisive victory
Liberia, 1989–94[i]	Yes	Yes	Decisive victory
Romania, 1989*	No	No	Decisive victory
Rwanda, 1990–94	Yes	Yes	Decisive victory
Georgia (Abkahzia), 1991–*	Yes	No	Unresolved
Georgia (S. Ossetia), 1991–*	Yes	No	Unresolved
Nagorno-Karabakh, 1991–*	Yes	No	Unresolved
Croatian Independence, 1991–92	Yes	Yes	Successful settlement
Turkey, 1991–*	Yes	No	Unresolved
Burundi, 1991–	Yes	No	Unresolved
Bosnia, 1992–95	Yes	Yes	Successful settlement
Tajikistan, 1992–94	Yes	No	Decisive victory[j]

*Borderline cases (see chapter 3 for details).

[a]Civil wars were considered unresolved if neither a negotiated settlement nor a decisive military victory had been reached by December 31, 1999.

[b]The Correlates of War database (COW) codes this as two separate wars, the first 1946–50, the second in 1947.

[c]COW codes this as two separate wars, the first in 1948, the second 1949–62.

[d]COW codes this as two separate wars, 1960–62 and 1963–73.

[e]COW codes this as three separate wars, 1966–72, 1970–71, and 1978–84.

[f]COW codes this as having ended in a decisive victory. Technically, however, the war ended inconclusively when Syrian troops occupied the country in 1976 and forced a peace.

[g]COW codes this as two separate wars, the first 1975–91, the second in 1992.

[h]More accurately, this war petered out after January 1993 elections restored self-government. Terrorism continued as of December 1999.

[i]COW codes this as two separate wars, the first 1989–90, the second ongoing since 1992.

[j]War temporarily ended in 1994 with a cease-fire enforced by fifteen thousand Russian soldiers.

APPENDIX 2

Here I explain the results behind model 1, the basic model; model 2, guaranteed power sharing; and model 3, which adds the possibility of a third party that enforces or verifies the agreement.

Model 1: The Basic Model

This game, shown in figure 2.1, can be solved using a backward induction process. Starting with the subgame at the start of phase 3, where both players choose simultaneously, we now know that if both choose to demobilize, the winner of the election will take full control of the state. Thus, if both players demobilize, their payoffs are $pS_g + (1 - p)H_g$ and $pH_r + (1 - p)S_r$. The subgame therefore has the normal form shown in table A.2.

From this, we see that for all p, the only Nash equilibrium is for both not to demobilize, so both players will prefer not to demobilize and the outcome is (W_g, W_r). As a result, when we look up the tree, we see that the only possible outcome is (W_g, W_r). Thus, the players are, in the first two phases, indifferent between negotiating or not and between signing a bargain or not. Hence, each player has four subgame perfect equilibrium strategies, for a total of sixteen subgame perfect equilibria. Despite this indeterminacy, there is only one possible outcome, (W_g, W_r).

Model 2: Guaranteed Power Sharing

This game can be solved as is model 1. Starting at the phase 3 subgame, we can see that both players have a dominant strategy to refuse to

TABLE A.2
Model 1: The Basic Model

	Rebels	
	Do Not Demobilize	*Demobilize*
Government		
Do Not Demobilize	W_g, W_r	H_g, S_r
Demobilize	S_g, H_r	$pS_g + (1-p)H_g,$ $pH_r + (1-p)S_r$

TABLE A.3
Model 2: Guaranteed Power Sharing

	Rebels	
	Do Not Demobilize	*Demobilize*
Government		
Do Not Demobilize	Wg, Wr	Hg, Sr
Demobilize	Sg, Hr	Pg, Pr

demobilize because $H > P$ and $W > S$. As in model 1, when we then move up the tree, we see again that the players will receive the payoff for war (W) no matter what they do. The players are, in the first two phases, indifferent between negotiating or not and between signing a bargain or not. Hence, each player has four subgame perfect equilibrium strategies, for a total of sixteen subgame perfect equilibria. Despite this indeterminacy, there is only one possible outcome, (W_g, W_r) (table A.3).

Model 3

Third Party Will Enforce or Verify a Bargain

We start again at the phase 3 subgame. As shown in figure 2.3, it differs because nature chooses whether to have a third party enforce or verify a bargain. Here we assume the government and rebels are certain a third party will actively enforce or verify demobilization once a settlement is signed, so $p = 1$. Given this, the subgame has the normal form shown in table A.4.

From this, we see that both parties have a dominant strategy to voluntarily demobilize in the final stage of the game in order to obtain power sharing (P). Voluntary demobilization is always preferred to coerced demobilization because a reluctant demobilizer will pay a cost ($P - c$) for having been coerced to do so, and $P > P - c$.

Working up the tree, since both players know that power sharing will result in phase 3, and since both prefer power sharing to continued war ($P > W$), both prefer to sign a bargain than not in phase 2, and they will both prefer to initiate negotiations in phase 1 rather than refuse to negotiate. Hence, knowing a third party will enforce or verify a bargain,

TABLE A.4
Model 3: Third Party Will Enforce or Verify a Bargain ($p = 1$)

	Rebels	
	Do Not Demobilize	Demobilize
Government		
Do Not Demobilize	$(P-c)_g, (P-c)_r$	$(P-c)_g, P_r$
Demobilize	$P_g, (P-c)_r$	P_g, P_r

the government and the rebels will negotiate in phase 1, sign a bargain in phase 2, and voluntarily demobilize in phase 3. This is a unique subgame perfect equilibrium.

Third Party Will Not Enforce or Verify a Bargain

In this version of Model 3, the parties know that the third party will not enforce demobilization ($p = 0$). Given this, the subgame has the normal form shown in table A.5.

From this, we can see that both the government and the rebels have a dominant strategy to not demobilize since both prefer hegemony to power sharing ($H > P$) and war to a sucker's payoff ($W > S$). The outcome of the final subgame, therefore, is war (W_g, W_r).

As in models 1 and 2, we again see that the players will receive the payoff for war (W) no matter what they do. The players are, in the first two phases, indifferent between negotiating or not and between signing a bargain or not. Hence, each player has four subgame perfect equilibrium strategies, for a total of sixteen subgame perfect equilibria. Despite this indeterminacy, there is only one possible outcome, (W_g, W_r).

TABLE A.5
Model 3: Third Party Will Not Enforce or Verify a Bargain ($p = 0$)

	Rebels	
	Do Not Demobilize	Demobilize
Government		
Do Not Demobilize	W_g, W_r	H_g, S_r
Demobilize	S_g, H_r	P_g, P_r

Model 3: Combatants Are Uncertain Whether Third Party Will Enforce or Verify

Here is the proof for figure 2.3, where it is now assumed that the players are uncertain whether a third party will enforce or verify a bargain when one or both parties fail to demobilize. The probability of enforcement is p, and nonenforcement is $1 - p$. The solution concept employed is subgame perfect equilibrium (SPE).

To solve this game, first consider the players' expected utilities from each of their strategies. Because the players receive the W payoff (war) if either one fails to negotiate or sign, we can simplify matters by collapsing the players' moves in the first two phases to constitute one move each. Thus, if G negotiates and signs a bargain, that is considered one move, $q = 1$, and either not negotiating or not signing is $q = 0$. Similarly for R, negotiating and signing is $z = 1$, while not negotiating or not signing is $z = 0$. In phase 3, G chooses to not demobilize or demobilize, represented by $x = 0$ and $x = 1$ respectively, and R chooses to not demobilize or demobilize, represented by $y = 0$ and $y = 1$ respectively. We thus have the EU equations for each player's respective strategies as shown below.

G's EU for its three pure strategies are as follows:

$$EU_G(q = 1, x = 1) = z[yP_g + (1 - y)\{pP_g + (1 - p)S_g\}] + (1 - z)W_g$$

$$EU_G(q = 1, x = 0) = z[y\{p(P_g - C_g) + (1 - p)H_g\} + (1 - y)\{p(P_g - C_g) + (1 - p)W_g\}] + (1 - z) W_g$$

$$EU_G (q = 0) = Wg$$

R's EU for its three pure strategies are as follows:

$$EU_R (z = 1, y = 1) = q[xP_r + (1 - x)\{pP_r + (1 - p)S_r\}] + (1 - q)W_r$$

$$EU_R(z = 1, y = 0) = q[x\{p(P_r - C_r) + (1 - p)H_r\} + (1 - x)\{p(P_r - C_r) + (1 - p)W_r\}] + (1 - q)W_r$$

$$EU_R (z = 0) = W_R$$

There are nine pure strategy combinations to test using the EU equations above, to see if they are in equilibrium.

1. $(q = 1, x = 1; z = 1, y = 1)$
2. $(q = 1, x = 1; z = 1, y = 0)$
3. $(q = 1, x = 1; z = 0)$
4. $(q = 1, x = 0; z = 1, y = 1)$

5. $(q = 1, x = 0; z = 1, y = 0)$
6. $(q = 1, x = 0; z = 0)$
7. $(q = 0; z = 1, y = 1)$
8. $(q = 0; z = 1, y = 0)$
9. $(q = 0; z = 0)$

Substituting into the EU equations above, we can deduce mathematical contradictions that eliminate four of the nine combinations as equilibria (numbers 3, 6, 7, 8). The other five are in equilibrium.

EQUILIBRIUM 1. An agreement is negotiated and signed, and both demobilize $(q = 1, x = 1; z = 1, y = 1)$. This exists if $p \geq (H_G - P_G)/(H_G - P_G + C_G)$ and if $p \geq (H_R - P_R)/(H_R - P_R + C_R)$.

EQUILIBRIUM 2. An agreement is negotiated and signed, but only G demobilizes $(q = 1, x = 1; z = 1, y = 0)$. This exists if $p \geq (W_G - S_G)/(W_G - S_G + C_G)$ and if $p \leq (H_R - P_R)/(H_R - P_R + C_R)$.

EQUILIBRIUM 3. An agreement is negotiated and signed, but only R demobilizes $(q = 1, x = 0; z = 1, y = 1)$. This exists if $p \leq (H_G - P_G)/(H_G - P_G + C_G)$ and if $p \geq (W_R - S_R)/(W_R - S_R + C_R)$.

EQUILIBRIUM 4. An agreement is negotiated and signed, but neither demobilizes $(q = 1, x = 0; z = 1, y = 0)$. This exists if $p \leq (W_G - S_G)/(W_G - S_G + C_G)$ and if $p \leq (W_R - S_R)/(W_R - S_R + C_R)$.

EQUILIBRIUM 5. No agreement is signed $(q = 0; z = 0)$. This exists for all values of p. (Note that because the moves in phases 1 and 2 were collapsed into one move for each player, this actually represents all the strategy combinations for the first two phases other than (Negotiate, Sign; Negotiate, Sign). Hence, there may or may not be negotiations, and if there are negotiations there will not be a signed deal.

BIBLIOGRAPHY

Adelman, Howard, and Astri Suhrke. "Early Warning and Response: Why the International Community Failed to Prevent the Genocide." *Disasters* 20, no. 4 (1996): 295–304.

Alden, Chris, and Mark Simpson. "Mozambique: A Delicate Peace." *Journal of Modern African Studies* 31, no. 1 (1993): 109–30.

Andemichael, Berhanykun. *Peaceful Settlement among African States: Roles of the United Nations and the Organization of African Unity.* New York: United Nations Institute for Training and Research, 1972.

Anstee, Margaret Joan. *Orphan of the Cold War: The Inside Story of the Collapse of the Angolan Peace Process, 1992–93.* New York: St. Martin's Press, 1996.

Anyidoho, Henry Kwami. *Guns over Kigali: The Rwandese Civil War, 1994.* Accra, Ghana: Woeli Publishing Services, 1997.

Arnold, Guy. *Wars in the Third World since 1945.* 2d ed. London: Cassell, 1995.

Art, Robert J., and Robert Jervis, eds. *International Politics: Enduring Concepts and Contemporary Issues.* New York: Harper Collins, 1992.

Asiwaju, A. I. *Partitioned Africans: Ethnic Relations across Africa's International Boundaries, 1884–1984.* New York: St. Martin's Press, 1985.

Assefa, Hiskias. *Mediation in Civil Wars: Approaches and Strategies: The Sudan Conflict.* Boulder: Westview Press, 1987.

Avenhaus, Rudolf, Hassane Karkar, and Michel Rudnianski, eds. *Defense Decision Making: Analytical Support and Crisis Management.* Berlin: Springer-Verlag, 1991.

Avenhaus, Rudolf, Reiner K. I. Huber, and John D. Kettelle, eds. *Modeling and Analysis in Arms Control.* Berlin: Springer-Verlag, 1986.

Axelrod, Robert. *The Evolution of Cooperation.* New York: Basic Books, 1984.

Bailey, Clinton. *Jordan's Palestinian Challenge, 1948–1983: A Political History.* Boulder: Westview Press, 1984.

Bailey, Sydney D. *How Wars End: The United Nations and the Termination of Armed Conflict, 1946–1964.* 2 vols. Oxford: Clarendon Press, 1982.

Baldwin, David, ed. *Neorealism and Neoliberalism: The Contemporary Debate.* New York: Columbia University Press, 1993.

Barber, James. *Rhodesia: The Road to Rebellion.* London: Oxford University Press, 1967.

Barry, Brian. "Political Accommodation and Consociational Democracy." *British Journal of Political Science* 5 (October 1975): 477–505.

Baumhoegger, Goswin. *The Struggle for Independence: Documents on the Recent Development of Zimbabwe (1975–1980).* 7 vols. Hamburg: Institute of African Studies, Africa Documentation Center, 1984.

Bell, J. Bowyer. "Societal Patterns and Lessons: The Irish Case." In *Civil Wars in the Twentieth Century,* ed. Robin Higham. Lexington: University Press of Kentucky, 1972.

Bendor, J., R. M. Kramer, and S. Stout. "When in Doubt: Cooperation in a Noisy Prisoner's Dilemma." *Journal of Conflict Resolution* 35, no. 4 (1991): 691–719.

Bercovitch, Jacob. *Social Conflicts and Third Parties: Strategies of Conflict Resolution.* Boulder: Westview Press, 1984.

———, ed. *Resolving International Conflicts: The Theory and Practice of Mediation.* Boulder: Lynne Rienner, 1996.

Bercovitch, Jacob, and Jeffrey Z. Rubin, eds. *Mediation in International Relations: Multiple Approaches to Conflict Management.* Boulder: Westview Press, 1984.

Berry, R. Albert, Ronald G. Hellman, and Mauricio Solaun. *Politics of Compromise: Coalition Government in Colombia.* New Brunswick, N.J.: Transaction Books, 1980.

Betts, Richard. "The Delusions of Impartial Intervention." *Foreign Affairs* 73, no. 6 (1994): 20–33.

Blainey, Geoffrey. *The Causes of War.* New York: Free Press, 1973.

Blake, Robert. *A History of Rhodesia.* New York: Alfred A. Knopf, 1978.

Bowman, Larry W. *Politics in Rhodesia: White Power in an African State.* Cambridge: Harvard University Press, 1973.

Bracey, Audrey. *Resolution of the Dominican Crisis, 1965: A Study in Mediation.* Washington, D.C.: Institute for the Study of Diplomacy, 1980.

Brams, Steven J., and Marc D. Kilgour. "Putting the Other Side 'On Notice' Can Induce Compliance in Arms Control." *Journal of Conflict Resolution* 36, no. 3 (1992): 395–414.

Brett, E. A. "Rebuilding Organisation Capacity in Uganda under the National Resistance Movement." *Journal of Modern African Studies* 32, no. 1 (1994): 53–80.

Brogan, Patrick. *The Fighting Never Stopped: A Comprehensive Guide to World Conflict since 1945.* New York: Vintage Books, 1990.

Brown, Michael D. *Ethnic Conflict and International Security.* Princeton: Princeton University Press, 1993.

———, ed. *The International Dimensions of Internal Conflict.* Cambridge: MIT Press, 1996.

Bueno de Mesquita, Bruce, and David Lalman. *The War Trap.* New Haven: Yale University Press, 1992.

Burton, John W. *Resolving Deep-Rooted Conflict: A Handbook.* Lanham, Md.: University Press of America, 1987.

———. "International Conflict Resolution Priorities." *Forum* (Peace Institute Reporter), June 1987.

Bushnell, David. *The Making of Modern Colombia: A Nation in Spite of Itself.* Berkeley: University of California Press, 1993.

Byrne, Hugh. *El Salvador's Civil War: A Study of Revolution.* Boulder: Lynne Rienner, 1996.

Calvocoressi, Peter. *World Politics since 1945.* 7th ed. London: Longman, 1996.

Carment, David, and Patrick James. "The Escalation of Ethnic Conflict: A Survey and Assessment." *International Politics* 35, no. 1 (1998): 65–82.

Carment, David, Dane Rowlands, and Patrick James. "Ethnic Conflict and Third Party Intervention: Riskiness, Rationality, and Commitment." Occasional Paper Series. Norman Paterson School of International Affairs, Ottawa, 1995.

Carnegie Commission on Preventing Deadly Conflict. *Preventing Deadly Conflict: Final Report.* New York: Carnegie Corporation of New York, December 1997.

Carrington, Peter. *Reflecting on Things Past: The Memoirs of Peter, Lord Carrington.* London: William Collins, 1988.

Charlton, Michael. *The Last Colony in Africa: Diplomacy and the Independence of Rhodesia.* Oxford: Basil Blackwell, 1990.

Chassin, Lionel Max. *The Communist Conquest of China: A History of the Civil War, 1945–1949.* Cambridge: Harvard University Press, 1965.

Child, Jack. *The Central American Peace Process, 1983–1991: Sheathing Swords, Building Confidence.* Boulder: Lynne Rienner, 1992.

Cimbala, Stephen J., and Keith A. Dunn, eds. *Conflict Termination and Military Strategy: Coercion, Persuasion, and War.* Boulder: Westview Press, 1987.

Claude, Inis L., Jr. *Power and International Relations.* New York: Random House, 1962.

Clubb, O. Edmund. *Twentieth Century China.* New York: Columbia University Press, 1964.

Cohen, Anthony P. *The Symbolic Construction of Community.* London: Routledge, 1989.

———, ed. *Symbolizing Boundaries: Identity and Diversity in British Cultures.* Manchester: Manchester University Press, 1986.

Collier, Paul. "Demobilization and Insecurity: A Study in the Economics of the Transition from War to Peace." *Journal of International Development* 6, no. 3 (1994): 343–51.

Collier, Paul, Anke Hoeffler, and Måns Söderbom. "On the Duration of Civil War and Postwar Peace." Centre for the Study of African Economies, University of Oxford, March 1998.

Commonwealth Observer Group. *The Report of the Commonwealth Observer Group on the Elections Leading to Independent Zimbabwe.* London: Commonwealth Secretariat, Marlborough House, 1980.

Cooper, Robert, and Mats Berdal. "Outside Interventions in Ethnic Conflicts." *Survival* 35, no. 1 (1993): 118–42.

Coser, Lewis. *The Functions of Social Conflict.* New York: Free Press, 1956.

Cowan, L. Gray. "Zimbabwe at a Crossroads." *CSIS Africa Notes,* no. 136 (1992)

Crocker, Chester A. *High Noon in Southern Africa: Making Peace in a Rough Neighborhood.* New York: W. W. Norton, 1992.

Crook, D. P. *Diplomacy during the American Civil War.* New York: John Wiley and Sons, 1975.

Dahl, Robert. *Polyarchy: Participation and Opposition.* New Haven: Yale University Press, 1971.

Daly, M. W., and Ahmad Alawad Sikainga. *Civil War in the Sudan.* London: British Academic Press, 1993.

Damrosch, Lori Fisler, and David J. Scheffer. *Law and Force in the New International Order.* Boulder: Westview Press, 1991.

Darnton, John. "Africa Tries Democracy, Finding Hope and Peril." *New York Times*, June 21, 1994.

Davidow, Jeffrey. *A Peace in Southern Africa: The Lancaster House Conference on Rhodesia, 1979.* Boulder: Westview Press, 1984.

Deeb, Marius. *The Lebanese Civil War.* New York: Praeger, 1980.

Deng, Francis M., and I. William Zartman, eds. *Conflict Resolution in Africa.* Washington, D.C.: Brookings Institute, 1991.

Department of State. *Peace Accords for Angola.* Trans. LS #134967. May 1991.

Des Forges, Alison L. "Alas, We Knew." *Foreign Affairs* 79, no. 3 (2000).

DeSilva, K. M. *A History of Sri Lanka.* Berkeley: University of California Press, 1981.

Despres, Leo A., ed. *Ethnicity and Resource Competition in Plural Societies.* The Hague: Mouton, 1975.

Deutsch, Morton. *The Resolution of Conflict: Constructive and Destructive Processes.* New Haven: Yale University Press, 1973.

Diamond, Larry, and Marc F. Plattner. *The Global Resurgence of Democracy.* Baltimore: Johns Hopkins University Press, 1993.

Diehl, Paul F. *International Peacekeeping.* Baltimore: Johns Hopkins University Press, 1993.

Diehl, Paul F., Jennifer Reifschneider, and Paul R. Hensel. "United Nations Intervention and Recurring Conflict." *International Organization* 50, no. 4 (1996): 683–700.

Dixon, William J. "Third-Party Techniques for Preventing Conflict Escalation and Promoting Peaceful Settlement." *International Organization* 50, no. 4 (1996): 653–81.

Dommen, Arthur. *Conflict in Laos.* New York: Praeger, 1964.

Downs, George W., and David M. Rocke. *Optimal Imperfection? Domestic Uncertainty and Institutions in International Relations.* Princeton: Princeton University Press, 1995.

Downs, George W., David M. Rocke, and Peter N. Arsoom. "Is the Good News about Compliance Good News about Cooperation?" *International Organization* 50, no. 3 (1996): 379–406.

Doyle, Michael W., Ian Johnstone, and Robert C. Orr, eds. *Keeping the Peace: Multidimensional UN Operations in Cambodia and El Salvador.* Cambridge: Cambridge University Press, 1997.

Doyle, Michael W., and Nicholas Sambanis. "International Peacebuilding: A Theoretical and Quantitative Analysis." *American Political Science Review* 94 (2000): 778–801.

Dragnich, Alex N. *Serbs and Croats: The Struggle in Yugoslavia.* New York: Harcourt Brace, 1992.

Duner, Bertil. *Military Intervention in Civil Wars: The 1970s.* New York: St. Martin's Press, 1985.

Dunnigan, James F., and William Martel. *How to Stop a War: The Lessons of Two Hundred Years of War and Peace.* New York: Doubleday, 1987.

Durch, William J. *The Evolution of UN Peacekeeping: Case Studies and Comparative Analysis.* New York: St. Martin's Press, 1993.

————, ed. *UN Peacekeeping, American Politics, and the UN Civil Wars of the 1990s*. New York: St. Martin's Press, 1996.

Du Toit, Pierre. *State Building and Democracy in Southern Africa: Botswana, Zimbabwe, and South Africa*. Washington, D.C.: U.S. Institute of Peace, 1995.

Eckstein, Harry, ed. *Internal War: Problems and Approaches*. New York: Free Press of Glencoe, 1964.

Elbadawi, Ibrahim A., and Nicholas Sambanis. "External Interventions and the Duration of Civil Wars." World Bank Policy Research Paper, July 25, 2000.

Elman, Colin, and Miriam Fendius Elman. "Diplomatic History and International Relations Theory: Respecting Difference and Crossing Boundaries." *International Security* 22, no. 1 (1997): 5–21.

Esman, Milton J., and Shibley Telhami, eds. *International Organizations and Ethnic Conflict*. Ithaca: Cornell University Press, 1995.

Fearon, James D. "Bargaining, Enforcement, and International Cooperation." *International Organization* 52, no. 2 (1998): 269–305.

————. "Domestic Political Audiences and the Escalation of International Disputes." *American Political Science Review* 88 (1994): 379–406.

————. "Ethnic War as a Commitment Problem." University of Chicago, 1993.

————. "Rationalist Explanations for War." *International Organization* 49, no. 3 (1995): 379–414.

Feis, Herbert. *The China Tangle: The American Effort in China from Pearl Harbor to the Marshall Mission*. Princeton: Princeton University Press, 1953.

Findlay, Trevor. *Cambodia: The Legacy and Lessons of UNTAC*. Oxford: Oxford University Press, 1995.

Finnegan, William. *A Complicated War: The Harrowing of Mozambique*. Berkeley: University of California, 1992.

Fortna, Virginia Page. "A Peace That Lasts: Agreements and the Durability of Peace." Ph.D. diss., Harvard University, 1998.

Fox, William T. R. *How Wars End*. Annals of the American Academy of Political and Social Science, vol. 392. Lancaster, Pa.: American Academy of Political and Social Science, 1970.

Francis, Dana, ed. *Mediating Deadly Conflict: Lessons from Afghanistan, Burundi, Cyprus, Ethiopia, Haiti, Israel/Palestine, Liberia, Sierra Leone, and Sri Lanka*. Cambridge: World Peace Foundation Report, 1998.

Galbraith, W. O. *Colombia: A General Survey*. Westport, Conn.: Greenwood Press, 1985.

Gann, Lewis H., and Thomas H. Henriksen. *The Struggle for Zimbabwe: Battle in the Bush*. New York: Praeger, 1981.

Gastrow, Peter. *Bargaining for Peace: South Africa and the National Peace Accord*. Washington, D.C.: U.S. Institute of Peace, 1995.

Gisselquist, Rachel M. *Sudan: Policy Options Amid Civil War*. Cambridge, Mass.: World Peace Foundation Report, 2000.

Glaser, Charles L. *Analyzing Strategic Nuclear Policy*. Princeton: Princeton University Press, 1990.

Gleditsch, Kristian S., and Michael D. Ward. "Double Take: A Reexamination of Democracy and Autocracy in Modern Polities." *Journal of Conflict Resolution* 41, no. 3 (1997): 361–82.

Glenny, Misha. *The Fall of Yugoslavia: The Third Balkan War*. New York: Penguin, 1992.

Goemans, H. E. *War and Punishment: The Causes of War Termination and the First World War*. Princeton: Princeton University Press, 2000.

Goldstein, Erik. *Wars and Peace Treaties, 1816–1991*. London: Routledge, 1992.

Goldstone, Jack A., Ted Robert Gurr, and Farrokh Moshiri. *Revolutions of the Late Twentieth Century*. Boulder: Westview Press, 1991.

Gurr, Ted Robert. *Minorities at Risk: A Global View of Ethnopolitical Conflicts*. Washington, D.C.: United States Institute of Peace Press, 1993.

Gurr, Ted, and Charles Ruttenberg. *Cross-National Studies of Civil Violence*. Washington, D.C.: Center for Research in Social Systems, 1969.

Hall, David K. "The Laos Crisis, 1960–1961." In *The Limits of Coercive Diplomacy: Laos, Cuba, Vietnam*, ed. Alexander L. George, David K. Hall, and William E. Simons. Boston: Little, Brown, 1971.

Hampson, Fen Osler. *Nurturing Peace: Why Peace Settlements Succeed or Fail*. Washington, D.C.: U.S. Institute of Peace Press, 1996.

Hansen, Holger Bernt, and Michael Twaddle, eds. *Changing Uganda: The Dilemmas of Structural Adjustment and Revolutionary Change*. London: James Currey, 1991.

————, eds. *From Chaos to Order: The Politics of Constitution-Making in Uganda*. London: James Currey, 1994.

Hardin, Russell. *Collective Action*. Baltimore: Johns Hopkins University Press, 1982.

Hare, Paul. *Angola's Last Best Chance for Peace: An Insider's Account of the Peace Process*. Washington, D.C.: U.S. Institute of Peace, 1998.

Hartlyn, Jonathan. *The Politics of Coalition Rule in Colombia*. Cambridge: Cambridge University Press, 1988.

Hartzell, Caroline A. "Explaining the Stability of Negotiated Settlements to Intrastate Wars." *Journal of Conflict Resolution* 43, no. 1 (1999): 3–22.

Hastings, Max. *The Korean War*. New York: Simon and Schuster, 1987.

Hellman, Joel S. "Winners Take All: The Politics of Partial Reform in Postcommunist Transitions." *World Politics* 50, no. 2 (1998): 203–34.

Herbst, Jeffrey. *State Politics in Zimbabwe*. Berkeley: University of California Press, 1990.

Higham, Robin, ed. *Civil Wars in the Twentieth Century*. Lexington: University of Kentucky, 1972.

Hills, Denis. *The Last Days of White Rhodesia*. London: Chatto and Windus, 1981.

Holiday, David, and William Stanley. "Building the Peace in El Salvador." *Journal of International Affairs* 46, no. 2 (1993): 415–38.

Holl, Jane. "When War Doesn't Work." In *Stopping the Killing: How Civil Wars End*, ed. Roy Licklider. New York: New York University Press, 1993.

Holsti, Kalevi J. *Peace and War: Armed Conflicts and International Order, 1648–1989*. Cambridge: Cambridge University Press, 1991.

Horowitz, Donald. *Ethnic Groups in Conflict*. Berkeley: University of California Press, 1985.

Howard, Michael. *The Causes of Wars*. Cambridge: Harvard University Press, 1983.

Hudson, Miles. *Triumph or Tragedy? Rhodesia to Zimbabwe*. London: Hamish Hamilton, 1981.

Hume, Cameron. *Ending Mozambique's War: The Role of Mediation and Good Offices*. Washington, D.C.: U.S. Institute of Peace, 1994.

Iatrides, John O. "Civil War, 1945–1949: National and International Aspects." In *Greece in the 1940s: A Nation in Crisis*, ed. John O. Iatrides. London: Hanover, 1981.

Ikle, Fred C. *Every War Must End*. 2d ed. New York: Columbia University Press, 1991.

Jaggers, Keith, and Ted Robert Gurr. "Tracking Democracy's Third Wave with the Polity III Data." *Journal of Peace Research* 32, no. 4 (1995): 469–82.

James, Alan. *Peacekeeping in International Politics*. London: Macmillan, 1990.

Janowsky, Oscar I. *Nationalities and National Minorities*. New York: Macmillan, 1945.

Jervis, Robert. "Cooperation under the Security Dilemma." *World Politics* 30, no. 2. (1978): 167–214.

———. *The Logic of Images in International Relations*. New York: Columbia University Press, 1989.

———. *Perception and Misperception in International Politics*. Princeton: Princeton University Press, 1976.

Job, Cvijeto. "Yugoslavia's Ethnic Furies." *Foreign Policy* 92 (1993): 52–74.

Joint Evaluation of Emergency Assistance to Rwanda. *The International Response to Conflict and Genocide: Lessons from the Rwanda Experience*. 5 vols. Copenhagen: Steering Committee of the Joint Evaluation of Emergency Assistance to Rwanda, 1996.

Jones, Bruce D. *The Best Laid Plans . . . Peace-Making in Rwanda and the Implications of Failure*. New York: Sage, 2001.

Joseph, Myron L., and Richard H. Willis. "An Experimental Analog to Two-Party Bargaining." *Behavioral Science* 8, no. 2 (1963): 117–127.

Kamukama, Dixon. *Rwanda Conflict: Its Roots and Regional Implications*. Kampala, Uganda: Fountain Publishers, 1997.

Karl, Terry Lynn. "El Salvador's Negotiated Revolution." *Foreign Affairs* 71, no. 2 (1992): 147–64.

Kaufmann, Chaim. "Possible and Impossible Solutions to Ethnic Civil Wars." *International Security* 20, no. 4 (1996): 136–75.

Keesing's Contemporary Archive. London. 1940–.

Kelly, George A., and Linda B. Miller. *Internal War and International Systems: Perspectives on Method*. Occasional Papers in International Affairs, no. 21. Center for International Affairs, Harvard University, 1969.

Keohane, Robert O. *After Hegemony: Cooperation and Discord in the World Political Economy*. Princeton: Princeton University Press, 1984.

Kessler, Richard J. *Rebellion and Repression in the Philippines*. New Haven: Yale University Press, 1989.

King, Charles. "Devolution of Power and Negotiated Settlements in Civil

Wars." Paper presented at the Second Annual Convention of the Association for the Study of Nationalities, New York, April 1997.

King, Gary, Robert O. Keohane, and Sidney Verba. *Designing Social Inquiry: Scientific Inference in Qualitative Research*. Princeton: Princeton University Press, 1994.

Kissinger, Henry. "The Vietnam Negotiations." *Foreign Affairs* 47, no. 2 (1969): 211–34.

Klinghoffer, Arthur Jay. *The International Dimension of Genocide in Rwanda*. London: Macmillan, 1998.

Kosut, Hal, ed. *Indonesia: The Sukarno Years*. New York: Facts on File, 1967.

Krasner, Stephen D., ed. *International Regimes*. Ithaca: Cornell University Press, 1983.

Krebs, David M. *A Course in Microeconomic Theory*. Princeton: Princeton University Press, 1990.

Krebs, David M., Paul Milgrom, John Roberts, and Robert Wilson. "Rational Cooperation in the Finitely Repeated Prisoner's Dilemma." *Journal of Economic Theory* 27, no. 2 (1982): 245–52.

Krebs, David M., and Robert Wilson. "Reputation and Imperfect Information." *Journal of Economic Theory* 27, no. 2 (1982): 253–79.

Kumar, Krishna, ed. *Rebuilding Societies after Civil War: Critical Roles for International Assistance*. Boulder: Lynne Rienner, 1997.

Kuperman, Alan J. "Rwanda in Retrospect." *Foreign Affairs* 79, no. 1 (2000): 94–118.

Kydd, Andrew. "Game Theory and the Spiral Model." *World Politics* 49, no. 3 (1997): 371–400.

———. "Mediation, Preferences, and Credibility." University of California, Riverside, August 2000.

Kydd, Andrew, and Barbara F. Walter. "Sabotaging the Peace: The Politics of Extremist Violence." International Organization (Spring 2002).

Lake, David. *Entangling Relations: American Foreign Policy in Its Century*. Princeton: Princeton University Press, 1999.

Lake, David, and Donald Rothchild. "Containing Fear: The Origins and Management of Ethnic Conflict." *International Security* 21, no. 2 (1996): 41–75.

———, eds. *The International Spread of Ethnic Conflict: Fear, Diffusion, and Escalation*. Princeton: Princeton University Press, 1998.

Langlois, Catherine C., and Jean-Pierre Langlois. "Engineering Cooperation: A Game Theoretic Analysis of Phased International Agreements." Georgetown University, September 1998.

Leeds, Brett Ashley. "Domestic Political Institutions, Credible Commitments, and International Cooperation." *American Journal of Political Science* 43, no. 4 (1999): 979–1002.

Lemarchand, Rene. *Burundi: Ethnic Conflict and Genocide*. Cambridge: Cambridge University Press, 1994.

———. "Managing Transition Anarchies: Rwanda, Burundi, and South Africa in Comparative Perspective." *Journal of Modern African Studies* 32, no. 4 (1994): 581–604.

Licklider, Roy. "The Consequences of Negotiated Settlement in Civil Wars, 1945–1993." *American Political Science Review* 89 (1995): 681–87.

———, ed. *Stopping the Killing: How Civil Wars End.* New York: New York University Press, 1993.

Lijphart, Arend. *Democracy in Plural Societies.* New Haven: Yale University Press, 1977.

Lipson, Charles. "International Cooperation in Economic and Security Affairs." *World Politics* 37, no. 1 (1984): 1–23.

Loh, Pichon P. Y., ed. *The Kuomingtang Debacle of 1949: Collapse or Conquest?* Boston: D. C. Heath, 1965.

Low, Stephen. "The Zimbabwe Settlement, 1976–1979." In *International Mediation in Theory and Practice,* ed. Saadia Touval and I. William Zartman. Boulder: Westview Press, 1985.

Madison, James. "Federalist No. 10." *The Federalist Papers.* New York: Penguin, 1961.

Martin, David, and Phyllis Johnson. *The Struggle for Zimbabwe: The Chimurenga War.* London: Faber and Faber, 1981.

Mason, T. David, and Patrick J. Fett. "How Civil Wars End: A Rational Choice Approach." *Journal of Conflict Resolution* 40, no. 4 (1996): 546–68.

Mason, T. David, Joseph P. Weingarten Jr., and Patrick J. Fett. "Win, Lose, or Draw: Predicting the Outcome of Civil Wars." *Political Research Quarterly* 52, no. 2 (1999): 239–68.

McFaul, Michael. "A Precarious Peace: Domestic Politics in the Making of Russian Foreign Policy." *International Security* 22, no. 3 (1997–98): 5–35.

McPherson, James. *Battle Cry of Freedom.* New York: Oxford University Press, 1988.

Mercer, Jonathan. *Reputation and International Politics.* Ithaca: Cornell University Press, 1996.

Meredith, Martin. *The Past Is Another Country: Rhodesia, 1890–1979.* London: Andre Deutsch, 1979.

Miall, Hugh. *The Peacemakers: Peaceful Settlement of Disputes since 1945.* New York: St. Martin's Press, 1992.

Mitchell, C. R. "Classifying Conflicts: Asymmetry and Resolution." In I. *Resolving Regional Conflicts: International Perspectives,* ed. I. William Zartman. Newbury Park, Calif.: Sage, 1991.

Mitchell, C. R., and K. Webb, eds. *New Approaches to International Mediation.* Westport, Conn.: Greenwood Press, 1988.

Modelski, George. "International Settlement of Internal War." In *International Aspects of Civil Strife,* ed. James Rosenau. Princeton: Princeton University Press, 1964.

Montgomery, Tommie Sue. *Revolution in El Salvador: From Civil Strife to Civil Peace.* Boulder: Westview Press, 1995.

Montville, Joseph V., ed. *Conflict and Peacemaking in Multiethnic Societies.* New York: Lexington Books, 1991.

Moore, William H., III. "Why Internal Wars End: The Decision to Fight, Negotiate, or Surrender." Ph.D. diss., University of Colorado at Boulder, 1991.

Morales, Waltraud Queiser. *Bolivia: Land of Struggle*. Boulder: Westview Press, 1992.

Morgan, T. Clifton, and Sally H. Campbell. "Domestic Structure, Decisional Constraints, and War: So Why Kant Democracies Fight?" *Journal of Conflict Resolution* 35, no. 2 (1991): 187–211.

Mudoola, Dan M. *Religion, Ethnicity, and Politics in Uganda*. Kampala, Uganda: Fountain Publishers, 1993.

Mutibwa, Phares. *Uganda since Independence: A Story of Unfulfilled Hopes*. London: Hurst and Company, 1992.

Naldi, Gino J. *The Organization of African Unity: An Analysis of Its Role*. London: Mansell, 1989.

Nash, Manning. *The Cauldron of Ethnicity in the Modern World*. Chicago: University of Chicago Press, 1989.

Nkomo, Joshua. *Nkomo: The Story of My Life*. London: Methuen, 1984.

Nolutshungu, Sam C. *Limits of Anarchy: Intervention and State Formation in Chad*. Charlottesville: University Press of Virginia, 1996.

North, Douglass C., and Barry R. Weingast. "Constitutions and Commitment: The Evolution of Institutions Governing Public Choice in Seventeenth-Century England." *Journal of Economic History* 49, no. 4 (1989): 803–32.

Nyangoni, Christopher, and Gideaon Nyandoro, eds. *Zimbabwe Independence Movements: Select Documents*. New York: Harper and Row, 1979.

Nydegger, R. V., and G. Owen. "Two-Person Bargaining: An Experimental Test of the Nash Axioms." *International Journal of Game Theory* 3, no. 4 (1974): 239–49.

Nzuwah, Mariyawanda. "Conflict Resolution in Zimbabwe: Superpower Determinants to the Peace Settlement." *Journal of Southern African Affairs* 4, no. 4 (1979): 389–400.

O'Ballance, Edgar. *The Greek Civil War, 1944–1949*. New York: Praeger, 1966.

———. *The War in the Yemen*. Hamden, Conn.: Archon Books, 1971.

O'Conner, Mike. "Bosnia Croats Resist Peace Accord." *New York Times*, February 13, 1996.

———. "Bosnia's Military Threat: Rival Police." *New York Times*, January 2, 1997.

Ofcansky, Thomas P. *Uganda: Tarnished Pearl of Africa*. Boulder: Westview Press, 1996.

Ohlson, Thomas, and Stephen Stedman, with Robert Davies. *The New Is Not Yet Born: Conflict Resolution in Southern Africa*. Washington, D.C.: Brookings Institution, 1994.

Omaar, Rakiya, and Alex de Waal. *Humanitarianism Unbound? Current Dilemmas Facing Multi-mandate Relief Operations in Political Emergencies*. London: Africa Rights, 1994.

Organski, A. F. K. *World Politics*. 2d ed. New York: Alfred A. Knopf, 1968.

Owen, David. *Balkan Odyssey*. New York: Harcourt, Brace, 1995.

Oye, Kenneth A., ed. *Cooperation under Anarchy*. Princeton: Princeton University Press, 1986.

Pazzanita, Anthony G. "The Conflict Resolution Process in Angola." *Journal of Modern African Studies* 29, no. 1 (1991): 3–114.

Pearson, Frederick S. "Foreign Military Interventions and Domestic Disputes." *International Studies Quarterly* 18, no. 3 (1974): 259–90.

Pillar, Paul R. *Negotiating Peace: War Termination as a Bargaining Process.* Princeton: Princeton University Press, 1983.

Pirouet, M. Louise. "The Achievement of Peace in Sudan." *Journal of East African Research and Development* 6 (1970).

Posen, Barry. "The Security Dilemma and Ethnic Conflict." In *Ethnic Conflict and International Security*, ed. Michael E. Brown. Princeton: Princeton University Press, 1993.

Powell, Robert. "The Theoretical Foundations of Strategic Nuclear Deterrence." *Political Science Quarterly* 100, no. 1 (1985): 75–96.

Premdas, Ralph R., S. W. R. de A. Samarisinghe, and Alan B. Anderson, eds. *Secessionist Movements in Comparative Perspective.* New York: St. Martin's Press, 1990.

Prunier, Gerard. *The Rwanda Crisis: History of a Genocide.* New York: Columbia University Press, 1995.

Przeworski, Adam. *Democracy and the Market: Political and Economic Reforms in Eastern Europe and Latin America.* Cambridge: Cambridge University Press, 1992.

Rabinovich, Itamar. *The War for Lebanon: 1970–1985.* Ithaca: Cornell University Press, 1985.

Randle, Robert F. *The Origins of Peace: A Study of Peacemaking and the Structure of Peace Settlements.* New York: Free Press, 1973.

Reed, Laura W., and Carl Kaysen, eds. *Emerging Norms of Justified Intervention.* Cambridge, Mass.: American Academy of Arts and Sciences, 1993.

Regan, Patrick M. *Civil Wars and Foreign Powers: Outside Intervention in Intrastate Conflict.* Ann Arbor: University of Michigan Press, 2000.

———. "Conditions of Successful Third-Party Intervention in Intrastate Conflicts." *Journal of Conflict Resolution* 40, no. 2 (1996): 336–59.

The Report of the Commonwealth Observer Group on the Elections Leading to Independent Zimbabwe. London: Commonwealth Secretariat, Marlborough House, 1980.

Report of the Constitutional Conference, Lancaster House London, September–December 1979. London: Her Majesty's Stationery Office, Cmnd. 7802, 1980.

Roett, Riordan, and Frank Smyth. *Dialogue and Armed Conflict: Negotiating the Civil War in El Salvador.* Foreign Policy Institute Case Studies no. 12, School of Advanced International Studies, Johns Hopkins University, 1988.

Rosenau, James N. ed. *International Aspects of Civil Strife.* Princeton: Princeton University Press, 1964.

Rotberg, Robert I. *Creating Peace in Sri Lanka: Civil War and Reconciliation.* Washington, D.C.: Brookings Institution Press, 1999.

Rotberg, Robert I., and Thomas G. Weiss. *From Massacres to Genocide: The Media, Public Policy, and Humanitarian Crises.* Washington, D.C.: Brookings Institution, 1996.

Rothchild, Donald, and Caroline Hartzell. "The Peace Process in the Sudan,

1971–1972." In *Stopping the Killing: How Civil Wars End*, ed. Roy Licklider. New York: New York University Press, 1993.

Rousseau, David L., Christopher Gelpi, Dan Reiter, and Paul K. Huth. "Assessing the Dyadic Nature of the Democratic Peace, 1918–1988." *American Political Science Review* 90 (1996): 512–33.

Rule, James B. *Theories of Civil Violence*. Berkeley: University of California Press, 1988.

Rupesinghe, Kumar. "Theories of Conflict Resolution and Their Applicability to Protracted Ethnic Conflicts." *Bulletin of Peace Proposals* 18, no. 4 (1987): 527–42.

———, ed. *Conflict Resolution in Uganda*. London: James Currey, 1989.

Schelling, Thomas C. *Arms and Influence*. New Haven: Yale University Press, 1966.

———. *The Strategy of Conflict*. Cambridge: Harvard University Press, 1980.

Schermerhorn, R. A. *Comparative Ethnic Relations*. Chicago: University of Chicago Press, 1978.

Schultz, Kenneth A. "Do Democratic Institutions Constrain or Inform? Contrasting Two Institutional Perspectives on Democracy and War." *International Organization* 53, no. 2 (1999): 233–66.

———. "Domestic Opposition and Signaling in International Crises." *American Political Science Review* 92, no. 4 (1998): 829–44.

Shaw, Chonghal Petey. *The Role of the United States in Chinese Civil Conflicts, 1944–1949*. Salt Lake City: Charles Schlacks, Jr., 1990.

Sisk, Timothy. *Power Sharing and International Mediation in Ethnic Conflict*. Washington, D.C.: United States Institute of Peace, 1996.

Sisson, Richard, and Leo E. Rose. *War and Secession: Pakistan, India, and the Creation of Bangladesh*. Berkeley: University of California Press, 1990.

Small, Melvin, and J. David Singer. *Resort to Arms: International and Civil Wars, 1816–1980*. Beverly Hills, Calif.: Sage, 1982.

Smith, David S., and Robert F. Randle, eds. *From War to Peace: Essays in Peacemaking and War Termination*. International Fellows Program Policy Series. New York: Columbia University Press, 1974.

Smith, David, and Colin Simpson. *Mugabe*. London: Sphere Books, 1981.

Smith, James D. D. *Stopping Wars: Defining the Obstacles to Cease-Fire*. Boulder: Westview Press, 1995.

Snyder, Glenn, and Paul Diesing. *Conflict among Nations*. Princeton: Princeton University Press, 1977.

Soames, Rt. Hon. Lord. "From Rhodesia to Zimbabwe." *International Affairs* 56, no. 3 (1980).

Sommerville, Keith. "The Failure of Democratic Reform in Angola and Zaire." *Survival* 35, no. 3 (1993).

Stack, John F., Jr., ed. *The Primordial Challenge: Ethnicity in the Contemporary World*. Westport, Conn.: Greenwood Press, 1986.

Stanley, William. "International Tutelage and Domestic Political Will: Building a New Civilian Police Force in El Salvador." *Studies in Comparative International Development* 30, no. 1 (1995).

Stedman, Stephen John. *Peacemaking in Civil War: International Mediation in Zimbabwe, 1974–1980*. Boulder: Lynne Rienner, 1991.

———. "Spoiler Problems in Peace Processes." *International Security* 22, no. 2 (1997): 5–53.

Stein, Arthur. *Why Nations Cooperate: Circumstances and Choice in International Relations.* Ithaca: Cornell University Press, 1990.

Stoneman, Colin, and Lionel Cliffe. *Zimbabwe: Politics, Economics, and Society.* London: Pinter, 1989.

Stookey, Robert W. *Yemen: The Politics of the Yemen Arab Republic.* Boulder: Westview Press, 1978.

Stremlau, John J. *The International Politics of the Nigerian Civil War: 1967–1970.* Princeton: Princeton University Press, 1977.

Stuart-Fox, Martin, ed. *Contemporary Laos: Studies in the Politics and Society of the Lao People's Democratic Republic.* New York: St. Martin's Press, 1982.

Tamarkin, M. *The Making of Zimbabwe: Decolonization in Regional and International Politics.* London: Frank Cass, 1990.

Tannenbaum, Frank. *Peace by Revolution: Mexico after 1910.* New York: Columbia University Press, 1966.

Taylor, Michael. *Anarchy and Cooperation.* New York: John Wiley and Sons, 1976.

———. *The Possibility of Cooperation.* Cambridge: Cambridge University Press, 1992.

Thompson, Virginia, and Richard Adloff. *Conflict in Chad.* Berkeley: University of California, 1981.

Tillema, Herbert K. *International Armed Conflict since 1945: A Bibliographic Handbook of Wars and Military Interventions.* Boulder: Westview Press, 1991.

Touval, Saadia, and I. William Zartman, eds. *International Mediation in Theory and Practice.* Conflict Management Studies, School of Advanced International Studies. Boulder: Westview Press, 1985.

Toye, Hugh. *Laos: Buffer State or Battleground?* London: Oxford University Press, 1968.

Treadgold, Donald W. *Twentieth Century Russia.* Boulder: Westview Press, 1990.

Tsou, Tang. *America's Failure in China: 1941–1950.* Chicago: University of Chicago Press, 1963.

United Nations. *El Salvador Agreements: The Path to Peace.* United Nations Department of Public Information, May 1992.

United Nations. *The Guatemala Peace Agreements.* Department of Public Information. New York. 1998.

The United Nations and El Salvador, 1990–1995. United Nations Blue Books Series, vol. 4. New York: United Nations, Department of Public Documents, 1995.

The United Nations and Rwanda, 1993–1996. United Nations Blue Books Series, vol. 10. New York: United Nations, Department of Public Documents, 1996.

United States Department of State. *The China White Paper.* Department of State publication 3573, Far Eastern Series 30. Stanford: Stanford University Press, August 1949.

Vambe, Lawrence. *An Ill-Fated People: Zimbabwe before and after Rhodes.* London: Heinemann, 1972.

Vance, Cyrus. *Hard Choices: Critical Years in America's Foreign Policy.* New York: Simon and Schuster, 1983.

Van den Berghe, Pierre L., ed. *State Violence and Ethnicity.* Niwot: University Press of Colorado, 1990.

Verrier, Anthony. *The Road to Zimbabwe: 1890–1980.* London: Jonathan Cape, 1986.

Wagner, R. Harrison. "The Causes of Peace." In *Stopping the Killing: How Civil Wars End,* ed. Roy Licklider. New York: New York University Press, 1993.

———. "Peace, War, and the Balance of Power." *American Political Science Review* 88 (1994): 593–607.

Wai, Dunstan M. *The African-Arab Conflict in the Sudan.* New York: Africana Publishing, 1981.

Walter, Barbara F. "The Critical Barrier to Civil War Settlement." *International Organization* 51, no. 3 (1997): 335–64.

———. "Designing Transitions from Civil War: Demobilization, Democratization, and Commitments to Peace." *International Security* 24, no. 1 (1999): 127–55.

———. "The Resolution of Civil Wars: Why Negotiations Fail." Ph.D. diss., University of Chicago, 1994.

Walter, Barbara F., and Jack Snyder, eds. *Civil Wars, Insecurity, and Intervention.* New York: Columbia University Press, 1999.

Weingast, Barry R. "Constructing Trust: The Political and Economic Roots of Ethnic and Regional Conflict." Hoover Institute, 1994.

———. "The Economic Role of Political Institutions: Market-Preserving Federalism and Economic Development." *Journal of Law, Economics, and Organization* 11, no. 1 (1995): 1–31.

Weinberger, Naomi Joy. *Syrian Intervention in Lebanon: The 1975–76 Civil War.* New York: Oxford University Press, 1986.

Weissman, Stephen R. "Preventing Genocide in Burundi: Lessons from International Diplomacy." United States Institute of Peace Peaceworks Paper No. 22, July 1998.

Werner, Suzanne. "Negotiating the Terms of Settlement: War Aims and Bargaining Leverage." *Journal of Conflict Resolution* 42, no. 3 (1998): 321–44.

Williamson, Oliver E. "Credible Commitments: Using Hostages to Support Exchange." *American Economic Review* 73 (September 1983): 519–40.

Wiseberg, Laurie S. "The Nigerian Civil War, 1967–1970: A Case Study in the Efficacy of International Law as a Regulator of Intrastate Violence." Student Series Paper for the Southern California Arms Control and Foreign Policy Seminar, May 1972.

Wiseman, Henry, and Alastair M. Taylor. *From Rhodesia to Zimbabwe: The Politics of Transition.* New York: Pergamon Press, 1981.

Wittman, Donald. "Arms Control Verification and Other Games Involving Imperfect Detection." *American Political Science Review* 83 (1989): 923–45.

Wood, Elisabeth Jean. *Forging Democracy from Below: Insurgent Transitions in South Africa and El Salvador.* Cambridge: Cambridge University Press, 2000.

Woodhouse, C. M. *The Struggle for Greece, 1941–1949.* New York: Beekman/ Esanu, 1976.

Wright, Quincy. *A Study of War.* Chicago: University of Chicago Press, 1965.

Wu, Jianzhong, and Robert Axelrod. "How to Cope with Noise in the Iterated Prisoner's Dilemma." *Journal of Conflict Resolution* 39, no. 1 (1995): 183–89.

Zartman, I. William. *The Negotiation Process: Theories and Applications.* Beverly Hills, Calif.: Sage, 1978.

———. *Ripe for Resolution: Conflict and Intervention in Africa.* Oxford: Oxford University Press, 1989.

———, ed. *Resolving Regional Conflicts: International Perspectives.* Newbury Park, Calif.: Sage, 1991.

———, ed. *Elusive Peace: Negotiating an End to Civil Wars.* Washington D.C.: Brookings Institution, 1995.

Zartman, I. William, and J. Lewis Rasmussen, eds. *Peacemaking in International Conflict: Methods and Techniques.* Washington, D.C.: U.S. Institute of Peace, 1997.

INDEX